T4-AJX-882

Heart of the Matter

THE ROLE OF ATTITUDE IN TEACHING

Arthur D. Willis

M.S. Secondary Education

Marcia M. Greenberg

M.S. Special Education

Illustrations by
Sandra Peterson

This book is dedicated to our grandchildren in
concern for the full life of their minds:

Ezra and Naomi Dulit-Greenberg; Noah, Jesse, and
Lena Cohen-Greenberg; Nathaniel Haist Greenberg;
Ezekiel Oliver; Lucas and Tate Yoder;
Aidan and Marlee Yoder; Isabella DeJoy;
and any others who may come along.

Copyright © 2007 by Arthur D. Willis and Marcia M. Greenberg.

Illustrations © 2007 by Sandra Peterson.

Packaged and co-published by Publishers Solutions, LLC. To order this book online or for additional information go to: www.publisherssolutions.com

Discounts on bulk quantities of this book are available to corporations, professional associations, and other organizations. For details and discount information, contact Arthur D. Willis at 518-895-8257.

Manufactured in the United States of America.

Library of Congress Cataloging-in-Publication Number: 2007939542

FIRST EDITION
10 9 8 7 6 5 4 3 2 1

ISBN-13: 978-0-9799475-0-6

Contents

Foreword

In the concluding words of his pessimistic *Civilization and Its Discontents*, the great Western philosopher Sigmund Freud remarked ruefully that humankind had already subdued "the forces of nature to such a pitch that by using them they could now very easily exterminate one another to the last man." He was suggesting that in the perennial struggle between Death and Eros over the right to direct the destiny of humankind, Death appeared to have the upper hand.

Herr Professor added that this burden had taken hold of the human psyche with such vehemence that it explained "a great part of their [humankind's] current unrest, their dejection, their mood of apprehension." But there was hope, he advised. We might expect "the other of the two 'heavenly forces,' eternal Eros, will put forth his strength so as to maintain himself alongside of his equally immortal adversary."

Of course the Eros he was referring to is not an abstraction, but reveals itself in the visions of life we dream, the social arrangements we design and reward each other for committing ourselves to, the acts of compassion we show to those who have sinned or failed in other ways to live up to the requirements Eros lays out: on the one hand, for the survival of the species; on the other, for the everyday human enjoyment of each of us.

I believe Arthur Willis and Marcia Greenberg's *Heart of the Matter* is one such act of Eros, a hope-filled celebration of being alive as well as an invitation to others to strip themselves of the trappings of Death—as it manifests itself in power and control in our school systems—and join in the celebration of life.

This near-seamless artifact of inspiration by two well-seasoned wisdom teachers is an invitation to other teachers—young and old alike—students, school officials, and parents concerned about the

well-being of children some of which, given the morbid political economic constrictions put on personhood in schools today, manifests
itself in perverse and morbid ways.

The "attitude" the authors talk about is really Hindu heart consciousness, maybe even the poetic consciousness of silence, a take on
the world that resides in a place of deep reflection and which is associated with feelings of love, universal compassion, and detachment.

Arthur and Marcia say that teachers who collaborate with students
through heart consciousness, who speak to students' needs as they
strive to find themselves, will not find the traditional control and "disciplines problems" that teachers and administrators worry about,
because students experience an awareness of self that is simultaneously extremely personal and highly collective, that is, is attuned to
the well-being of the entire community, inside and outside the classroom. Fear not, they say, for even "scattered energies in the classroom
will turn into a symmetry that is unexpected and delightful."

This is not a how-to book but more of a what-kind-of-tools-does-
the-humanist-teacher-need-in-his/her-tool-box book. Their aims agree
with those of the great twentieth-century psychotherapist Carl Rogers
and Danish philosopher Soren Kierkegaard, who maintain that life is
not worth living unless a person "is that self one truly is," which means
for teachers and students alike creating spaces, relationships, ideas,
concepts where they can cast off their masks of Death—and examine
their perverse commitment to them.

John Heckewelder, a missionary who lived among the Delaware
Indians during the late seventeenth and early eighteenth centuries,
witnessed a community ritual that gave young people a chance to find
their calling in life as they sludge through that "no person's land"
called adolescence into adulthood. Heckewelder says that when a
young person is to be initiated:

> he [sic] is put under an alternate course of physic and fasting, either tak-
> ing no food whatever, or swallowing the most powerful and nauseous
> medicines, and occasionally he is made to drink decoctions of an intoxi-
> cating nature, until his mind becomes sufficiently bewildered, so that he
> sees visions and has extraordinary dreams, for which, of course, he has
> been prepared beforehand. He will fancy himself flying through the air,
> walking under ground, stepping from one ridge or hill to the other across
> the valley beneath, fighting and conquering giants and monsters and
> defeating whole hosts by his single arm. . . . When a boy has been initiat-
> ed, a name is given to him analogous to the visions he has seen, and to the
> destiny that is supposed to be prepared for him. The boy, imagining all

that happened to him while under perturbation to have been real, sets out in the world with lofty notions of himself, and animated with courage for the most desperate undertakings.

What a wonderful celebration of our heritage! Obviously U.S.-American culture has no such practice today. Indeed the opposite is true, as childhood is extended far into adulthood, and yes, an adulthood that stifles the true self through its support of the purchase of packaged accessories of self, needs that are market-conceived, manufactured, wrapped, hawked, bought, and consumed as commodities.

In *Heart of the Matter* Arthur Willis and Marcia Greenberg call for the creation of spaces, venues, relationships in which the Delaware would find themselves at home, that is, a school or classroom designed to encourage young people to develop into caring stewards. There a young man and a young woman can test their visions of well-being among a community of similarly situated others—young people engaged in the struggle to be human—what Parker Palmer calls a "community of truth."

What a relief this book will be for teachers who feel trapped and see dwindling opportunities for a creative life. Imagine: it calls for curricular materials (primary categories) to be the source of debate; shows how such debate might be handled; even telling students to be defiant, yes defiant, encouraging them to refuse labels that corner and dismantle their brilliant inner-diamond selves maybe for the sake of a state-certifying standardized test. *Heart of the Matter* is a work driven on passion, but it allows room to breathe.

Years ago Neil Postman (with Charles Weingartner), in his cutting-edge work *Teaching as a Subversive Activity* (1969), claimed that all students "develop built-in shockproof crap detectors as basic equipment in their survival kits" (p. 220) so that any time a teacher, fellow student, school administrator, or anyone assigned the task of passing on the wisdom of the ages, sends forth lessons that are crapola, the crap detector goes off like a fire alarm.

As we know, this means that every student, which means all of us, has a built-in authenticity detector as well because, at all levels of consciousness, we know that without authenticity we are consigned to be a shadow of ourselves, and feel treasonous because we have let Death have the upper hand.

My authenticity detector—perhaps yours too—has been well honed for years and it sees that this work on heart consciousness is the real McCoy—Eros! By having examined its tenets I am already different;

that is what courage-teachers Willis and Greenberg hope for, transformation. They are looking for a world—like Peter Maurin co-founder (with Dorothy Day) of the Catholic Worker movement used to say—in which it is easier for people to be good, easier for people to enjoy each other's company because we have committed ourselves to authentic life. When wrangling arises, we don't panic because we have learned to go directly to the heart of the matter.

Dennis Sullivan
Editor-in-Chief
The Contemporary Justice Review

Preface

The authors began the extended conversation that is embodied in this book in 1982, when Arthur was already twenty-three years into a teaching career and Marcia had just completed her teaching credentials. From the beginning, our discussions revolved around the themes of how we experience human nature and what we imagine to be the elements that constitute a human being. In 1993 Arthur took a sabbatical during which he explored in greater depth educational and philosophical literature dealing with these topics. By 2000 Arthur had retired and Marcia was working part-time as a graduate student supervisor. With this increased spare time, we began to write chapters expressing the conclusions we had come to through our professional experiences, conversations, and research.

The structure of the book and how we came upon it is discussed at length in the first chapter. We discovered that each person comprises four faculties that are progressively more inclusive. We call these faculties Behavior or Persona, Thinking or Understanding, Feeling or Knowing, and Personal Awareness. It is our contention that most modern schools in the United States address only two of these dimensions: Behavior and Thinking. Many fine teachers—such as Parker Palmer, Jonathan Kozol, and Frank McCourt—have published books on the subject that include discussion of the Feeling or Knowing faculty. Other educators, personally known to us, have also influenced this book; among those who have contributed their wisdom are Mark Diefendorf, Frank Faber, Mary Garrett, Karen Griffin, Brian Hunt, Ken Kirik, Tom Kurkjian, Chris Mastro, John Perry, John Piechnick, Carol Rasowsky, Richard Searles, Nina Sher, Lydia Tobler, Ed Welch, and Jennifer Wolfe.

The faculty of Personal Awareness is the largest and most inclusive of the four faculties. We suspect that some teachers regularly access this faculty, this largest and most inclusive human dimension, but only indirectly or unconsciously. This is understandable, because Awareness is a state in which a person is paying close attention, in a nonjudgmental frame of mind, to everything that is going on around him or her. Awareness often occurs in brief flashes that go unnoticed. This state is completely perceptual or "phenomenological" (in one interpretation of that philosophical term), without any interference by evaluation or judgment. Things simply are as they are. It is inevitable that impressions from this faculty will be made on the sensory system in such a way that they will imprint a wash of images on the Feeling arena, images that in turn will focus and organize as thoughts and, subsequently, as behaviors in judgmental responses to these impressions. Thus, each inclusive perceptual situation will yield to the demands of increasingly concentrated or reductive patterns of judgment, in a flowing alignment that loops back and contributes its conclusions to a broadened personal awareness. We believe that this aligned flow is crucial to any authentic learning experience.

The problem is one of conscious duration: How long are we able to hold our Awareness open, as if it were a camera lens, so that the imaginative impressions formed on our Feeling faculty are as conscious, complete, and accurate a registry of Awareness as possible? There is almost always, because of the time constraints of the classroom, a rush to judgment and an urgent need for action. Trouble arises with students because this urgency leads to an incomplete, vastly reduced registry of those faculties that comprise their humanness. Continuing with the metaphor of the camera lens, if the exposure is too brief, images will be indistinct and inaccurate; if too long, images will be washed out and darkened, like an overexposed negative. When discussing these ideas, we have often been dismissed as cockeyed idealists and criticized as unrealistic regarding actual classroom situations. However, this effort to align the human faculties in our teaching approaches, in as accurate and timely a manner with our students as possible, has been central to our pedagogy, with greatly enhanced professional results.

We believe it is possible to train beginning educators in these perceptual and evaluative capacities; for example, Marcia experimented with training exercises directed toward the acquisition of such skills during the supervision and university faculty adjunct phase of her career just before retirement. Gradually, the guided practice of paying close attention to their students, with as little hasty judgment as possible allowed the imprints from the trainees' Awareness to become more conscious, accurate, and purposefully useful in the classroom. This practice also led some of her trainees to notice the reciprocal nature of this effort: as they paid closer, more neutral attention to the faculties of their students, they attended to the alignment of their own awareness and made important discoveries through constant written reflections on how their attitudes either enhanced or subverted the classroom situation. In another example, Arthur used projection and introjection exercises in his psychology classes to emphasize how judgmental attitudes arise. Over time we both found that behavior management issues became negligible, the presentation of lessons more coherent, and the fear factor decreased.

When we shared this theory of alignment with colleagues, they often responded with objections, such as: "I couldn't have done that as a new teacher—I was too concentrated on classroom control, lesson preparation, supervision issues, whether the kids liked me or not, whether I would get tenure, and so on. I was very afraid of making mistakes in all these areas." We noticed that, though valid, these objections are focused on "me-the-teacher" and are largely self-referential. Fear, and overcoming fear, are the implied themes of early professional practice.

Discipline and behavior modification imposed from the outside do not necessarily translate into self-discipline. To make us feel less anxious, we need to turn our fear into alertness that will foster the student's need for self-regulation. We say "alertness" because students represent a very wide developmental spectrum of skills, temperament, interests, and compliance with educational expectations. As we become alert to students, we pick up on their nuances and bring attention to individual and shared capacities. As we cultivate this attitude of greater attentiveness, we increase our chances of making the leap to Awareness of our students' actual selves, their "just-so-ness." We begin to feel a real joy in their actuality, rather than a mere toleration of it. This elation is inexpressible, but completely palpable, and is experienced by any good teacher from time to time; one of the purposes of this book is to suggest that one can train oneself to experience more frequently this feeling of "all's right with the world." Our accuracy and our energy for the task of teaching will have made a quantum leap.

Perhaps what we most fear is anything that contradicts our identity, that is, who we think we are. Getting to know oneself is intimidating. With this in mind, we offer two chapters on Jungian typology and its moral and ethical ramifications for our actions. Typology offers a fairly neutral way of approaching our own shadow material, some of which we project onto others or onto our own unacknowledged capacities. It holds out the possibility of becoming more inclusive of those whom we might otherwise dismiss as being unlike ourselves. What is called for is a courage that upholds our right to make mistakes and to proceed according to the evidence we glean from them. We must ground our actions in our own reservoir of experience as we correct our mistakes and gain increasing accuracy in "actual occasions" (Alfred North Whitehead's term for the real situations we find ourselves in). We call this courageous insistence on the integrity of one's own evidence "defiance." We recognize that the themes addressed in our book may cause some readers to experience dissonance, because becoming more cognizant of one's own rejected shadow aspects, while at the same time building a healthy defiant confidence, seems a daunting task. We hope readers will look at the structured process that this book offers as a means to gain steady, long-range, increasing inclusiveness by way of transforming the energies of fear to alertness, to deep attentiveness, and ultimately to Awareness.

To suggest that there are current crises in our public schools is simply a matter of pointing out the obvious: high dropout rates; violence; too many students in classrooms; dilapidated buildings; teachers lacking legacy and subject preparation; cutbacks in the arts and humanities; curriculum bound to standardized testing; curriculum tied to pat, constrictive evaluation; behavior management that doesn't work; sound-byte lessons that acquiesce to limited attention spans; students bereft of any sense of historical process, and so on. There is clearly an urgent need for problem solving in our society.

We believe that cultivating an attitude toward expanding the four faculties in our students and ourselves, and transforming fear-based, self-protective approaches to perceptive, conscious teaching, would go a long way toward encouraging new directions in education, because attitude plays an overarching influence on educational outcomes. This book is about cultivating a specific attitude in teaching, an attitude of waiting upon Awareness. Goal setting, curriculum design, mission statements, behavior management approaches, and replicable teaching strategies, although important, are not what this book is about. It is not a how-to book. Rather, we pay close, differentiated, and systematic attention to two factors that shape attitude: first, the nature and cultivation of human faculties in the determination of what and how much we learn; and second, the role fear plays in both students and educators.

Arthur Willis
Marcia Greenberg

Acknowledgments

This book encompasses the experiences of almost thirty years of research, discussion, and professional work. The manuscript itself was written during a seven-year process. In the course of this time there have been many who have given significant assistance. Colleagues who have contributed their wisdom and teaching stories must include: Sue Cullen, Mark Diefendorf, Dirk DeJong, Bill Dodge, Frank Faber, Dick Freyer, Bill Furdon, Don Fyfe, Lynn Gelzheiser, Kim Greiner, Karen Griffin, Brian Hunt, Ken Kirik, Tom Kurkjuan, Chris Mastro, Rich Mele, Nina Sher, Chris and Rachel Theodorou, Lydia Tobler, Jennifer Wolfe, Linda Wolkenbreit, and Jan Wysocki.

These former students provided us with valuable insights: Christian Clark, Fanny Delaporte, Randi Dell'Acqua, Melissa Edmunds, Don Houk, Sonja Phinney, Kara Relyea, Bertrand Romagne, Dan Schreiber, Matt Schreiber, Mike Stanton, and Cheryl Weeks. We thank our friends for listening to our themes without rolling their eyes, and for adding their unique perspectives: Dr. Lorraine Davis, Arthur Jarvis, Hazel Jarvis, Joyce Johnson, Pete Looker, John and Helen Perry, John and Nikki Piechnik, Tony and Jean Tartaglia, Ken and Pax Vogt, and Linda Witkowski.

Our children and their spouses, through propinquity, have been subjected to endless discursive probing: Hannah Willis, Annie Willis, Tom and Colleen Yoder, Ted and Michelle Yoder, Jennifer and Derek DeJoy; Josh Greenberg and Kate Dulit, Adam Greenberg and Kate Cohen, Ben Greenberg, and Elizabeth Greenberg. All hail! It is finished. And to Dr. Lyon Greenberg for his patient indulgence, we send our gratitude.

To Marcia's friend, jungian analyst, Leah Gindoff Berne, who first taught her about the ramifications of typology. And to Art and Jessie MacDonald—thanks mom and dad for underwriting this book.

To our greatly appreciated editors, we owe a heavy debt: Judi Willis, the initial reader, for consistency; Kate Cohen, our primary copy editor and esteemed daughter-in-law; Richard Searles, our champion proofreader and indexer; Dennis Sullivan, for germane and essential commentary and further editing; and Linda DeMasi and Bruce Sherwin of Publishers Solutions for their talented assistance in the preparation and publication of our manuscript. And for the final edit we are indebted to Nancy Crompton for her outstanding contribution of legacy and structure.

About the Authors

Arthur D. Willis received his BA in political science and English from Northwestern University and a MAT in history from the University at Albany, SUNY. He has taught social studies and English at Arlington Heights High School in Illinois and at the Oakwood Friends School in Poughkeepsie, New York. He was one of the first organizers of the Leysin American School in Leysin, Switzerland, where he designed curriculum for both the English and Social Studies departments. He has chaired social studies departments in the public schools of Vorrheesville, New York and Rhinebeck, New York.

Art has been a consultant at the University at Albany, SUNY, training teachers in writing and literary ideology. These two groups spawned the Capital District Writers' Project and the Literary Ideology Project, respectively. He has also worked with the education department at the University at Massachusetts, Amherst, where he helped establish the National Alternative Schools Program.

Art currently resides in the capital region of New York State, and has five children and six grandchildren. He is also a published poet.

Marcia M. Greenberg received her BA in early early modern European history from Mount Holyoke College and has an MS in special education from the University at Albany, SUNY. She has worked for St. Ann's School in Albany, New York, teaching math and GED preparation to emotionally challenged students. She has also helped create programs for developmentally delayed infants and toddlers; tutored all four core subjects for grades 7–12; and helped establish a gifted and talented program for elementary school students, as well as working in the Reading Partners project, an after-school reading program designed to help elementary students with reading problems.

Marcia has also worked at the University at Albany, SUNY, graduate program in special education as an adjunct professor, where she helped develop a practicum course for uncertified graduate students based on the Reading Partners model.

Marcia resides in the capital region of New York State and she and her husband have four children and six grandchildren.

About the Illustrator

Sandra Peterson received her formal training at the American Academy of Art in Chicago and at Northern Illinois University. Her paintings have been shown at many juried and group exhibitions, including the Art Institute of Chicago, the Cudahy Gallery of Wisconsin Art at the Milwaukee Art Museum and the Bradley Gallery in Milwaukee, Wisconsin. Sandra has also taught at Gateway Technical Institute and at McHenry County College.

Sandra and her family reside in Door County, Wisconsin. She can be contacted by email at ckpeterson@itol.com.

Heart of the Matter

THE ROLE OF ATTITUDE IN TEACHING

AS IF
EVERYTHNG
IN LIFE ONLY
HAPPENED ONCE

CHAPTER ONE

Introduction

"Quick now, here, now, always—"
— T. S. Eliot

WE ARE HERE FOR THE KIDS

One of the dictums most often heard among those who educate children is: "We are here for the kids. Whatever else may concern us, we can agree that we are here, first and foremost, for the kids." But what does this mean, to "be here for the kids"? And what, other than a young goat, is a kid, anyway?

WHAT IS A KID?

Our answer to that question is different from those offered by the dominant models of our time: behaviorism, cognitive constructivism, and social constructivism. Briefly, behaviorists see students as seemingly intelligent, but potentially unruly organisms that need to be controlled, conditioned, and shaped (through means of stimulus/response) into socially desirable objects, as well-expressed by B. F. Skinner in *Walden II*. Behaviorist educators seem to say "Give me the child, tell me what the culture wants him or her to be, and I, like a master potter, will mold that child into the predetermined cultural shape."

Cognitive constructivists say "Children, like all of us, exhibit characteristic patterns of thinking, feeling, and behaving, and possess both nurture and nature components and limits. Each child is borne along in discrete stages, as determined by nature (bio-design) and nurture (environment)." They say that we must design our curriculum according to demonstrable cognitive stages through which children pass.

1

A reliable testing program will indicate a given child's level of mastery of Piaget's stages of intellectual development.

Social constructivists believe that, whatever else a student is, she or he is, at center, a personality located in relationship to other personalities, during which the student is constantly altering his or her personality to reflect the dynamics of the observer and his or her own perspective. The self is contextual, oscillating in relation to others, says Vygotsky. The educator must become a master of defining social context for the benefit of the student through group learning, the development of language skills, and other forms of interdependence. The emphasis here is on the development of personality, which can competently navigate social relationships within desired cultural norms. Curriculum means teaching kids to behave along certain acceptable lines and to think within a certain design. In this model, Thinking is considered the leader and Behavior the follower. Result: seriously depressed, dispirited, unmotivated, bored kids! Why? Because a kid is far more than an amalgam of thought and behavior. As with Procrustes' bed, in these models we are pulled and shrunk in conformity with the assumptive program.

After about two decades of teaching, I began to realize that these three models are not so much wrong as they are only *partly* right. To see kids in these terms is to see incompletely, because not only does each model make gross assumptions about the nature of the child, but it offers little more understanding of that nature except that it is young and malleable. If I know my students as individuals, what is it that I know: their names, their personalities, their interests, their friends, their academic records, their abilities to conform to expected standards? Are your students safely tucked into these models, knowable only by these descriptions? Are you the custodian of their surface existence? Or are these impressions important, but secondary, ways of knowing your students?

When I began my teaching career in Cook County, Illinois, students appeared to me as adversarial demons; some were properly cowed, others were just waiting for an opportunity to attack and render me useless, if not helpless. I wasn't necessarily misreading their mood: I was replacing a teacher whom they had driven off, who reportedly had lost control of both the classroom and himself, and suffered a nervous breakdown.

It took a few years to know that that was, indeed, the mood of the students that first day, but that was all it was—a mood. Over the next several years I came to realize that student persuasion was usually consonant with my persuasion, and that my attitude toward them sculpted their attitude toward me.

And what is attitude? The *Oxford English Dictionary* defines it as "a habitual mode of regarding anything"; also, a "settled behavior or manner of acting, as representative of feeling or opinion." And *Webster's* definition, "a position or bearing as indicating action, feeling, or mood," describes attitude in stark relief. What lies beneath this behavior, this habitual mode of regarding? Clearly my early teaching attitudes had been shaped by the cultural preferences within which I had been educated.

What *are* students made of, then? Are they simply bodies—organisms—as the behaviorists assume, with mental workings that are inscrutable and therefore unknowable, experienced by us only as behaviors that are shaped by stimulus and response? Or are they organisms with mental properties, which can be duly examined through standardized testing procedure? Psychometricians (human measurers), following a model called cognitive psychology, base their studies on the idea that students are testable, measurable entities that can be reasonably shown to possess a mind or mental life at demonstrable levels. Are students in your midst a mix of body and mind? If that is all you experience, then you are justified in assuming an attitude of condescending objectivity. You are there to educate—which can be described as *educere*, "to lead out," in a process Van Cleve Morris notes, or *educare*, "to rear or nurture, working with what is already given in a child's nature" (p. 105). But what is already given? A body reduced to its automatic functions? A mind shrunk to its organizational agency? And if we see our students as a combination of only body and mind, we are reverting back to our Puritan roots and earlier, wherein young people can be habitually modeled as depraved or disabled. Beware: these are strong words, but this is how many in society, and especially older, embittered teachers, customarily regard the young. Marcia also notes that in the field of special education, where "functional skills" are the desired and well-meant outcomes, the body/mind models are the ones exclusively concentrated on in teacher-training programs.

Rather than seeing students as bipartite beings (body/mind), we suggest adding a third part to your experience, namely spirit, thereby granting to human nature a tripartite status: body and spirit can meet in mind with often salubrious results. Sarvepalli Radhakrishnan's advice in *Indian Philosophy* is instructive:

> We generally identify ourselves with our narrow limited selves and refer to spiritual experience as something given or revealed to us, as though it did not belong to us. We separate the power of spiritual apprehension from the rest of our nature and refer to it as something divine. Such a separation is unfair to humanity. The insight of the best moments reveals the

deepest in us. It is wrong to regard human nature as its very self when it is least inspired and not its true self when it is most. If our self finds in these moments of vision its supreme satisfaction, and is intensely alive while they last, then that self is our true self. We cannot limit our being to the physical or vital, the customary or conventional. (p. 628)

Therefore, we need to recognize the spirit as well as the body and mind. But in the words of Aline D. Wolf, "Unlike the teaching of academic subjects, spiritual nurturing cannot be approached with detailed steps that tell the teacher exactly how to present specific concepts with appropriate materials. The effort to nurture spirit must flow freely from the teacher's own inner essence and from his or her belief that each child is truly a spiritual being." (p ii). In other words, this effort must flow from the teacher's authentic self, through an attitude of attention to the tripartite nature of a child.

As my career lengthened and deepened, I passed through a sort of progressive expansion of notions about what a student is. At first, I saw students as behaving personalities that needed to be shaped and controlled. After a few years, I began to see them as having an interior life of feelings and thoughts that needed to be acknowledged, motivated, and directed. Gradually, I began to feel that kids are more than human objects or *others* with distinctive patterns—rather, I became impressed by an elusive element, something that was beyond the uniqueness of each individual. That something seemed embedded in the nature of each person as an amalgam of the elements of body, mind, and spirit, which we see as soul. Whenever all three of these elements were recognized, students and teacher became mutually animated. I found myself more and more present in the company of students, both in and out of the classroom.

In this regard, Marcia's account of becoming present to her student Melanie is resonant with my experience:

Marcia and Melanie

Melanie joined my caseload when she was about ten months old. She had been referred for early intervention services because of failure to meet developmental milestones across all domains. Difficulties in her functioning had been noticed from birth, but her failure to make any significant progress had become pronounced by ten months and neurological tests indicated that she might have a severe, progressive disability. Within weeks of beginning services it was obvious to me that she was the most handicapped child on my caseload, with little hope of making much progress, even with intensive therapeutic intervention.

Melanie lived with her teenaged single mother in a working-class neighborhood; her father was serving a short sentence in prison. When her mom was at work, Melanie was frequently cared for by her great-grandmother, who lived in a rundown, crime-ridden area of the city. Melanie's great-grandmother presented as a large, unkempt woman, who, because of leg-vein problems, had difficulty moving around her home and, as a result, conducted her domestic business from a couch in the living room. Consequently, Melanie was confined to a small area of the couch, surrounded by pillows, so that great-grandmother could feed her and change her diapers without having to get up. It was in this setting that her other therapists and I made many visits during the two years Melanie was with our program.

I hated going to that place. My fastidious, middle-class nose was offended by the stale cooking odors, by the smell of Melanie's unbathed body and by the stench of dogs and cats that wandered through the room and occasionally left their deposits in the long entrance hallway that was stacked with boxes of cast-off items. I felt uncomfortable around the rough-looking male family members who streamed into and out of the house in steady waves all day. I loathed the cockroaches that skittered across my pant legs while I engaged in floor time play with Melanie. Great-grandma rambled on throughout the sessions, and I acknowledged her chatter with polite, but detached attention, just as nice girls of my generation are expected to do.

Because of my strong work ethic, inculcated by Depression-era parents at a young age, I dutifully kept going—twice a week, week after week. Periods of respite occurred when her grandmother cared for Melanie in a much less chaotic home setting in a nicer part of town.

Around the beginning of the last six months I worked with Melanie, I had the following dream:

I go to great-grandmother's house for my regularly scheduled visit with Melanie and knock on the door. Great-grandmother opens the door. She is wearing a bright, pretty housedress, all starchy and ironed, and her shiny white hair is in a little bun on top of her head—a vision of the archetypal grandmother or fairy godmother. The hardwood floor of the long hallway is polished and glowing. On a credenza against the wall is a vase of large, colorful flowers. She welcomes me warmly and invites me in.

Just then Melanie comes running down the hallway. She flings herself into my arms, calling out, "Hi, Marcia!" In the dream I feel astounded: both Melanie and her great-grandmother are walking! Melanie can talk! The house is beautiful!

When I awoke, my first rueful thought was that the dream was some sort of compensation for helping me get through another tedious visit that day. That afternoon, when I entered the house and picked Melanie up, I physically felt a shock, a thunderbolt of awareness. I looked into Melanie's eyes and fell completely in love. To this day, I can't explain how that process of coming to see her spirit and soul instead of just her unkempt little body and disabled mind occurred. She was to me no longer a handicapped child with almost nonexistent skills that needed improving. She was simply Melanie, just who she was. That process must have had something to do with persisting, of gradually becoming attentive—what Arthur calls "staying in the room"—long enough to face and wear down my own judgmental nature and fears and pass beyond them. My dream had apparently showed me what the souls of Melanie and her great-grandmother looked like and if I entered that wider space, they would welcome me. Seeing them in a context greater than their hard lives and disabilities allowed me to step past my own limits to human connection.

In the following months, Melanie began to move around more independently and exploratively with her little bunny-hop crawl and attempted to stand up to play with toys on the coffee table. Her brand-new glasses and leg braces helped a lot. I began to notice certain subtleties in her communication system—eye glances, crawling toward desired objects, use of a word that sounded like "dhat"—that indicated her interest in pictures and photographs as she looked toward them. I accompanied Melanie and her mother on several trips to the neurologist's office and became her vocal advocate there, once literally grabbing her off the examining table and playing with her on the floor so the doctor could see her movement patterns beyond the routine and rather dismissive examination. The doctor began to question the progressive nature of her disabilities.

I took to listening closely to great-grandmother's stories and found out a lot about her interests and not-easy life. Regarded attentively, she began to register as the interesting person she was, a woman with a jolly sense of humor and good stories to tell. The rough guys no longer bothered me and, in fact, turned out to be helpful and motivational during visits, because Melanie liked them; one would regularly escort me to my car car-

*rying my supply bag and making sure I left the neighborhood
safely. In short, a hard-won change in my fearful, judgmental
attitude—one that led to increased attentiveness and to a more
expansive view of Melanie and her great-grandmother as based-
in-soul-touching-my-soul—seemed to make my teaching more
effective, to Melanie's benefit.*

As a result of starting to experience students as based-in-soul, as
Marcia came to experience Melanie, I slowly developed a habitual attitude of patience. My knowledge of kids took on a dynamic that seemed
to proceed in the following way: I found myself simply awaiting their
respective presences and forming no judgments, either intellectual or
aesthetic. Then I would allow my vision of them to transform from
looking to seeing. I would again try to not pass judgment on what I
saw. The students would initiate some sort of response to this waiting
and seeing, and I would respond in turn out of what I saw and heard,
again permitting myself as little affective and cognitive evaluation as
possible. Both Marcia and I found this process awkward, requiring
long-term, often painful, patience, because it forced us to become
more open and receptive than our training had prepared us to be.
Finally, I would "await" all over again, and the process would repeat
itself in an expanding circularity that led to deepening and more *accurate* responses on both sides. This circularity can occur rapidly or
slowly and in any context. In this "awaiting," I could become alert to
students and begin to bring an increased attention to them.

Just as Marcia experienced this process in a one-to-one situation
with a young child, so it can occur in a group context with teenagers. I
am thinking, for example, of a tenth-grade social studies class in which
several of my more-focused students demanded that I shut down what
they considered to be too many disruptive comments from other students. I put to the whole class the question: "Is there too much confusion and thoughtless commentary here, or should we allow people in
good faith to say whatever comes into their minds?" The less-focused
students spoke up, saying, in effect, that this was the first class in which
they felt free to be themselves and hence, the first class to keep their
interest. After glowering a bit, the more-focused students agreed that it
would be useful to hear all points of view. After several weeks a kind of
mutual tolerance evolved, in which students of all types could find their
rhythm and pacing. If I had dealt with this by "laying down the law"
(what I shall later call the "justice response"), this mutuality of attention would never have occurred. What I did instead was to suspend
judgment in the service of Presence: We await the presence of others

and bring our own presence out in the bargain. It is an attitude of patient intuition, which helps us cultivate the firm intention to regard ourselves and our students in the larger context of our souls, of "going out to meet" them with greater accuracy. As W. H. Hudson wrote, "unless the soul goes out to meet what we see, we do not see it; nothing do we see, not a beetle, not a blade of grass" (p. 224). It is permitting the core of the student and the core of the teacher to meet in the immediacy of the educational moment. It is a witnessing of each other. It is unattached, not detached. It is present, not dissociated. In my experience, this cycle of pause-respond-pause-respond produces mutual attention and respect in ways that no other manner of communicating can. It allows teachers and students to be present to each other. We observe; we follow the students' lead; we expand on that lead; and start over again—all in a context of suspending judgment. In the example of the tenth-grade social studies class, we see that the students are perturbed with each other; we feel out those concerns; we allow the students to work with those concerns; and then we come to a new perspective for all concerned. Moreover, this process took place within the time and curricular constraints of the classroom as a whole.

THE FOUR EDUCATIONS

As our conversations proceeded with respect to the tripartite nature of kids, and the more expansive attitude that we as educators needed to encompass it, we began to develop ideas about a general sort of curriculum that could contain these more capacious notions of nature and attitude. We posited four organizing faculties that we called, simply, "educations," and that occur in all educational settings, either strongly or inadequately rendered. Our thoughts about these four educations came to us during one of those odd synchronistic events when everything suddenly falls into place: Arthur was skimming through an old copy of the *Tao Te Ching* by Lao Tsu when he came across reading 38:

> Therefore when Tao is lost, there is Goodness
> When Goodness is lost, there is Kindness
> When Kindness is lost, there is Justice
> When Justice is lost, there is Ritual

This little aphoristic verse seemed to capture not only our ideas about the increasing inclusiveness of attitude (as opposed to a linear, hierarchical arrangement), as needed to encompass the tripartite human being, but also suggested an alternate vocabulary that we could use to describe the four educations.

For the purposes of this book, we understand Tao as Absolute Awareness, beyond the capacity of the human mind to grasp fully and therefore beyond the purview of education. It is the All, which includes all the dynamic phenomena of the universe and informs everything. Although it traditionally has been the subject of spiritual inquiry, it lies beyond human ken. It is Infinite Inclusion and is given various names across cultures: Tao, God, Goddess, Yahweh, Allah, Love, Buddha. As Woody Allen so pithily notes, "I'm astounded by people who want to 'know' the universe when it's hard enough to find your way around Chinatown."

Personal Awareness

In our model, Tao is not so much completely unavailable to human ken as it is filtered or glimpsed in order to inform human perception and contemplation to the greatest extent possible in our world of limits. As Wordsworth writes in *Intimations of Immortality*, these filters are like the "clouds of glory" that we trail when we enter the world at birth. They give us the presentiment of the infinitely inclusive dimension of Absolute Awareness throughout our lives—the presentiment that there is *Something* rather than *Nothing* and that this inclusive Something presents itself to us as both the One (form) and the Many (content). The cloudy wisps are as much of Tao as the human being can take in. So, while it is not possible for any given individual (or species) to be Absolutely Aware, each of us has the capacity to simply observe, to see or witness the phenomena before us, in a state often called Socratic Unlearning. Lao Tsu calls this filtering bridge Goodness; we refer to it as Personal Awareness, the most inclusive of the four educations. At once the simplest and most baffling education, Personal Awareness is the experience of perception in the absence of any judgment whatsoever. In this education we struggle to see all that we can see and only afterward run these phenomena through their exercises to evaluate whether they are credible and accurate as played through our human bodily perception. The lifelong cultivation of Personal Awareness might be conceptually similar to the psychological processes that Abraham Maslow and Carl Jung call Self-Actualization and Individuation, respectively. Although open access to Personal Awareness historically has been the purview of select groups of adepts—Christian mystics, Sufis, Kabbalists, Shamans, Hindu gurus, enlightened Buddhists—it is our contention that it can be regarded as an "education" and consciously taught without attaching to it any mystical, occult, or theological significance.

When we hold others in Personal Awareness, we allow ourselves to include the presence of everyone in our midst, here and now, including ourselves. We are all "here" to each other. The only precondition to this awareness is the *intention* to hold others in awareness. No mood, no attitude, no circumstance excludes one from Personal Awareness. It is a state of being that is as abundant, available, and reflexive as breathing air. In less lofty terms, Personal Awareness encompasses such presentiments as fullness, enlarging context, ever-bigger picture, multicontextualism, and content. It is religious only in the sense that *religio* implies connection. When we seek greater relevance and begin to see ourselves as interconnecting with everyone and everything in an immediate and global context without imposing exclusionary doctrines, in an attitude of attention, then we can be said to be practicing *religio*. We reject placing others outside and away from our behaving, feeling, and thinking life. Our sense of Personal Awareness is like the foundation and stage set for the other educations: Knowing/Feeling; Understanding/Thinking and Personality/Behaving—all three can come into harmonic play in the plenum of Personal Awareness.

Knowing/Feeling

Corresponding to the arena of Kindness in the *Tao Te Ching* verse is the education of Knowing/Feeling in our construct. In his philosophy Plato posed one great human antipode: Idea/Form/Design on the one hand and Life/Movement/Content on the other. It is the latter which informs the education we call Knowing/Feeling. Knowing/Feeling is the experience of the multifarious, the diverse; it is the arena in which diversity promotes novel combinations and evolutionary urges; it is the container of our biographical, subjective experiences—what we have undergone and the arrangements we have made within ourselves in response to our experiences. The Knowing/Feeling domain is like a multiplex system where many signals can be carried on the same wire, traveling in either or both directions simultaneously, a busy venue full of the comings and goings of our pre-symbolic, image-making faculty. It is a bridge between Personal Awareness and the organizing function of thought. In curricular terms, Knowing/Feeling informs humanities programs. At the end of the humanities bridge that touches Personal Awareness, music, graphic arts, poetry, and dance connect the Knowing life, with its source in open-ended Awareness. At the other end of the bridge, Knowing/Feeling joins with the organizing function of Understanding/Thinking. Here the humanities emphasize philosophy (which subsumes science and logic), drama, and literature. For very small children, a concrete Knowing/Feeling curriculum is essential. It helps kids build a rich, imaginative, experiential base from which future development emerges: field trips to neighborhood places (fire-houses, police stations, museums, and post offices), theme-based activities and projects, use of a wide variety of materials and tools (art supplies, blocks, playground equipment, musical instruments), and an appreciation of books.

By itself, the Knowing life would be a bottled-up flood of perceptions with nowhere to go and nothing to inform. This situation might present in students as inattentiveness or extreme distraction. When integrated with the other three organizing structures, it becomes the place where body, mind, and spirit freely cross paths and meld as Soul. It becomes the artist-citizen, the instrument of connection and meaning.

There is limited place for the humanities in our current public school curricula, and this affects the two educations we have discussed so far (Personal Awareness and Knowing/Feeling). This is especially true where the bridge touches Personal Awareness—arts programs are the first to go in a climate of funding cutbacks. We don't recognize Personal Awareness at all. Although many good teachers tap into Personal Awareness intuitively, most do not recognize it as an education, let alone consciously cultivate it or teach it to their students.

Understanding/Thinking

When we cross the bridge from Knowing/Feeling to Understanding/Thinking, we enter the domain that corresponds to Justice in the *Tao Te Ching* reading. It is the task of Understanding/Thinking to interpret and explain life as objects; to make things manifest, ordered, and measurable in both the natural and human sciences. It is a synonym for intellect, ruled by logic, and is thought to reside in the cerebral cortex. It is subject to constantly revising measures and tests. Understanding/Thinking as an organizing structure ("education") comprises and encompasses most of any school's curriculum. When taken by itself and not informed by Personal Awareness via the Knowing/Feeling bridge, Understanding/Thinking reduces all the perceptions flowing from Personal Awareness to testable formulae, or at least to measurable propositions. Any perception that is not amenable is set aside or denied. In other words, the open flow from Personal Awareness may be constricted to a phenomenological dribble. This is what occurs when our materialistic, objective, science-based curriculum acts as a sort of bypass around Knowing/Feeling and leads directly to thinking. If we bypass Plato's life-in-movement antipode and focus only on the idea or form, the form will exclude novelty and become even more static and rigid than it already is because of the exclusion of unacceptable perceptions. Educational systems based on this approach will then produce adequate, sometimes brilliant, technicians, but no truly creative, imaginative minds.

How many scientists, let alone students, can make the imaginative leap that Barbara McClintock did while peering through a microscope and *becoming the process* (Knowing/Feeling) of the chromosomes she was observing (Keller, chs. 7–8)? It was *after* she made this leap that she engaged in the logical structuring of her observations of process and formulated a more comprehensive genetic theory than had previously existed. In its proper place, Understanding/Thinking acts as a follower, not a leader. It performs as a fine recording secretary, keeping the complex record straight, but not predetermining its content. When bridged widely and openly to Personal Awareness via the Knowing life, Understanding/Thinking becomes the agent of great intellectual creativity, exploration, and precision. When Archimedes cried "Eureka!" he was expressing the relief he felt when his Understanding became commensurate with his experience.

Personality

Finally we come to the last bridge from Understanding/Thinking to the education of Personality, which correlates to Ritual in the *Tao Te Ching* verse. Personality behaves, acts out, and determines how we interface with our social context. The personality is made up of the protective and situational characteristics that we fashion to help us cope, and hopefully thrive, with our peers, our superiors and our greater social environment. It is the one element of self that is outside our skins, attached to us like circumscribing weather balloons, bobbing and weaving in response to the human climate.

When Personality becomes dominant or central at the expense of the other three educations, as frequently occurs in our media-driven society, then people feel confused and hollow, falling well short of a sense of accurate and full relationships to others. When personality becomes overblown, a disproportionate *shadow zone* can be formed in the psyche. That is, large sectors of the self, deemed unworthy or unhelpful to the necessities of social interaction, remain embedded and embittered in the soul and are actively, if not consciously, projected onto others. When Personality is underdeveloped, we have all kinds of social friction due to lack of reciprocity and good manners.

Much of teacher training and teaching itself is devoted to Personality display or entertainment, called Communications: we teach teachers to be actors and actresses, as a central means of grabbing and holding attention. We become bobbing objects to each other, each seeking self-esteem, which is a process of settling for a diminished and twisted sense of self that commiserates with the Personalities of others. We deal with each other on the level of behavior, mutually conditioning each other in a gabble of stimulus/response.

Often we model our personality upon others—even upon celebrities—leaving us ignorant of our fuller nature and liable to seek sensation through acting out: We may present as eccentric, crazy, or extremist. These reduced, ritualized responses often lead people to believe that Personality alone is more important than it really is. When Personality is integrated with the other three educations, it becomes an agent of openness, grace, and humor. Good manners and graceful behavior aid and abet the best aspects within us.

If Understanding and Personality are the only faculties emphasized in our schools, then the illusion arises that Personality equates with self, served by the facilitating intellect; this leaves students and teachers feeling empty, bored, and inauthentic.

The four educations, when in full operation, are connected by three reciprocating bridges, mutually informing their constituent parts: Personal Awareness, as it glimpses the Absolute, flows as unjudged perception of phenomena over one bridge to Knowing/Feeling, which then conveys its novel configurations of "life and movement" over a second bridge to Understanding/Thinking. In this model, those configurations are given idea, category, and design so that we can talk about them. Understanding/Thinking then transfers these structures over the third bridge to Personality, which now can take fully informed actions. Conversely, Personality conveys back to Understanding/Thinking the outcomes of interaction, Understanding/Thinking conveys modeled or ordered notions to Knowing/Feeling, which in turn conveys the efficacy or accuracy of any given transaction to Personal Awareness, where it adds to our species' phenomenological storehouse. The emphasis here is on *full operation, alignment, and inclusiveness,* rather than hierarchical levels of importance, which are inherently exclusive. Rendered schematically, the four educations in dynamic full play might look like Figure 1–1.

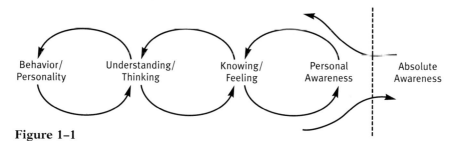

| Behavior/ | Understanding/ | Knowing/ | Personal | Absolute |
| Personality | Thinking | Feeling | Awareness | Awareness |

Figure 1–1

Except in rare places and circumstances, the complete circularity/ reciprocity of all our parts is not in full play in our public schools. Instead, the single bridge between Personality (the behaving body) and Understanding/Thinking (mind) is given most or all of the attention. The rest of our faculties are considered extraneous, even superfluous. Such an absence, such a lack, strikes us as truly depressing.

It is our experience and conviction that education should promote the alignment of and open flow among these four educations in students. In this book we are particularly concerned with serving the Knowing/Feeling life richly, because it is the gateway to Personal Awareness, our human contact with the Absolute, which informs the life of all souls with its infinite abundance. In order to do this, teachers must develop a more inclusive attitude, an effort that often feels awkward and requires openness to students that we are not used to. This effort can make us feel downright scared, especially when we are beginning teachers faced with many other anxiety-producing factors: accountability demands, classroom management, lesson planning, interactions with colleagues and administrators, dealings with parents, and all the rest that makes up a teacher's busy day. A colleague, proofreading this section, said, "I couldn't have done this when I first started teaching; there were just too many practical details that overwhelmed me at first. I was totally concentrated on my performance. It took several years before I felt comfortable with being open to the kids, and I think I am just now, after thirty years of teaching, becoming truly attentive. I like how that attentiveness feels; I was beginning to feel bored with the same old routine, but on the days when I am attentive my lessons are exciting to both the kids and me. The kids are so interesting! I just love them!"

How then, might we put this fear to some sort of positive, robust use? How could we use it to generate an attitude of Attentiveness (a term we use that corresponds with Kindness in the Chinese aphorism), rather than restricting ourselves to punitive Justice responses or, worse yet, resorting to coercive Rituals?

Fear and the Cultivation of Attentiveness

When we started to articulate this topic, we found ourselves harking back to the language of the *Tao Te Ching*, which provided us with a way to talk in more effective terms about the progression of fear toward Attentiveness, and which paralleled the language of our "educations" model. Thus the two discussions (regarding the "educations" and the uses of fear) became subtly linked; the evolution of fear toward Attentiveness takes place in the domain of Kindness, which in turn relates to the Knowing/Feeling education. The following comparison may serve to refresh readers' memories regarding the parallel terminology:

Terms Used in the *Tao Te Ching*	Terms Used to Describe the Four Educations
Goodness (Wakefulness)	Personal Awareness
Kindness (Attentiveness)	Knowing/Feeling
Justice	Understanding/Thinking
Ritual	Personality/Behavior

For the purposes of education, it is desirable to cultivate right-mindedness so that there is an attitude of Fair Play or Justice in the classroom. However, Justice responses can become quite restrictive and punitive ("get thee to the principal's office") if they are not informed by a more capacious attitude. It is in the field of Kindness (parallel to Knowing/Feeling) that early fear evolves in stages toward Attentiveness. Just as the Knowing/Feeling domain of the four "educations" is one of life-in-motion, so the related arena of Kindness/Attentiveness is where fear can morph in a motion of its own toward fearless attention. The stages of this metamorphosis, which we have identified from our own teaching experiences, are as follows.

Wariness: As we first begin to become present to our students and admit their presences to us, we often feel wary. Our fear revolves around dealing with people who function differently than we do and, as our friend commented above, on concerns about our performance. This unfamiliar territory can seem to threaten our authority and make us vulnerable to attack. Those first tentative intentions to become somewhat present to others can be intimidating because of the multi-contextual nature of the Kindness arena; here we can no longer indulge in dismissiveness and other categorical defenses. If looked at from the perspective of the four educations model, wariness is our first encounter with Personal Awareness and teaches us something about it. It shows us what the nature of our contact with all those around us is; that, like it or not, everyone around us is a "neighbor," both on the outside and the inside.

Alertness: As we become more acclimated to those human differences and more confident in the face of the mystery of others, we have less difficulty with Socratic moments. "I don't know" becomes a function of our confidence and newfound alertness and focus. We have become more willing to bypass judgment in order to access perception and seek its accuracy. Rather than startling us, the uniqueness of our students begins to strike us as interesting, even intriguing.

Attentiveness: We begin to vanish as a personality and become more fully present as we disappear into the milieu of others. We become attentive to the actual occasions, as described by Whitehead in *Process and Reality*, to the people who are with us, and we are increasingly more delighted by who they are in their own skins. We do not lose our identity in a morass of collective singularities; on the contrary, we find ourselves in our presence in juxtaposition to the presence of students. In the Attentive state we are relating to others, not as masks and objects, but as I/Thou, or even Thee/I, as Emmanuel Levinas (*Alterity and Transcendence*) would have it. In such relating, we find ourselves in full play, in full motion, in the arena of Kindness. Here we begin to truly *enjoy* ourselves and reverse the process of burnout, or vitiation that normally attends American education. A teacher who achieves Attentiveness stands in the gateway to his or her own Personal Awareness; she or he will not have control problems, because students will answer Attentiveness with their presence. The teacher is there; the students are there. Isolation and a felt lack of authenticity are intolerable to people. We need, we demand, attention to what we are—there is no living without it. Attentiveness brings both attention and the real being behind the attention. Only the more seriously wounded students will not be immediately responsive, but given time, copious amounts of time, they too will begin to thrive. Everyone sits up and takes notice when held in Personal Awareness through the agency of Kindness/Attentiveness.

Just as the beginning teacher typically experiences initial wariness of the unfamiliar beings before him or her, so the children may experience wariness of their new teacher. As Marcia and I were thinking about the behaviors that children demonstrate when they feel threatened and anxious, we began to chuckle a bit about the reactions to anxiety that we have observed in very young children. The behavior of wary little ones is direct, overt, and often contextually comprehensible, which makes it easier to track the evolution of fear in their responses and apply it to what we observe in older students.

For example, when we first started writing this book, we often met at Marcia's home. Her grandson, Noah, was a toddler at the time and sometimes stopped by to visit during our writing sessions. The first time he saw me he stared at my face, burst into tears, buried his face in his father's shoulder and clung to him inconsolably. His father remarked that he had recently done the same thing with another male family friend; the only similarity we could determine was that both of us had mustaches. Noah was not used to seeing mustaches on the faces of his male relatives; they were unfamiliar and he did not have enough information or experience to process "mustache." Crying and clinging to his dad was his wary reaction. At this stage the child may exhibit some overt or distancing behavior that says, "I just can't take this new information in yet; it feels threatening; I need to rely on someone or something safe; I don't trust this situation at all." Older kids might handle this initial fear by putting some distance between themselves and what they experience as threatening, perhaps acting out in class and getting sent to detention where they know the monitor!

As time went on and I kept showing up at Marcia's house, I became a more familiar figure. Noah could see that his dad, mom, grandma and grandpa liked and welcomed me. Although he would stay near his parents while independently playing with his toys, he no longer cried or clung. He maintained his distance, but he was no longer terrified. This is what an alert child looks like; Noah was indicating that he might be able to include this mustachioed adult in his world. Alertness says, "Things seem OK, but I'll just wait a little longer and see if this person remains trustworthy." By this time he was also treating the other family friend in the same manner; Noah wouldn't let the friend hold him, but he would sit quietly near him when he came to dinner. Older kids might maintain a certain reserve with their teacher, but comply with classroom demands.

Noah and I have now arrived at the attentiveness stage with each other and have delightful conversations about his toys, books, and activities. At this point the attentive child is asking, "I want to include this person, but how or in what way?" Marcia reports, for example, that the family friend has become Noah's "train buddy," because they discovered a shared interest in trains of all kinds. They talk about subways and play together on the floor with Thomas the Tank Engine paraphernalia. Whenever his parents have a dinner party he asks, "Is Aaron coming?" At this stage, an elementary- or middle-school-aged child might delight in running errands for her teacher, helping with classroom bulletin boards or seeking out his teacher for help with homework. I have had similar experiences on the journey toward attentiveness with my own grandchildren: For Aidan I am a roughhousing playmate, and for Bella I am a weekly telephone partner with whom she can discuss her activities and talk about her worldview. Just as these small people have found creative ways to include initially unfamiliar adults in their world, so will teachers and older students learn to include each other in lively ways in the classroom by cultivating attentiveness.

Personal Awareness is, in the long run, irresistible, whether it deals softly or toughly, because it is accurate witnessing of others—accurate because judgments are held in abeyance while the actual manifests itself. Kindness/Attentiveness lets others speak for themselves in an attitude that, as it reports outside itself, is also reporting within.

As indicated earlier, we consider that Tao, or Absolute Awareness, is well beyond the parameters of consideration, but the *Tao Te Ching's* Goodness, or Wakefulness, in a teacher is certainly worth the journey through the stages of fear. While the authors of this book make no claim to have traveled extensively on this path, we pose a question: Why not intend to move in the direction of human fullness, trying to become so awake to what we and everyone around us are, that we begin to welcome such an attitude even as such a practice slips beyond description? It is this Wakefulness that we call Personal Awareness.

SPIRITUALITY, PERCEPTION, AND JUDGMENT

When educators speak of spirituality as just one among many elements of the self that needs to be cultivated—among them intellectual, physical, affective, social and moral skills—they are right, insofar as being human involves constant judgments outside the purely perceptual domain of Personal Awareness. Of necessity, our thinking life, our feeling life, and our social life are all exercises of choices, of establishing limits, of curtailing movement. To judge is to exclude this and include that, whereas to perceive is to register what is. Even the effort to exercise unqualified acceptance is an act of the hedging nature of judgment, for example, "you are included because I say so." Perception alone—the function of Personal Awareness—allows us to step beyond the limits of time and space and simply record occasions "as is." It yields a big picture without which living seems boring, redundant, and finally, insufferable.

Why insufferable? We subscribe to an axiom and a corollary with regard to judgment and exclusion: "Everyone is unique, but no one is special" and the corollary, "The root of all evil is exclusion." Marcia made the first observation during a conversation with our friend Joyce Waddell Johnson, who made the second. These canny observations bespeak both the ontology and epistemology of this book: Because judgments are intrinsic to our very nature, we cannot grow beyond our knowledge and the models of our knowledge without the assistance of Personal Awareness. Short of the inevitable relief (both for us and others) granted by our own mortality, in which these limitations are circumscribed biologically, the only education that prevents us from painting ourselves into an exclusionary corner is the cultivation in ourselves and in our students of Personal Awareness. "Seeing, he saw," wrote Aeschylus in admiration. He did not write, "Seeing, he thought," or "Seeing, he felt," or "Seeing, he postured." One cannot convincingly tell a child that she or he is just fine as a judgment call; one *can* tell her or him that she or he is fine as a perception, as happened in the case of Marcia with Melanie. It is in the act of perceiving someone that we register that she or he is fine, not in the act of thinking about that someone. Presence to presence, body to body—you are fine. Almost immediately after birth, people are going to cut us off from unmediated perception and tell us to sit in serried ranks and visit upon us a thousand caveats. Children know when we walk through the door whether or not we are bringing something they can move into. The rest becomes insufferable as their lives stretch out, because there is no substance in it. T. S. Eliot combines the poignant sense of being and nothingness in the perceptions of children in the last seven lines of *Burnt Norton*:

> Sudden in a shaft of sunlight
> Even while the dust moves
> There rises the hidden laughter
> Of children in the foliage
> Quick now, here, now, always—
> Ridiculous the waste sad time
> Stretching before and after.

RESPECT

Most educators in the United States have asserted and agreed at one time or another that we must respect students as individuals, and no small number of these pedagogues suggest that some sort of love should be felt and projected. And, as will be discussed later, without respect and love, an educator is debris in the water. But where does this respect, and its issue, love, come from within the teacher? Can we learn to respect and eventually love our students as behaving organisms, as mental products?

After a somewhat painful evolution, I came to experience my students as young folks with a spiritual core—a body and mind connected to spirit through their souls. I saw the soul in most of my students confounded in various degrees as public schools attempted to divert and even subvert their compelling desire for meaning. I came to thoroughly appreciate Elliot Eisner's observation that "schools are educational churches, and our gods, judging from the altars we build, are economy and efficiency. Hardly a nod is given to the spirit" (p. 97). In another context Eisner wrote, "practical judgments based in ineffable forms of understanding should not be regarded as irrational. It may reflect the highest forms of human rationality"

(p. 365). This observation about rationality merits a lengthy discussion of its own, and is the subject of Chapter 7.

One of several ways I came to think about the word *spirit* was precisely the realm of higher cognition, as yet untreated, undifferentiated and unexplicated by educators. Could there be cognitive stages beyond Piaget's "formal operations," falling outside our cultural norms? Ken Wilbur has called a fifth stage of cognitive development "vision logic," and some of us have referred to it as multicontextualism. How does experience outside of our cultural norms affect attitude? When we have an alert and expansive outlook regarding our students and their possibilities, we feel at once respect, love, and openness toward them, and, in the main, they will respond in kind, both toward each other and toward their teachers. This is in stark contrast to the reductionist, nonexploratory attitude that so many educators have adopted under the rationale of practicality and realism.

Hence, as in Marcia's description of Melanie, attitude quite determines what we experience, how we configure that experience, expectations revolving around what we think people are and what we think we are. *What we make of things* is largely self-fulfilling. As Frank Faber, a master teacher colleague of mine, once remarked, "Your attitude is your life. It doesn't change in or outside the classroom." But, of course, attitude changes as one grows. One of the best criteria I have found in marking what one's attitude is in the present is in Robert L. Fried's book, *The Passionate Teacher*, when he quotes Jay Shapiro's method for defining and exploring one's educational stance:

1. What are the five most important beliefs in my life? What are the ideas and ideals I try my best to live by?
2. What are the five core beliefs I hold about children and adolescents?
3. If I were a boss of the whole school, what words would I like to see greet everyone who entered the building and every student who walks into the classroom?
4. What is it about the subject(s) I teach that connects with my core values and beliefs? Why have I chosen to devote my professional life to this field?
5. What might my students produce or demonstrate to prove to me that they really benefited from my role as teacher?

ATTITUDE AND DESIRE

As you, the teacher, find your vocation in education, your attitude or experience often pivots upon the claims of both the individual and the community. Your autonomy demands independence, individuality, self-development, agency, and even transcendence, while your context seeks inclusion, connection, relationship, and even immanence. Integrating these two desires constitutes a major challenge not only for you, but also for the school in which you work. As community seeks to impose its culture on the generations, you feel the friction as goals, ideals, and experiences imperceptibly shift and change. Education attempts to accommodate this commotion while maintaining correspondence between autonomy and community. Your attitude needs a similar balance and congruence. An attentive and open participation in this dynamic will serve to keep you whole. This book will explore the means of doing this, of following your own path while meeting the needs of a disparate community. How to keep your students' growth alive, keep your own intense need to grow alive, and yet keep alive the spiritual chemistry of groups and community, will serve as an attitudinal *leitmotif* through the topical chapters.

EXCITEMENT

There is for students, and for most of us, nothing comparable to being perceived beneath the level of personality, beneath the level of the behaving body, beneath the level of the contriving mind—to the core wherein the soul resides and the spirit is glimpsed. It is pleasant when our personhood is appreciated, it is fun when our body language is accurately interpreted, and it is stimulating when our mind's thoughts are actually addressed. But it is far more affirmative and exciting than any of the above when our soul's journeying is witnessed attentively, because it is only then that we begin to know who we are. It is only then that we begin to experience the many dimensions of our being. We long for this, we yearn to be so perceived; it is the basis of our desires. If you, as a teacher, can mirror for even one instant the majesty of your students' inmost lives, you will have introduced them to themselves and to the subject matter of their own natures. You will have participated in an excitement like no other. You will have helped bring them to the highest standard—their own legacy of spirit. And this kind of witnessing is conveyed through your experience of yourself and of them as beings—through your attitude. This is what it means to be there for the kids.

CHAPTER TWO

Behavior and Being

The best teachers I have known throughout my years as a student and as a teacher have all shared one characteristic: defiance. They have displayed that plucky, sometimes jaunty, refusal to be anything but true to themselves, true to their inmost lights, true to what they believed is true. No authority, no coercion, no convention could diminish that adamant intent. From day to night, their temperaments differed—some cheerful, some quiet and reserved, some affectionate, some sarcastic, some relentlessly logical, some sour and curmudgeonly. But they all listened within and obeyed their core promptings. They all were profoundly undivertible, and they often were the bane of their superiors' existences. A few were fired, but most were central to the collective spirit of their respective institutions and communities. They were also the ones who grew in an expanding spiral emotionally, intellectually, morally, socially, and spiritually, because when they made mistakes, the mistakes were their own, taken to heart, and then forged into genuine transformation.

DEFIANCE

One of the fundamental jobs of the teacher is to cultivate, model, nurture, and protect this quality of undivertibility, which I call defiance, in their students as well as in themselves, even if it is often directed toward themselves. It is the jaunty, adamant, spirited authenticity of the student that provides the opening to a kind of learning that is central to his or her soul. Books on teaching overflow with caveats and admonitions about dealing with unproductive and antisocial behaviors. Teachers are repeatedly forewarned that these issues loom largest in our day-to-day experiences of the classroom, and that learning cannot occur in an atmosphere of poor control and disorder. But control and order will not be compelling issues in a classroom that speaks to the students' needs to pursue their own journeys and rejoices in their growing ability to do that. If the teacher embodies this stance, control and order will arrange themselves even in very disruptive situations. Like bright pieces of stained glass in a kaleidoscope, scattered energies in the classroom will turn into a symmetry that is unexpected and delightful. To illustrate this point, Marcia told me about the experience of a friend who once taught in a middle school with a large population of students from economically, emotionally, and educationally impoverished backgrounds.

Nina

My friend Nina, a superb teacher of foreign languages, is a person who believes to the depths of her being that there is something decent, affectionate, and teachable in the being of every child, and she is relentless in her attempts to nurture these potentials. Several years ago she was given a class full of kids who had "ability," but who were struggling academically and bordering on failure. Some displayed behaviors that were often quite offensive, to the point of threatening: they were physically and verbally abusive, sassy, disruptive, inattentive. Looking past these behaviors, as she always does, Nina came to the conclusion that although their life problems appeared overwhelming, they were not as intellectually challenged as their bad reputations, labels, and IEPs would lead one to believe. Could she ameliorate any of the environmental problems they struggled with and make some sort of meaningful learning accessible to them? She started going in to school an hour early in the morning and offered tutoring help for unfinished homework. She listened empathetically as they described their home lives: parents working multiple jobs; physical abuse; parental arguments that kept them awake all night; lack of food; undereducated parents who could not help them with their work—the litany of social problems we hear about all too often these days. She began to bring in food, at first only things she could slip into her big purse, like breakfast bars and orange juice. Later she got a school grant to provide more extensive breakfasts (bagels, cream cheese, peanut butter.) She initiated a series of parent-child activities, such as luncheons, orientations, and field trips, which she set up at convenient between-job hours; the parents who attended expressed gratitude that someone was not only caring about their children but doing something constructive to alleviate their stresses. She enlisted the aid of several other teachers to provide extra academic help. She talked to the children constantly about how they could change their self-defeating behaviors and modeled good manners and effective communication for them.

Little by little, her informal program got results: the kids' behavior improved and an orderly classroom came into being of its own accord. Their grades started to climb, sometimes a lot, and they began to express excited interest in a variety of subjects. The food seemed to help them get a better start in the morning because they were no longer trying to do challenging academic work on empty stomachs.

However, there is a down side to this story that all beginning teachers with defiant spirits should take note of. Colleagues complained that Nina's kind of undivertibility set a precedent for taking on additional, noncontractual responsibilities without compensation. They also felt threatened because Nina had developed a rapport with these students to the extent that their behavior was dramatically better in her class than in theirs. Hence, the kids still met with almost daily instances of thoughtless unkindness from staff and students, which undermined their positive, but still fragile behavioral changes. In addition a new administration not only failed to follow through on the enthusiastic support given by the previous one, but actively undermined efforts to improve the program. Although her eventual decision to resign from this position was difficult, Nina felt the changed school situation as an assault on her soul. She did not wish to be "obedient" as a teacher in order to "fit in," as every strategy that she tried to make the program work met with increasing resistance. Sometimes the quality of undiveribility and staying true to oneself will lead to leaving an untenable situation.

When you were a student, did defiance ever dictate your moves, in any manner? As a teacher I became concerned when the soul of a student seemed to capitulate, discarding all of its weapons—disobedience, tricksterism, refusal, mockery, and confrontation, to name just a few. I became worried that this student had begun to trade his or her soul for academic game-playing, bogus negotiation, for a lifetime of roles bearing little or no resemblance to his or her self. I also rejoiced when I caught a glint in the eye of a student, telling me she was alive and well, when I saw her set herself in opposition to my truth with a gaze that said, "So? I'll wait and see." This attitude of defiance ensures that this being—this student or this teacher—intends to follow his or her journey of context, connection, and meaning. Defiance says, "I will not be diverted into believing that disconnection, alien context, and no meaning are real for me. I will not become a shade for anyone or for any collectivity." We may be players strutting upon a stage, but our soul requires that we strut toward spirit.

A SCHOOL IN MOSCOW, 1946–47

In the summer of 1946 when I was eleven years old, my father took our family to Moscow. As the first American cultural attaché to the U.S.S.R., he was charged with the task of cultural and scientific exchanges between the United States and the Soviet Union. Part of his concept of exchange was to enter my nine-year-old sister, Lesley, and me into the Soviet school system. In those times, boys and girls attended separate schools. The only shred of the Russian language Lesley and I possessed was, "I don't understand. I'm an American." Aside from being pelted with spitballs the first morning (this was the first contact for these Russian kids with an evil capitalist, and spitballs were an excellent device to test American mettle), I received nothing but kindness. Within two weeks, Lesley and I could understand most of what was said in class; within three months, we were essentially fluent in Russian, as is standard with most nine- and eleven-year-olds when totally immersed in another language.

My memories of that year frame for me the best school year of my life, before or after. I have been at great pains to account for this, since the physical environment was anything but ideal: the classroom was cold, with discolored peeling paint, the smell of the urinals and toilets wafting down the halls and into the rooms, and the leering smile of Stalin over my teacher's desk. But my teacher, call her Anya, rendered all these disadvantages insignificant. What presence she had! Of medium height, she had wisps of fine, curly, dirty-blond hair that was usually in disarray. Her pale blue eyes looked right at you and into you, and her full, small, round mouth, was nearly always in the shape of amusement. She wore a gray professional uniform that sported two military medals for heroism as a tank driver at the battle of Stalingrad. Always direct, never couched, always feminine, never frail, she conveyed to me a towering figure of intelligence, warmth, and strength. I simply knew I could be myself, and so could everyone else in the class. I once shouted at her, "We don't study Euclidian geometry in the seventh grade in the United States!" "Well," she replied to this interruption, "when do you study Euclid?" "In the tenth grade!" She walked in the studied fashion of a ballet dancer over to my desk, peered closely into my emphatic eyes and said, "Well we do . . . and you will . . . and . . . you will succeed admirably." Instantly I believed her. I had no doubt my awakening brain would follow her, and Euclid, toward mastery of the subject.

Another time, our class was being taught that the United States had been one of several imperialist powers that had invaded the Soviet Union in 1918, but had been driven off by the Red Army in 1921. I stood up abruptly and informed the entire class that this was typical of Communist propaganda; there wasn't a word of truth in it. Anya commented lightly, "Well, perhaps, but why don't you ask your father tonight at home and tell us tomorrow what he said." Of course, my father affirmed the historic fact, and the next day I apologized to the class and to Anya for having spoken out of turn, and erroneously at that. No one acted smug about it, or made me feel foolish, and I was allowed to take responsibility for correcting my own behavior.

Still another time, my ample lunch (a sandwich, apple, and chips) was stolen from inside my desk. The rest of the class was allowed one hard roll at lunch and all the water they could drink as the only refreshment in an eight-hour school day. I reported the theft to Anya, and she announced solemnly, "The lunch will appear in Artur's desk at the end of the day, yes?" And sure enough, there it was at the end of recess that afternoon, untouched. My father scolded me for reporting the theft and I was thereafter allotted one hard roll per day with the others. Anya asked me a few days later, "Are you so very hungry, Artur Amondovitch?" "Yes," I replied, "but so is everyone else." I still remember her wonderful teasing smile.

Whenever the principal came into our classroom, about three times a week, teacher and students stood up respectfully at the side of their desks. The principal would inquire how we were prospering and walked around relating to each student with a marvelous ruffling sort of banter. She seemed a great mountain of a woman who firmly and respectfully adored us. We adored her back. Once, while I was absorbed with my penmanship exercise book, she came up behind me and jiggled my arm so that my pen darted across the page. She looked aghast and shouted to the class, "Good heavens, Mr. Willis made this mess on purpose!" Everyone fell about laughing, while I told her to give me a new exercise book for her naughty behavior. I think we all laughed for some time before Anya brought us back to task. My sister flourished also, and we both started loving school.

We returned to the United States in the fall of 1947 and were enrolled in a middle school in the Midwest. The first day back, my teacher Mrs. Granite (call her that) said, "Arthur, now come up to the front of the room and tell the students about your experience in a communist school," which I gladly did. As I was enthusiastically narrating a heartfelt report, Mrs. Granite interrupted loudly, "Arthur Willis, we will have no such lies in this classroom. Go to the back of the room and put your face to the wall." My shock and hesitation were interpreted as defiance, and Mrs. Granite tugged me angrily to the appointed wall. After this public exposure, I experienced what used to be called "Red baiting" on the way home from school, with kids throwing stones at the "commie," a much harsher rebuke than the Russian spitballs had been. Leaving the "commie school" for my school in the United States was like going from a warm, well-lit place into a dark refrigerator. I soon decided that real defiance would have to replace shock and hesitation. And I realized that, whereas the United States was a political democracy and the Soviet Union a political dictatorship, the United States was a social dictatorship and the Soviet Union a social democracy, at least as far as children were concerned. In high school, I wondered if a society could be a democracy in both areas. Which is more important to a kid—the political or social reality? As a result of negotiating that hostile social reality when I returned from Russia, I began to understand full well the importance of a defiant attitude in its sense of undivertibility, of staying true to myself and to the things that were meaningful to me.

A FUNDAMENTAL DISTINCTION

Looking back as a teacher, one of several lessons that the Russian school taught me was to always distinguish between the being of a student and his behavior. A teacher can be quite within her spiritual and professional right mind to love, hate, be amused by, be angered by, or be shocked by any given student behavior, as long as it is the behavior and not the student herself that is so entertained. "Louise, I think your behavior is really nasty, but (and) I respect you." Opprobrium directed deep into the psyche or at the soul of a student is unloving, unwise, and unwarranted. Rewards and punishments that do not allow for this distinction may *shape* behavior, but will leave everyone involved feeling empty, shallow, and unrelated. The trained bear likes its pleasures, hates its pains, and suffers stupefying boredom at center. Furthermore, many, if not most, American public school strategies for shaping student behavior are oriented toward creating a more efficient, compliant individual who will behave "appropriately." If we ask what purpose these individuals might serve in society, the most obvious answer seems to be that American education aims to turn out productive workers for a competitive, market-driven economic system. This system assesses candidates on their ability to look the part and possess the necessary skills to fill a slot in that system, much as the trained bear is part of his circus.

The problem, which arises from this orientation, is the confusion of behavior with being. We gradually begin to accept these compliant poses as the reality of the student, although they are only masks. One indicator that this confusion has occurred is the use of labels—labeling people in ever more discrete ways and hence, not focusing on the soul-process of each student. As a means of organization and control, labels set each individual apart from others, and engage students in competition with each other toward winning accolades or losing status. In both cases, labels are distractions from seeing and learning what is really going on in each student. "Flake, slow, wise-guy, lazy, disruptive, liar, sneaky, bully, shy, withdrawn, arrogant, geek, nerd, bookworm, manipulative, brown nose, punk"—these are all labels for behaviors unaligned with the soul's process. In the words of Eliot Eisner, "Operationalism and Measurement have focused so heavily on behavior that the quality of the student's experience has generally been ignored or seriously neglected" (p. 361). And when the quality of a student's experience is disregarded, one can expect behaviors that reflect the state of being confounded, often leading to boredom and shame and sometimes, even to violence. On the teacher's side, the use of labels may be convenient projections of their own unaligned soul-process: Whenever we find ourselves assigning labels, whether positive or negative, we should explore how we deal with these issues in ourselves before laying them as burdens on our students.

In my experience, students are largely innocent of the actual sources of their own parboil. Except in rare cases, young people seldom appreciate the one-to-one origin of their souls rubbed wrong. They act out in ways learned throughout childhood from the dynamic of their own unique composite of polar temperamental elements—extraversion/introversion, thinking/feeling, intuition/sensing, judging/perceiving—and from behavior learned from family, friends, and peers. Their displeasure can be expressed in a variety of ways: engaging in covert disruptions, such as whispering to another student when the teacher has required silence; seeking direct attention from the teacher and other students; defending against boredom, tedium, or a feeling of emptiness by creating excitement; seeking confrontation with authority and testing brinkmanship as a cool person in the eyes of peers; and outright avoiding any sort of compliant work, thus escaping any risk of overt failure. Kids are perfectly well aware that they are being disruptive, but seldom have an idea how this disruption is configured within their selves. Their behavior is distinct from their being, but is connected to and revealing of it. Their behavior can cue us to what is going on in their inner world, to the frameworks of the negotiating personality, and to the circumstances in which they and we find ourselves, the class and/or the school climate. In this Case Study, Marcia observes and describes cues in her student Max.

Max

Max was a young man I worked with in an after-school reading/mentoring program for fourth graders. I had been told that he was something of an enigma as a reader: bright with excellent vocabulary and comprehension skills, but unable to decode even the simplest words, a profile not usually associated with poor readers. His behaviors were purported to be difficult and he appeared to challenge authority in a passive-aggressive sort of way. He was taking medication for attention difficulties. There were family problems involving the serious illness of a parent and a second marriage with small half-siblings. Moreover, his inability to read was preventing him from keeping up with the increased academic expectations of fourth grade. When asked how he felt about any of this, Max's gaze would go blank and he would assert that he had no feelings about any of these issues. These bits of personal history, which I gleaned from testing results, parents, and teachers, suggested that Max might be in a high-stress situation with limited positive attention that he couldn't do much about. Any attention he was getting seemed to be based on negative, rather passive, covert behaviors, which helped him to escape from difficult tasks as well as annoy and distance himself from authority figures. Any teacher who has faced this kind of attitude on the part of a student knows how profoundly frustrating it is.

Max made a strong, physical impression on me the first time we met. He was well dressed, neatly groomed, and seemed to take pride in his appearance. He had the shiny clear skin of pre-adolescence and blue-green eyes as deep and old as the sea, but flat and impenetrable as a becalmed ocean is to a stranded sailor. Whenever we made eye contact, his expression seemed to be daring me to dive in and offer myself up as shark food. Deep, chal-

lenging, defiant eyes, but not dead ones. His shiny outward vitality indicated that his spirit was alive and well, but gone deep and defiant.

Several weeks went by. Nothing much occurred in reading improvement and Max's avoidance tactics ruled the sessions: he needed another drink of water; he negotiated who would read each and every paragraph of our shared reading; he needed a pen from his book bag; he fiddled with objects on the table; he insisted on excessive amounts of time to look at the pictures; he was a clock watcher who could mentally reduce a forty-minute period to twenty minutes while he shrugged into his coat and prematurely packed his book bag.

Max was getting to me. In general, I have a good deal of patience with and acceptance of children, but he was pushing my perfectionist, achievement-oriented side toward a judgmental, impatient response to his behaviors. One afternoon I finally turned to him and said, "Max, I drive all the way over here two times a week to read with you. I expect you to use this time productively and to stop fooling around with all these distractions. That's just a waste of my time."

He looked at me with a sparkle of triumph in those jaded eyes and said, "Well, I guess you come over here for nothing, then." This was a moment of opening between us. The gauntlet was down. We were finally engaged. After waiting him out for so long, the challenge became more apparent; he had finally let me hear a crucial piece of information, albeit one girded round by sassiness: "Working with me is a waste of time; I'm a lost cause."

Confronted with the matter-of-fact observation about his avoidant behavior and my continued appearance at the after-school program, Max slowly began to look at words on the page instead of at me or at his fiddling-around objects. We concentrated on looking for repetitive word parts and on reading lists of word stems with different beginning sounds. Soon Max developed an increased repertoire of sight words and his reading fluidity picked up a little.

But he also kept up the challenges, the implicit question being was he worth the trip. Prove it. These continued covert interactions, instead of annoying me any longer, began to strike me as kind of funny and led to the "being strategy" that proved most beneficial in working with Max. One afternoon another mentor saw Max leaving school to get on the early bus. Max also saw the mentor. When he lowered his eyes and kept moving, the

mentor knew Max was skipping out and reported it to our super-
visor, who quickly collared him and brought him to the reading
room. My offended ego was beginning to seethe when suddenly
that moment of Awareness, that great Pause, came over me. I
said to Max, looking him in those sea-green eyes, very matter-of-
factly, "I heard you were trying to skip out of class, but they
caught you before you made the bus." Long pause. Big grin. "But
it was a nice try!" Max's eyes flew open. He gave me a little
acknowledging smile that seemed to say, "She's not mad even
though she knows exactly what I was doing—I didn't get to her."

Another time, in the spring, Max entered the reading room
and refused to return my greeting in what was by this time an
unusual burst of outright surliness. Using my strategy of non-
judgmental forthrightness, I said to him, "Hey, Bud, what did I
ever do to you to deserve that kind of rude treatment?" His
whole body deflated; his head went down; his shoulders
slumped. He said, "You didn't do anything. It's just so hot
today, and I don't feel like reading." "Well, maybe we can solve
some of the problem," I responded. "Let's go in the library
where they have that nice big fan. We'll sit on the floor where
it's cooler and I'll do a big chunk of the reading." We did just
that, and Max was cooperative and did his share of the work
without further complaint. Although a regular classroom situ-
ation might not lend itself to this particular settlement, solu-
tions to problems are sometimes simple when a teacher can
address them on the level of student being, rather than on stu-
dent behavior.

Little by little Max came to understand that I adamantly
refused to identify him with his off-putting behaviors. To the
contrary, I learned how to respond to him attentively, forthright-
ly, humorously, and respectfully in the dynamic of the teacher-
student relationship. Gradually he began to assert his growing
competence in reading and prove to himself how "worth it" he
was.

In Max, Marcia clearly describes the behavioral clues to his means
of processing the world as distinct from his being. Had she spent the
year constantly admonishing Max about his often-frustrating behaviors, instead of directing her attention to the needs of his being, his
manipulations would probably have hardened and he would not have
improved his reading to the degree he did.

WHAT IS GOING ON WITHIN ADOLESCENTS? THE FRAMEWORKS OF THE NEGOTIATING PERSONALITY

By the time children reach the adolescent stage of development, their distinctive behavioral adaptations for managing their worlds are well in place, with little self-awareness of their origins. In his book *The Ego and the Dynamic Ground*, Michael Washburn explores these origins in terms of two powerful anxieties working within the developing self, rather than influences acting from the outside (pp. 98–101, 103). He calls one the anxiety of nothingness and the other the anxiety of guilt. An understanding of how these two anxieties work provides teachers with yet another way to discriminate being from behavior and help us become attentive to our students.

As the result of the rapid rise in adolescence of our sense of who we are (ego self-consciousness), children often feel so confused and anxious about their changing sense of identity that they may experience it as a void, a nothingness. Washburn says, "One way in which the adolescent's anxiety of nothingness is evident is in compulsive internal dialogue. If the mental ego cannot see itself through introspection, it can at least, or so it assumes, *hear* itself." So often and in so many contexts, I have heard students express concern over whether or not it is actually they themselves who did a given act, positive or negative: "Oh man, Mr. Willis, I don't know what got into me (is it myself or am I nothing?) when I did that. What do you think?" They seemed to want me to mirror their internal dialogue (the expression of being) as they did something (the expression of behavior)—and perhaps even justify it, as well.

Washburn says of this internal sense of nothingness as it turns outward into behavior: "The anxiety of nothingness also plays an important role in the adolescent's concern with identity. They are acutely conscious of how they present themselves to others. Adolescents are concerned with these matters, I suggest, because identity recognition carries with it a sense of being. To have a recognized identity is to be something in the eyes of the world" (p. 100). In other words, the adolescent's ego identity, as yet unable to reflect on itself inwardly, likes being seen in its outward projection as validation for its existence. How others see the adolescent strengthens his or her as-yet fragile sense of inner being. For nearly forty years I have observed students collecting around each other to reinforce their shaky sense of being, through being seen by peers and witnessed by trusted adults. It is part of the gaggle of noises in class and hall and cafeteria, indeed, in any locale where teens gather. Their socializing behaviors express an intense need to identify themselves in the matrix of "I am seen; therefore I exist" (Washburn p.100).

In turning away from the conventional world of their parents and other immediate authority figures, Washburn notes that

> Adolescents, then, are prone to experience a sense of guilt, both because they commit an "unjustified" act of turning away from parents and because they divorce themselves from norms of selfhood implicit in the superego, the inner voice of conscience. This sense of guilt is a strong driving force that impels adolescents to search or strive for distinctions that might confer warrant on their existence. Accordingly, adolescents are driven, not only in flight from "nothingness," to forge a sense of being, but also in flight from "guilt," to seek a justification for being. (p. 102)

This flight from guilt takes attitudinal and behavioral forms that are similar to those of the flight from nothingness. Teens use internal dialogue and fantasy scenarios to confirm their value as human beings as well as their existence. According to Washburn their dialogues and fantasies focus on three main themes: their uniqueness and desire to be liked for who they are; their present personal accomplishments, such as being chosen for a part in the class play; and fantasies of an ideal future selfhood when they will, for example, be admired practitioners of their chosen career. This basic need for justification, within a shaky framework of identification toward being, accounts for no little amount of the notoriously irregular behaviors among teenagers. They cannot call up a rationale to defend their internal search for certainty, so they turn to each other and to anyone they feel they can trust.

I am reminded of my sixteen-year-old student Bill who continuously sought me out to discuss his home situation with a tough, critical, dismissive stepfather and whether his behavior toward the man was appropriate. One day he confided, "I hit my stepfather, Mr. Willis, but he was pushing me around and nagging at me about all his rules. I just walked out. Is that OK?" Such confidences may be taken as an expression of the student's inner dialogue and an attempt to hear himself through the teacher's responses. The teacher is sought out as an instrument of self-awareness to affirm the student's experience, and explore ways to handle problems that are not self-destructive. Bill already possessed a good deal of wit and detachment in the situation, so helping him to imagine alternative scenarios for dealing with his difficult stepfather was relatively easy.

From the framework and practice of the educator, *fairness* in these conditions involves a number of dimensions: being able to suffer fools gladly; suspending one's ego in the service of perception; stopping destructive behavior while making it clear how the destroyer may rejoin the group; finding in every student something worthy of respect; learning to convey to these students, in the words of Robert L. Fried, that the "supreme penalty for not learning something should be that one has, in fact, still to learn it, no matter how long it takes" (p. 261). Fay and Funk also write: "Knowing that fair is not equal treatment, but rather, giving what is needed" (p. 101). This kind of fairness is in the spirit of Paulo Freire's observation that education must begin with the solution of the teacher-student contradiction, by reconciling the poles of the contradiction so that both are simultaneously teacher and student (*Pedagogy of the Oppressed*, pp. 73–74) When, as teachers, we are able to give what is needed, as Nina did in the previous example, we reduce the implicit power inequities between teacher and student, while still insisting on academic growth and good manners. When we put the emphasis on being—both the students' and our own—the behaviors follow.

THE CIRCUMSTANCES IN WHICH WE MUTUALLY FIND OURSELVES

But how do we reconcile this student-teacher contradiction, wherein power and prestige largely lie with the teacher, so that, like disgruntled helots, students regularly cast their lot from the various regions of the self against the teacher? There are three orientations possible in a classroom. In his book *Education and Democracy*, Anthony O'Hear argues that learning is not a democratic affair, because the learner lacks what the teacher provides. It is a teacher-centered classroom with the teacher as master and student as dependent. Parker J. Palmer argues that education should be *subject-centered*, wherein teacher and student collaborate in a *community of truth*, an essentially level playing field in which both constituencies labor to discover both the internal and external facts of existence (pp. 99–100). And the holistic movement prefers the *student-* or *child-centered* learning environment, the central purpose of which "is to nourish the growth of every person's intellectual, emotional, social, physical, artistic, and spiritual potentials," according to Aline D. Wolf (p. 47)—the teacher must put herself in the service of her students' unfolding.

In the teacher-centered orientation, students respect the teacher's greater mastery of the content area; for example, a T'ai Chi master enjoys the respectful deportment of his or her students. In the community-based orientation, knowledge itself is the object of respect by teacher and student alike; in other words, the mastery of T'ai Chi is held in high regard by both master and students. In the student-centered orientation, the teacher respects the students as worthy of his complete attention, as when the T'ai Chi master bows to his or her students at the beginning of class because they are the *raison d'etre* for his or her pedagogy.

We believe that these three approaches can be synthesized successfully in the classroom, and if they are, the result is respectful behavior on the part of all constituents. Any deviant behavior then becomes discordantly obvious to anyone involved and tends to correct itself; none of the constituents enjoys discourteous behavior. Likewise, in the absence of synthesis of these three orientations, none of the constituents has an investment in maintaining a graceful alignment of behavior, and Freire's challenge—the solution of the teacher-student contradiction—remains unmet.

And synthesis *is* possible: the three stances are not, as some of their advocates would argue, mutually exclusive. If one's attitude is capacious enough, all three centers can be vibrant lifelines in the cycles of the school year.

Teacher-centered, as the teacher evolves in all the ways he would have his students grow, as she shares her wisdom and experience with them, as she represents elements of both transmission and transformation of culture. The teacher's presence is a mighty and subtle affair, from soul to souls, and requires authenticity and modeling. If students respect and love her back, they are vastly more likely to join Parker Palmer's "community of truth" (pp. 99–106).

Subject-centered, in the words of Parker Palmer: "As we try to understand the subject in the community of truth, we enter into complex patterns of communications—sharing observations, correcting and complementing each other, torn by conflict in this moment and joined by consensus in the next. The community of truth, far from being linear and static and hierarchical is circular, interactive and dynamic" (p. 103). Asymmetric and run by fits and starts, the subject-centered classroom is clearly the community dimension of education. It is one of the fundamental ways in which we honor all the constituencies of the circumstances in which we mutually find ourselves: students, teachers, administrators, parents, board members, and community, and the overarching influences such as media and government. All these are knowers, shaping data around the subject. A subject-centered classroom can thrill every participant with the possibility of relationship, connection, and meaning, and help us define our respective journeys.

Child-centered classrooms are paradoxically the most common and the most rare of the centers in our experience. They are common in the sense that we are constantly enjoined to practice cooperative learning; to be aware of students' rights and our subsequent liabilities; to heed the learning styles of all students, as indicated by such educators as Howard Gardiner, Grant Wiggens, and Alfie Kohn; and to bring each student's learning up to a standard dictated by school board, state, and national governments. Simultaneously, they are rare, in the sense that the models we use for the psychology of child development, as indicated in Chapter 1, are inadequate. Behaviorism, cognitive constructivism, and social constructivism, taken separately or together, add little to seeing the whole child. And these are the models most schools of education project on their teachers-in-training. If student teachers, in addition to cultivating their own nascent talent for seeing, were trained in the works of A. N. Whitehead, Carl Jung, A. H. Almaas, Ken Wilber, Stanislav Grof, Rudolph Steiner, Ron Miller, Maria Montessori, and many other explorers of a broader developmental psychology, our student centers would come alive. Our pupils would display increased vitality as they responded to the excitement of being perceived as actually possessing souls and bodies, and reflecting universal spirit. Ken Wilber defines this universal spirit in terms of higher states of cognition, which he calls "vision logic" or "multicontextualism," beyond the present orthodox views of cognitive psychology. Our accuracy and our arena of perception would be improved as we were able to see the I and the We and the It and the They of each student. What are the circumstances in which we, students and teachers, find ourselves interacting and hence behaving? We propose three elements that determine these circumstances:

1. The constituencies of students, teachers, administrators, school board members, parents, immediate community, colleges of education, media, and local-state-national governments are configured to and interact in the overall scheme of things that constitute your school.
2. The typical mixes of teacher-centered, subject-centered, and child-centered classrooms in your school.
3. The re-inventions, if any, that are occurring in the United States and in your locale as you enter teaching. Is your school actually and consistently trying to reinvent itself, as the media periodically announce? Or is it simply buzzing around, endlessly retranslating Frederick W. Taylor's *Principles of Scientific Management*, in which students continue to be regarded as products nudged toward efficiency in the marketplace?

These circumstances in which we find ourselves underlie a variety of behaviors from all the constituencies, which may range from complacency to consternation. None of these behaviors should deter us from integrating the three orientations operating in the classroom.

DISCIPLINE AS ENTHUSIASM

Larry Tift, John Sullivan, and Dennis Sullivan, in their *Entry in the Recent Discussion on the Moral Development of Children* (1997), remind us compellingly of the relationship of behaviors to the external world in which we live: "Character means responding to the world without controlling others and not allowing oneself to be controlled by others" (pp. 13–14). This is indeed what constitutes the practice of *satyagraha*. The person who practices satyagraha "lives according to his or her own lights" and does not cooperate with what seems wrong. It entails attempting "to accept whatever may be right and just" in the views and actions of those with whom one disagrees" (pp. 13–14).

The authors continue by linking behavior directly to the inmost motivation of the soul, saying that compliance dictated from the outside kills that part of the self that yearns for connection with the external world and with other people. They call this desire for connection an "enthusiasm" so strong that it promotes self-discipline, that is, discipline from the inside out. Self-discipline is constantly created and nourished through full participation in a process that honors the needs of both individuals and community.

In my first thirty-five years of teaching, I never had occasion to remove a student from class, because I never experienced someone so destroyed in that part of the self to justify ejection. In my thirty-sixth year, I did remove five students for showing disrespect to a visiting Mexican educator. At the end of class, they appeared at the classroom door, shamefaced and apologetic, indicating that it had not occurred to them that our Mexican friend was connected to them. With that understanding, they offered a sincere apology, and it was sincerely accepted.

Tift, Sullivan, and Sullivan establish a bridge between *entheos* and self-discipline: "If we wish children to develop moral character and self-control, that is, a sense of self that is autonomous, yet inseparable from the feelings, ideas, and needs of others, children must value the social world in which they live and interact" (pp. 13–14). Reciprocally, children must experience membership in a community that is just; a community in which everyone, the young and the old alike, join together in creating patterns of interaction and in defining and responding to the problems that arise in their shared life (pp. 13–14).

It is through membership in such a participatory community, one in which the needs of all are taken into account, that the young can experience that part of themselves that Ralph Waldo Emerson described as "the active soul." Given birth in community, "the eyes of the spirit would become one with the eyes of the body, and god would be in us, not outside. God in us, *entheos*; enthusiasm. . . . " (pp. 13–14).

SHADOW ZONE

One of Carl Jung's many outstanding contributions to developmental psychology is the theory of *the shadow*, a place in our psyche where we obscure those traits and behaviors that we find most alien to our waking identity. These traits and behaviors lurk in the lunar-like darkness of our personal dungeons, and like unwelcome inmates are largely forgotten, until we encounter the same traits and behaviors in another, whereupon we project (cast) our shadow on him, or her, or them, oblivious to our own self-division and estrangement. While I have not yet read of this singularly common phenomenon in any literature concerning the "reflective practitioner," a clear knowledge of one's own shadow zone is indispensable to getting to know one's self as a teacher. Most teachers I have known, including myself, will defend to the utmost their inalienable right to their own alienation. Our projections are often our dearest and nearest rights.

Several years ago, I was criticizing a student (behind his back) to a fellow teacher and friend who responded as a true dialectical comrade: "You tend to not appreciate talkative, social kids," he said. "You like the sensitive, intellectual types, and tend to be put off by extraverted, outgoing students whose first priority is to noisily relate to others." His comment had about it "the tap of sanity," as Mary Oliver wrote. I saw at once, and more lucidly than I would wish, the truth of his statement. The pain of it set me working on that previously twilight attitude to bring it to the light of Awareness. Apparently, I was not so very fond of my noisy, social self. How does one come to self-knowledge and hence into an expanding attitude of greater tolerance and accommodation? We can only contain the *entheos* (and the behaviors which emerge from that *entheos*) of each student if we acknowledge our own shadow zone.

BEING AND THE BEHAVIOR OF ATTENTION

The recurring theme of this chapter has been the differentiation of behavior from being. Using our own experiences and those of our colleagues, we have attempted to illustrate how effective relationships with students come about when "attentiveness to what is needed" is brought to bear in teaching situations. This effort helps us place student behavior in a broader context so that we can go out to meet the souls—the tripartite natures, the true selves—of the youngsters we teach. Furthermore, the greater the depth of reflection we bring to our own being, the fewer judgmental projections we will make on our students. When behavior becomes *aligned behavior* by means of an attentive attitude, it supports the beings of everyone in the educational environment. As discussed in Chapter I, alignment means that the bridges between Awareness and personality are open and functional.

It is the perspective of this book that a healthy, whole human being functions in a fluid four-fold process: personality reflects what behavior absorbs from understanding; understanding formulates what thinking delineates from knowing; knowing configures what feeling discriminates from personal awareness of actual occasions. If these four parts are in alignment, constantly oscillating like the movements of respiration, we humans behave well because our total being is accurately reflected in the doings of our personality. Our understanding and its thinking, our knowledge and its feeling, and our personal awareness with its connection to Awareness are played out faithfully by our behaving personality.

But personality rarely shows such congruence with thinking, feeling and personal awareness. Much of the time we are at a loss to behave "correctly" because we are disconnected from our other faculties. If students are interpreted solely on the basis of their behavioral incongruity, they are not only misinterpreted, but they are also taken as vastly less than they are. The tail does not wag the dog. But unlike dogs, we humans can demonstrate exceptionally ambiguous behavior. Body language in dogs is a good indicator of the feeling content of the dogs. However, in human students the behaving personality is capable of remarkable dissimulation.

For the teacher, it is essential for her to become attentive to all four faculties in her students. She must cultivate her own awareness of each student, she must allow her feeling to expand out through awareness and translate that discrimination into real knowledge of her students, she must move her thinking toward a proper understanding of how those students actually function, and she must be unimpressed by the urgencies of behavioral postures. The collage that comprises each student will then compel her attention.

Students, reciprocally, have a powerful need for their teachers to experience them as whole beings: as beings with a vast reach of Awareness; an intense but not refined feeling life; a vivid, if unrefined, thinking life; and a typological behavioral life not yet discriminated into a complete personality. The teacher is by necessity the person who will have to lead the way and model this behavior of attentiveness to all four faculties. In so doing he or she will synthesize the child-, subject-, and teacher-centered classrooms.

At the end of this chapter we are left with the question: How do I become attentive and aligned in my own behavior and how do I model this process for students? In the next chapters we will discuss some approaches that we have used to help ourselves and our students develop this behavior of attentiveness.

CHAPTER THREE

Teaching and Thuggery

The extreme dark side of behavior often reflects the afflicted side of being. No matter where we choose to teach or learn, some behaviors are much more immediately threatening than others, to the point of being thuggery, and we inevitably must face our own fears when we confront them. Thuggery encompasses behaviors that reflect a confounded spirit and a wounded feeling life, working through an understanding that is militant and constricted. Though all students may at times exhibit behaviors of the type discussed in the last chapter, some require more than the consistent respectful attentiveness of the teacher to reach them. The behaviors of these "hard-case" students do not reflect the centrality of a human being's soul, but those who behave in this extreme way wish us ill and intend to do something about it. Sometimes we encounter hard cases that are other teachers. In these situations, it is valid to feel afraid.

At base, problems of ill will are problems of control. Thugs, be they teacher thugs or student thugs, use fear as their central means of intimidation. They know and understand the world in terms of power and control. To thugs, either you are in control or they are. We use the plural here, because thuggery functions through networking in numbers. The lone thug is better understood as a bully whose bullying is curtailed by lack of means for a protracted siege; serious thugs need cohorts.

We have identified five genera of thugs, derived from composite portraits of students we have encountered, whose native habitats have as much to do with socioeconomic class as with habit. There are as many species of malice within each genus as there are locales to produce variants. But when people play the power game, variation is primarily of interest to the sociologist and anthropologist. For our purposes, it is enough to identify each genus of thuggery and penetrate the internal dynamic, in order to cope and work with it in a manner that corresponds to our philosophy. This dynamic is projected in terms of our criteria in Chapter 1: Personality/Behavior, Understanding/Thinking, Knowing/Feeling, and Awareness/Perception. In most cases of thuggery, one or more of the educations is underdeveloped (rather than merely out of alignment) in the self, and is asking to be helped.

The immediate threat of these behaviors in no way obviates an attitude of alertness turning to attentiveness, whether one is dealing with gang membership in city schools or the sociopathic memberships that form in elite private schools. It still behooves us to become attentive to the beings of these students with every expectation that this attentive attitude will eventually find its mark in their hearts. In addition, particular scrutiny should be directed to the *quality* of attentiveness brought to bear in each case cited. In Chapter 9 we elucidate our responses to fear, ranging from a ritual response to a justice response to an evolving gamut of alertness toward attentiveness. Ritual responses to thuggery are not only inept, but often tragic. Justice responses to thuggery are ineffective in the long run. But attentiveness responses to thuggery frequently succeed.

THE URBAN THUG AND THE RURAL THUG

Lester

As the third child of six kids in an African American family on the south side of Chicago, fourteen-year-old Lester knew all about the streets. He had seen his eldest brother shot dead in a vacant lot while trying to exchange bogus gems for cocaine. Lester was tall and muscular for his age, but he did not participate in school sports. Instead, he and his friends used their energy to plunder hall and gym lockers and sometimes steal from teachers' desks. Lester and his gang were known as people to avoid by all the students and teachers in the school, except for Mrs. Jackson, his English teacher, who had remained with him since he was left back to repeat sixth grade.

Mrs. Jackson was his eighth-grade core teacher, and she connected with Lester on the basis of a shared interest in snakes. Mrs. Jackson became for Lester a kind of female Steve Irwin, the great Australian naturalist and educator, whose illustrated books she shared with him. They would take regular trips to the Brookfield Zoo on weekends, where Lester particularly liked the serpentarium: "Everyone hates snakes, just like they hate me," he once observed to Mrs. Jackson, thus giving her a direct insight into the state of his being. The zoo was Lester's only contact with wildlife; he felt caged, too, and lashed out against anyone he deemed threatening. Just as Steve Irwin had caught poisonous snakes around the world and resettled them in less threatening environments, Mrs. Jackson let her charge know that she would remain with him until they could find a happier place for Lester, the caged snake. He began to see her as a friend he could trust—she understood snakes, thus she understood Lester.

Louis

Fifteen-year-old Louis knew firsthand how important it was to stay on the good side of his tenant-farmer father. Louis's mother had run off when his father had insisted that the whole family eat only popcorn and venison, which his father provided during the winter, because they had very little money for groceries. His dad wasn't about to accept "no damn handouts from anyone, including food stamps"—they could damn well eat what he provided. "Good enough for you pigs," he would say, then kick over a chair if anyone appeared to disagree. His father hit anyone in the family who fell out of his good graces.

At school Louis had collected a tough bunch of pals who extorted lunch money from younger and weaker kids. Like his father, Louis planned to quit school as soon as he turned sixteen and maybe enlist in the army. He was a good shot in the woods and got some fun out of bringing in dead squirrels and rabbits and placing them in surprising locations around the school, especially in the cafeteria. Most students were afraid of him, and most teachers were waiting for Louis to leave school someday.

One day Doris, a teacher aide, brought in a cookbook entitled Cooking Wild Game *and showed it to Louis. "We can cook up just about anything you bring in, Louis," she said. Despite laughter from his tough buddies (no one could prove Louis had brought in those mutilated animals), and although he turned red from embarrassment, she sat down next to him, went through some recipes in his full view, and offered to work with him on preparing tasty wild game. All the while she pretended to be oblivious to his blushing, which no one had witnessed before. Luckily, the principal understood what Doris was doing.*

In terms of the criteria presented in Chapter 1, both of the urban and rural thugs described above have energetic, developed Personalities and broad contact with Awareness. In the streets and in the outback, there is sufficient stimulation to cause even the most obtuse to take notice, to become *gewaer*, or wary, of dangers, excitements and myriad activities. The speed with which this Awareness advances is commensurate with the mysteries and menaces found out there. Personality is challenged to survive these perceptions in a flexible and necessarily amoral manner.

The presentiments of the Personality have little latitude for error: Is the wagging, snarling dog going for my leg, my hand, or my throat? Are those guys going to cross the street and intercept me in the alleyway? The life of the mind and my feeling life, my judgments, and my considered opinion, are utterly subordinate to the workings of my Personality as it absorbs the details and patterns of the environment. There is a will to survive, even though there may not be a belief in the enduring quality of that desire, and so I coordinate my wariness with a developing alertness, which is necessary to secure my immediate safety. I join a gang; they can protect me to some degree. I hive with my clan; they will protect me but also destroy me both within and without, by subjecting me to harassment or assigning me dangerous tasks. Others, who are found at school, on the streets, or in the woods, simply don't matter and have no connection to me. They can and will be controlled, exploited, and defended against. The police label me, both as what I am and what I am not. They control, we control—the devil take anyone else. Family not only can't protect me, but they might be and often are direct threats in themselves.

The urban and rural thugs, while initially presenting the most daunting experience for young teachers, are actually the easiest to serve in the long term. Lacking anything resembling a larger Understanding and a greater Knowing, they crave the benefits of a feeling and thinking life. Because such possibilities are first perceived as increasing their chances of survival and gaining control over their circumstances, the promise of a full Understanding of how things work, and of a Knowing that includes all experiences, are inducements that the urban and rural thugs cannot resist. The perceptual hookup to Awareness is already present for them as they reach out to the teacher's offering of the methods of Understanding and the connections of Knowing. The teacher's job is to help these students to connect their already formidable Awareness with their undeveloped feeling life. If you can do this—that is, bring their judgment functions of thought and feeling into a stage of development comparable to their perceptual functions of sensation and intuition—you will have students who will thrive and produce a rigor of scholarship difficult to duplicate elsewhere.

Mrs. Jackson made a decision to remain with Lester for a sufficient duration so she could witness how he thought of himself and what his family situation was, and thus she became attentive to his actual needs. She helped connect his feelings with his understanding by linking his appreciation for the threatened situation of snakes with their resettlement into a safer environment. By doing this, she helped him become conscious of the projection of his own situation onto snakes and held out the same possibilities for Lester to change his life. Eventually, with a recommendation from Mrs. Jackson, Lester got a job at a local animal shelter, and then an internship at the zoo; he began to pay attention to his schoolwork and got himself off the streets for good. His performance in these positions was exemplary and his mentors at the zoo helped him find scholarships to attend the state university. Lester is now a graduate student in ecology and environmental studies, and Mrs. Jackson reports that he still contacts her regularly via e-mail.

Likewise, Doris accurately observed a pattern of behavior in Louis that reflected his background and strengths, and then helped him connect these strengths with new possibilities. Through Doris' direction, Louis was able to coordinate with the local BOCES cooking classes and learn more about the preparation of wild game. Louis began to see the possibilities of a vocation oriented around a specialty, which was charged with significance for him. Both Mrs. Jackson and Doris acted out of attention to each boy's being, rather than using ritual or justice responses to behavior.

My own experiences with these students began in the late 1950s, when I was challenged by a group of fraternity brothers to practice what I was preaching. I sought out a middle school in South Chicago and asked the principal to let me start a basketball team for his hardest cases—mostly African American, eighth-grade boys. I met with them on the playground for a couple of days at lunchtime and we circled each other like sparring partners. I was beaned by the basketball several times, and I returned the favor, but we also exchanged ideas about basketball, about my university life, about my family, about their school, and about their family and friends. I wasn't so much afraid at this point as I was eager to "mix it up" and get the kids involved in activities in which they already had an interest. I began to come to their school on Saturday mornings, collect the willing (about fifteen students in all), and travel on the subway to a gym at a Presbyterian church. We gradually put together a formidable basketball team, but it was in the process of exchanging ideas and sharing feelings, that thugs were turned into thinkers. It was beautiful to behold.

At about the same time in my life, at Bear Mountain State Park, I watched a camp director essentially turn thugs into complete human beings through an attentiveness on his part to the Being in each of his charges, both boys and girls. Daughters and sons of prostitutes and criminals, they came to know their own feelings and develop their thinking lives through interacting with him. His strict discipline (no swearing, no tardiness to any camp function, cleanliness) was made effective by his constant attention to everyone in camp. How can this be done with fifty children by one teacher? I watched him as we gathered around the dining-hall table and he yelled out encouragement and admonishment to the kids: "Celia, that's fantastic, how did you manage to hit the target with that arrow, it was so far away?" "Logan, how will you ever get clean after you've rolled in all that dirt?" "Gloria, help Louise string up that net!" He was up and down in his seat without ever losing the thread of our conversation, while the kids were grinning, laughing, and eagerly participating in various activities.

By intending to be Aware of each child, you will be; by allowing yourself to enjoy the play of this attention, you will be energized— not enervated—by the activity of your own perception. If your judgments (your thinking and feeling) are not allowed to tell you otherwise, you will come to thrive in such a place, where you can help so many young people come to find their own souls and minds. This camp director accurately saw his campers, and they accurately perceived that he did. This clear, unobstructed attentiveness circulates and is contagious; it is a loving action no matter what the bark or bite.

Try to remember a time in your life when you felt your soul benumbed and your mind in service to your personality. You will then know what it feels like to be a thug—aware, but blank, an actor on cloven hooves. And then try to remember how exciting it was to fill in the blanks. James Garbarino feels that the mere access to material well-being cannot stabilize violent boys, "but a sense of meaningfulness rooted in higher purpose and a more enduring reality can" (p. 152). To harness this force they must come to experience their own feelings as the conduit between their nonjudging perception (Awareness) and their thoughts. In so doing, they find a way that envelops the conditioned and deterministic paths they have hitherto been traveling. Shame, anger, revenge—thuggery—will in time be seen as energies that are not worth the bother in their expanded view of the human journey.

SUBURBAN THUGS

Michael

Sixteen-year-old Michael was drawn to gatherings of his cohorts in the tenth-grade wing of a suburban high school where, together, they would ogle girls and harass nerds. He learned that his blond, six-foot frame could both thrill and scare females, and about which nerds would try to join his power group, and which ones avoided them like the plague. Male teachers were greeted with, "Yo, Mr. Turner, how goes it, man!" while female teachers were swept with what were meant to be suggestive glances. Michael and his group planned to go to college, of course, because "that is where the babes are, and how else do you get a good job and make big bucks?" He studied, lightly, for Cs and Bs and a good junior college, so he might later gain admission to a decent four-year school. "You're either a winner or a loser," he and his group all agreed. They intended to be the former.

Mr. Ricelli, Michael's global studies teacher, helped Michael know that there are abundant other ways to feel than the fleeting satisfaction of intimidating girls or playing superior to other boys. Mr. Ricelli's passion for graphic arts in particular and humanities in general served as his vehicle to introduce students to a feeling life that was vastly greater than thug assemblies in the hall. He routinely talked with students about any humanities topic—Renoir, Sartre, Charlie Parker, Kline, Whitman, and so on. Michael was much taken with Mr. Ricelli's many introductions to a seemingly endless array of fascinating artists. Michael couldn't help being drawn toward his nascent interests and jumped into discussions about Socrates'

statement "I know nothing," as readily as he entered into bait-
ing nerds.

One day, Mr. Ricelli suggested that Michael might want to go
next year during the winter break on an art history trip to Flo-
rence. Could Michael afford it? Could Mr. Ricelli help? Mr. Ricel-
li was at once attentive to Michael's intellectual and aesthetic
proclivities and to his need for an experience well outside his
own cultural context, with which to contrast his own environ-
ment. There is life outside the suburban cohort.

The suburban thug is at a greater remove from his roots than either the
urban or rural thug, and hence represents a greater challenge for the
empathic teacher. Whereas the urban or rural thug displays an immediate threat, they do possess experiences of nonjudgmental perception
to which they owe their immediate survival. Through Awareness, the
urban or rural thug has at least an accurate read on what is going on in
the byways. The suburban thug often has no ready reference to such
bodily and environmental peril, and is, on the contrary, often effectively protected against the exigencies of gangs, compulsory felonies, and
abandoning families. Savvy deportment and well-trained minds are frequently cultivated in these kids early on, in the service of incipient pro-
fessionalism, but often at the expense of the development of their
feeling lives and their connecting souls.

Suburban thugs come to believe that they are—in combination
with their highly accented minds and personalities—very important.
The self-esteem they develop is shallow, naïve, and provincial—a pride
in nothing substantial. Indeed, suburban communities are often not
communities at all, but rather housing for socially and materially
ambitious people. And the toxicity here does not even contain the benefits of shocks to Awareness, or the cultivation of a discerning aesthetic. Lacking a cultivated feeling life with which to hone their
perceptions, suburban thugs are left clueless to the ineffectuality of
their actual powers. They become susceptible to predation by both the
lower- and upper-class thugs. Without the enhancements of Awareness
and Soul, the domains of Understanding and Personality, they are left
to their own devices and can become every bit as alienated as the
urban or rural thugs, except that in suburbia, we must add boredom
and illusion to the equation.

Lacking a soulful feeling life, the suburban thug has no way to
connect to Awareness, his or her primary legacy. A savvy Persona leads
to its own kind of despair. And so it behooves the effective teacher to

introduce *sensibility* to the sense of suburban anomie or disconnection. Close attention to the thug's dimly experienced aesthetics is the
most helpful here. A curriculum rich in humanities and arts would be
a tremendous boost, along with excursions into developing personal
philosophy and poetry, so that philosophy might link thinking with
feeling, and poetry might link feeling with thinking. Actually, any ideas
and any poetry would help, because the suburban thug, except
through the use of hallucinogens, is utterly unaware of "the doors of
perception." Note the progression: *thinking* they *know*, they do not
know (experience) Awareness, and hence have no notion of humility
of mind and openness of heart. Their feeling life flounders in a false
sense of security based on being surrounded by like minds and personalities, to which their conformity is nearly total. Their felt emptiness is often projected as mockery of any sensibility or aesthetic
divergent from their behaving thoughts.

Thus deprived of essential human empathy, they take refuge in
unfeeling behaviors, which, if less directly menacing than their urban
or rural counterparts, are punishing and reboant in the subtle and
destructive effects they have on an open learning environment.
These thugs, above all, need to develop the "rationality of the feeling
life," discussed at length in Chapter 7. They need what they are
attempting to deprive others of, namely the ways and means of
exploring an unfolding life of the heart. They want a soul, their very
own souls, so that the larger life they instinctively sense can be tied
to operations of thought and persona, so that their egos might have
passion, instead of robotic summation. If teachers can help them
find their way into the unembarrassed contents of their feeling lives,
they will begin to forgo jackassing and mockery for the greater
promise of actual meaning. They will begin to surprise and delight
themselves with their own realizations and expressions, well beyond
the purview of their previous assumptions.

These middle- and upper-middle-class kids represent the hopes
and fears of their families. These families, these communities, and
these kids reduce their own nature to what they understand as the Big
Two, clever minds and competitive personalities, and thus deprive
themselves of a large feeling life and ready access to Awareness. In
these conditions, the *compleat* teacher is, of necessity, at odds with the
community if she or he wishes to develop a knowing sensibility in her
or his charges. Go ahead! Be at odds! The families and communities
won't resist your efforts, because your thuggish students will begin to
shed their unconscious bitterness.

ELITE THUGS

Bonnie

Eighteen-year-old Bonnie, vivacious and attractive, had a secret that she shared with no one at her all-female boarding school. If she couldn't have an affect on her powerful parents, she could certainly find the means to have an influence over future arrangements. She had traveled extensively to Brazil, France, England, and Australia. And her well-connected mother and father had shown her the value of who you know, in contrast with what you know. Her mother seemed particularly skilled in making people notice her entrances and exits during social occasions. Bonnie was her observant daughter and was expert in the art of seduction. No young man had yet proven worthy of her, socially or sexually. She enjoyed shaming any peer audacious enough to challenge her supremacy as leader and trendsetter in her circle, aided and abetted by a chorus of admiring girlfriends. Even faculty members were daunted by her considerable manipulative skills. On occasion, when she felt rather empty, she indulged in instant spiritual trips conveyed by peyote buttons and sometimes LSD.

Bonnie's spring challenge was Andrew, her comparative literature teacher, toward whom she began to direct all her powers of empathy, analysis, and charm. Andrew observed her efforts, but rose to the challenge: he sought ways to divert her sexuality into more spiritual directions, while at the same time not making her feel spurned or rejected. For Andrew, Bonnie was a reclamation project of sorts, and the opposite of a sexual diversion.

Andrew began by encouraging Bonnie to attend an IONS colloquium at the Institute of Noetic Sciences, founded by Edgar Mitchell after his space flight, dealing with the nature of philanthropy. There she would meet people who would not be easily impressed or suborned by her ego power, and who were primarily concerned with personal and collective growth.

But by far the best card up Andrew's sleeve was his friendship with a great soul, Maya Angelou. In the late spring of her senior year, Bonnie spent an intense and memorable evening with Maya and Andrew at his faculty apartment, where they discussed whatever was prompted by Bonnie's feelings and thoughts. She experienced the first inkling of intelligent exchanges that were more satisfying than the pleasures of con-

trolling others, and her first experience of being seen as a soul by the souls of others. Andrew became her mentor, rather than her intended, subordinated lover.

Even though the elite thug is sometimes stamped *preppie,* she or he seems to be the only thug respected by all other groups of thugs, if grudgingly. If this is true, perhaps it is in part because of the greater development of faculties that is offered to these elite members. Elite private schools tend to acknowledge all four educations, and considerable effort is given to the cultivation of Personality, Understanding, Knowing, and Awareness. Service to and hegemony over society are the underlying suppositions of an upper-class education. It is expected that graduates will benignly rule.

The elite thug is intoxicated by a power trip in which Knowing, Understanding, and Personality are used to manipulate and control others. There is a psychopathic quality to this particular kind of thuggery, with narcissism at its core. The elite thug uses her or his highly developed knowing life to anticipate the feelings of others, the better to manipulate them; her or his intellect to accurately analyze the circumstances of others, the better to manipulate them to her or his own interests; and her or his facile and flexible persona to charm others into her or his control. Their own power, prestige, and property are their only real concern, rather than advancement of the well-being of others. This condition of expert self-service is a tough nut to crack, and we have very few, if any, ready answers.

Because these thugs are so charming, intelligent, and copacetic, they appear to pose no menace whatsoever; but, in fact, they are the most threatening of all thugs if crossed or effectively confronted, because they have the greatest access and reference to the powers of their own natures. About the only way one could nudge them away from narcissism and beyond their own power-frame would be to expose them to a greater Awareness, exemplified by people who are of great service, who are luminaries and extraordinary souls. Direct introduction to such people is the most effective detoxificant; indirect studies of exemplary Awareness, through books, for example, is the second best method. For example, in the infamous 1920s murder of Bobby Frank at the hands of Leopold and Loeb, two elite, wealthy, university students, Leopold was deeply influenced by Loeb in partnering this crime. Later Leopold was profoundly transformed through his connections with the crimiologist Bill Byron and his defense lawyer, Clarence Darrow, who saved him from the death penalty by making a plea for a possible rehabilitation. Leopold was eventually released from prison after he had reorganized the entire Illinois prison system library, an effort that had given his life a meaninful purpose. After his release, he went to Puerto Rico, where he set up a similarly enlightened library system. Unfortunately, a similar result did not occur for Loeb, who was killed during a prison brawl. The elite thug benefits most from direct and authentic experiences with individuals who personify an integration of Awareness, Knowing, Understanding, and Personality. Lacking these models, the upper-class thug seems little susceptible to her or his own integration.

THE EDUCATOR THUG

George

George, a twenty-year survivor of teaching earth science and biology, also had secrets he never shared: control of one's students was all that mattered in education; administrators cared most about being left undisturbed and with an intact illusion of their own importance; sarcasm, unpredictability, or mystery kept both contingents at bay; each person is fundamentally self-centered and self-serving. He certainly didn't commence his career with these attitudes, instead beginning with what he later called profoundly naïve notions: that all kids are curious and eager to learn and need only attentive and mature guidance, and that one's colleagues and superiors, while uneven in performance, are sincere educators doing their best for all concerned. "Hah," he would occasionally divulge to his department chairperson, "imagine such ideas!" They would both have a good chuckle. George became a master at enlisting cynical assistance from colleagues through sarcasm and dismissive comments on both students and recalcitrant faculty.

George's reserved manner and quietly scathing humor kept the vast majority of potential adversaries at a safe distance. "Intimations of fear and intimidation are what motivate most folks," he told himself (he had read Wordsworth). "Education has nothing to do with learning and collegiality."

Why is George a teacher if he doesn't like kids? He is not secure and he is looking for surcease from anxiety through control. His obvious disillusionment with administrators, due to having been "shot down" in his earlier, creative days and told to go back to the classroom and keep the kids under control, would seem to be a disincentive for remaining in education. He hasn't departed because what he is doing and the role he is playing are working. He has learned to intimidate kids, with the help of similarly obnoxious colleagues. Together they agree that we need, consistently and uniformly, to enforce the rules. These teachers, like younger thugs, work in groups. They may resemble a good team, but the students, their charges, are perceived as the enemy.

Marjorie, an algebra and calculus teacher, gradually and perhaps inadvertently helped George to see otherwise—she was direct, curious, and somewhat prone to letting her feelings show. George had initially tried to help her protect herself against students and faculty. "Don't be so open with everyone, Marjorie. Don't let people see how you feel and think. They'll cut your legs off." In the faculty room, he called her Ms. Pollyanna, but somehow didn't enjoy his own flip put-downs of her idealistic assessment of students ("mall rats" is what he called them). But after many months of sharing lunchtime together, and having surreptitiously observed her interacting with kids in and out of class, he was compelled to conclude that Marjorie enjoyed (actually liked) students. What a concept! How the hell to get there? How to talk to her about that?

Whoever patrols the halls of learning expects order: Power, control, authority are the trinity of the expected result. Good order is the main and central concern of educators, and a teacher's orderliness is the standard upon which he or she is primarily judged. If the buzz from a classroom is too pronounced, if the "bang and blab" is too loud, then the teacher must not be in control. And so every educator is motivated to develop his or her own special sort of thuggery. Some choose to form circular defenses, wherein favorites are included and the unanointed are excluded. Shaming or humiliation is another sort of thuggery, with weapons of wisecracking and intellectual putdowns— I'm large, you're small; I'm powerful, you're vulnerable; I know, you don't. These hierarchical thuggeries reinforce thuggish behavior in susceptible students and subject other students to being the targets of bullying.

If one recognizes the thug in oneself, and how it plays itself out, then one is in a position to either transfer an unfavored student into another teacher's better care, or, better yet, witness one's uncaring and modify it toward caring. An educator could also invite intervention by an advocate for the student. To see the menace in oneself is to go a long way toward changing directions. On the other hand, you might become aware of a colleague or another student who is bullying one of your students. In that case, you might help the beleaguered student to understand that it is the thug who has a character defect and is projecting it onto his or her victim. Role play can sometimes assist both thugs and victims to see the absurd and destructive nature of intimidation. Perhaps you could help your student say to the offending teacher variations on the theme of "Maybe you're having a bad day; it's okay, get it out of your system." You are assisting the student by modeling your own fallibilities, foibles, and humanness, which takes the bite out of the self-righteous shadow in oneself. Remind the victim that she or he is not powerless as to how one interprets thuggery; she or he might be physically or socially weaker, but is never weaker in Awareness and perception. The victim is in a position to be an observer of destructive behavior, which is a power unto itself. Thugs can be intimidated by being observed or caught in the act of their destructiveness. Bending, not breaking, is a skill and a power that the victim can learn. It can also be instructive to help besieged students understand that thugs operate in a network. A loner, bent on inducing fear and intimidating others, is a bully, not a thug. Thugs depend on cohorts for validation and support. Thuggery, be it perpetrated by students or professionals, thrives in company and carries the day only with compliant members and conforming victims. In the absence of either, menace has no context or meaning.

MODELING AND PAUSING

While this book is decidedly not a treatise on replicable strategies for classroom management, we nevertheless posit certain effective attitudes that can boost wariness into alertness and on to attentiveness. Modeling—how to take or experience thugs through your own responses to menace in real situations—can do more than almost anything else to teach your students coping skills. Perhaps the most compelling response one can model is the Pause—your students witnessing your experiencing a thug without judgment. When you pause and witness thuggish behavior without judgment, you establish for your students an attentive base from which all students can function. In the quiet moment of the Pause, students usually feel held in the embrace of who they are, in the occasion, as it happens to be. They are prompted to self-reflection and to reciprocate all the attentions around them.

Kids have said to me, "Boy, Mr. Willis, we were really getting out of hand there." Or, "Wow, we were over the top, weren't we?" These self-reflections were initiated by my intentional pausing and waiting. On the other hand, quiet observation is not meant to be oppressive. As Theodore Roethke says, "Most teaching is visceral, and the genial uproar that constitutes a verse class, especially so. It is as ephemeral as the dance, and as hard to localize or define. It is what is left after all the reading and thinking and reciting: the residue, the illumination" (p. 51). A teacher must be able to discriminate between a genial uproar and thuggishness. What is called for is attentiveness, not justice.

CHAPTER FOUR

Know Thyself
Part I

The discussions that led to my collaboration on this book with
Arthur Willis began over twenty-five years ago. Arthur was an
experienced classroom teacher in the social studies department of a
high school where I had just begun a midlife career as a tutor for district teenagers who were home- or hospital-bound due to chronic ill-
nesses, physical traumas, or mental/emotional problems. I usually
turned in my daily records at the school during lunchtime and fell into
the habit of talking with Arthur during his break. We quickly discovered each other to be kindred spirits. We agreed on what teaching and
children meant to us and the importance of an intuitive awareness of
our students. We shared a common interest in philosophy and trans-
personal/Jungian psychology, and a mutual excitement in exploring
these areas that has persisted and deepened for over two decades.

In 1990 I finished my graduate work in special education and
began working full-time with developmentally delayed infants and
toddlers, once again doing itinerant teaching, now in daycare centers
as well as in homes. For the next five years Arthur and I talked only
sporadically, catching up during vacations. While I gained expertise in
early childhood development, Arthur was winding down his classroom
career and nearing retirement. The pace of our conversation picked
up again at the turn of the century; Arthur had retired and I was working only part-time, supervising special education graduate students
and teaching a practicum course at the state university. As Art's idea
for a "book about teaching for teachers in training" emerged, I had the
following dream:

Art and I are sitting outdoors on a porch or deck under a tree where
birds are flitting about in the leaves. He is building—very competently—

a birdhouse and I am awkwardly trying to form a large, unwieldy clump
of suet, peanut butter, and birdseed into a ball. The idea is that when
the birdhouse is finished the suet ball will fit into it to feed the birds
that will nest there.

When I woke up, it was obvious to me that Arthur would construct
the philosophical basis for our project and I would struggle to articulate and give round, full shape to the ideas. Our shared interests are in
an area of teaching that is not covered in most of the professional literature (Aline D. Wolf's *Nurturing the Spirit in Nonsectarian Classrooms* is one exception), and includes ideas that have grown out of my
personal teaching experience: namely, for meaningful learning to take
place, spirit and materiality must not be separated from each other.

The Western educational tradition has promoted an exaggerated
split between spirit and materiality. There is a divide between religious
fundamentalism that disdains all bodily pleasure on one hand, and
rampant consumerist materialism that degrades the spirit on the
other. The images in my dream seemed to suggest the possibility of
their merging into what Arthur and I refer to as soul: birds (the transcendent aspect of spirit) in house (material), with seeds (the imma-
nent or life-potential aspect of spirit) in suet and peanut butter
(material). The spirit cannot shelter or nourish itself without food, as
my friend Nina discovered in her mentoring program. Likewise, shelter and nourishment are meaningless if there is no spirit to be fed, as
we see in the burgeoning population of dis-spirited children in our
schools: depressed, drugged into compliance, affectively flat, or, conversely, outrageously noncompliant and distracted. Our hope is that
this book presents a structure filled with intimations of existential
reality; that it shows what an educational process that supports the
unity of body and spirit might resemble; that it gets readers thinking
about ways to accommodate this merger, in spite of the overwhelming
pressures of modern-day teaching.

OH, MY SOUL AND BODY

During one of our conversations, Arthur and I asked one another to
retrieve a memory of a truly superb, inspiring classroom teacher.
Arthur remembers his Russian teacher, Anya, vividly, and although I
can recall some fine, competent instructors, overall, school after the
fifth grade and through college was primarily an anxious, rote, flat,
and compliant experience. I remember my education much as Carol

Gilligan describes it for girls after puberty in her book *In a Different Voice*. Most of my meaningful learning experiences took place after school and on weekends. By eleventh grade I had organized a system for homework completion that involved complete utilization of study halls, often foregoing elective classes such as typing to gain an extra study period, or completing French II in half a year in order to reduce my homework load. At the end of the day, I headed for the library and completed any outstanding assignments. By 5:00 P.M. my books and papers were stowed in my locker, and I was liberated to explore the things that really interested me. For two years I never took a textbook home and I began to develop a lifelong habit of self-teaching. Repercussions of these high school choices occurred in college, when typing papers became a tortuous, time-consuming task; I spent more time typing and erasing mistakes on carbon paper copies than I did on research. Furthermore, the half-year without French language practice slowed down my foreign language acquisition, and I never fully participated in the vital give-and-take of classroom discussion or gained real depth in academic subjects.

Probably the very best teacher I ever had was my paternal grandmother; my busy mother and maternal grandmother provided excellent additional support for the way I learned best. If I had to identify what made their teaching exceptional, just as Arthur identifies defiance as his touchstone for great teaching, it would be that they collectively provided environments and experiences where body, mind, and spirit were allowed full play with little interference. And I do mean play!

Because I grew up in a small, rural, Erie Canal port-town in western New York State, I had the benefit of a close extended family. My grandmothers lived within safe walking distance, even for small children in the late 1940s. Moreover, they lived back-to-back on parallel streets, with their yards abutting. From the time we were toddlers, our parents allowed my younger brother and me to spend weekends with one or the other grandmother.

Although we freely roamed back and forth between grandmas, my brother usually stayed with my maternal Grandmother Lobbett, a somewhat reclusive, cultured, aesthetically inclined person. Her house was filled with books; some were velvet-covered gift books of poetry that I liked, literally, to caress. Others were the colorfully illustrated adventure classics of DeFoe, Scott, and Stevenson. She enjoyed playing chess and card games, and on Saturday afternoons she tuned her big, curvy Stromberg-Carlson radio to the Metropolitan Opera broadcasts.

Meanwhile, Grandma MacDonald and I spent our Saturday mornings baking the weekly treats she doled out to family members. Her kitchen was a magical, alchemical place for me, where we turned flour, sugar, eggs, farm butter and cream, molasses, yeast, apples, pumpkins, and nuts into cookies, pies, cakes, and bread. It was as if every Saturday Gretel got lost in the woods and was found by a good witch, who wafted in on the aromas of cinnamon and nutmeg. To this day memories of my Grandmother MacDonald are often called up by the smells of baking.

In the afternoon we would rest. Cuddled into her capacious lap, I would look through her big, illustrated Bible to find the story I wanted her to read. There were many favorites: Samson and Delilah, Daniel in the Lions' Den, Nebuchadnezzar's Dream, King Saul going crazy, King Solomon telling the disputatious mothers that he had decided to cut the baby in half. But most compelling to me was the one about David and Goliath, which Grandma must have read—patiently—a hundred times over the years I stayed with her.

After our rest, we would set out for a walk around the village, like Little Red Riding Hood and her Grandma (not a wolf in sight), with a basket full of goodies and knitted things for shut-ins, new babies, new neighbors, or church suppers. During visits to her elderly friends, I heard wonderful stories about their childhoods and immigrant beginnings. I learned to sit and listen, my imagination totally engaged, my mind eager for all the existential details. Afterward, our load lighter, we would stop at the local dry goods store to replenish supplies of yarn, embroidery thread, and yard goods. Near the door was the rack of comic books, and Grandma was always good for the latest issue of the original postwar Wonder Woman series. The mythological settings and physical derring-do of the heroine added a feminist dimension to my motley collection of archetypal gleanings picked up from the Bible, fairy tales, Greek myths, and comic books. These activities and themes formed the foundation for all the subjects that have most interested me since childhood: the nexus of archetypal psychology and religion; the caring for and nurturing of one's community and the individuals within it; a sense for historical roots and influences; the arts, especially writing and music; and most of all, a love of the natural world that growing up rural inspired.

In the evening, Grandma would help me knit or crochet simple pieces by placing her large, competent hands over mine, teaching me, kinesthetically and viscerally, the motions the needles and hooks took in their pattern-making. If a mistake was made, she would carefully drop the stitch back and reweave it, showing me that errors happen and that patterns are reconstructable. We might listen to a radio pro-gram or she might set me up at her desk with a collection of fountain pens, bottled ink, and flowered stationery to write letters to her sis-ters, my great aunts. Inkblots and all, she would mail them to the "Michiganders" as she called them, and they always wrote me back. I learned to write in an epistolary, newsy sort of style through these let-ters to relatives that both my mother and grandmother encouraged.

After a nice, warm bath, tucked into her big bed and snuggled up against her, she would lull me to sleep with stories about her child-hood mischief on a farm in Michigan and at a German Lutheran school where she completed eighth grade. I learned a basic German vocabulary and a prayer about guardian angels in these pre-sleep for-eign language classes.

Whenever Grandma MacDonald became happily excited or pleas-antly surprised about something, genuinely moved by some experi-ence—an unexpected visit from an old friend or a special gift, perhaps—she would throw her hands in the air and exclaim, "Oh, my soul and body!" Now that I am an adult and a teacher, her spirited expression has come to have a particular meaning for me: the impor-tant things that people learn for their soul's delight are learned best in a context of attentive regard for their "actual occasions," as described by Whitehead, with all the senses engaged.

GETTING TO KNOW YOU AND ME

It goes without saying that we will all have different stories to tell about what constitutes vibrant, meaningful learning for each of us. Our stories will be filtered through our life experiences, our distinctive personalities and our differentiated adaptations for perceiving and evaluating the world in which we live. My own unsatisfying experi-ence of school, like Art's, especially at the college level, made me ques-tion my ability to learn and resulted in years of low academic self-confidence; as a teacher I began to see many perfectly bright, capable youngsters similarly afflicted, and I became curious about the attitudes, internal or externally imposed, and circumstances that might have held us back. These days, supervisors require teachers-in-training to write formal *reflections* on both their written lesson plans and their implementations. Such reflecting rarely goes beyond think-ing over the mechanics of the lesson—timing, pacing, sequencing, interest level of materials and projects, behavior management strate-gies—in order for the teacher to become more adept at the perform-ance next time around. These are surely worthy skills for a beginning teacher to develop, but in my opinion, true reflection shines a wider light and requires the teacher to beam it inwardly on their own preferred ways of functioning, as well as outwardly on to their demonstration of professional competence.

Operating from this point of view, I began to pay closer attention to my own mental workings and how they had come into conflict with my experiences of school. As you may have noticed from my memories of time spent with Grandma MacDonald, I was interested in everything, a mental magpie that pecked around among a variety of interests that seemed to my family and all but a handful of teachers somewhat beside the common point. My parents thought me easily distracted; my professors saw me as a student who jumped to conclusions based on what struck them as scant evidence. I seemed to have private insights into how all these seemingly unrelated bits and pieces merged into meaningful, imagistic, coherent patterns for me, but were extremely difficult to articulate or to put into logical steps backed up by details—sloppy suet balls, indeed! My thinking tended to be analogical and metaphorical—I saw the world in terms of the stories it had to tell and how all those stories related to each other. Hence, my ideas tended to remain generalized and unexpressed. Whenever I did attempt to express them, my listeners seemed to be uncomfortable. They rolled their eyes, looked away, or dismissed outright what I was trying to say, usually by insisting that I use a more precise vocabulary. They also disappointed me by not "getting it," and my coping strategy was to simply (resentfully) keep it to myself. My favorite teachers were those who delighted in how my odd bits fell together in original ways and kindly helped structure my oral and written explanations. Some found unusual tasks for me to do, which called on my strengths in interesting ways: One year I was asked to be the ringmaster of a circus our school put on; another time, my seventh-grade English teacher put me in charge of pronouncing the words and sentences of the annual spelling bee, which I did every year until I graduated. I liked being privy to the entire production, rather than an individual performer in it.

Being called on in class was torture, especially if quick, rather rote, decisive answers were expected, as was often the case in math classes. I loved math, but the classroom experience of it made me feel edgy and unsure; I gave it up as a possible college major after enduring one semester with a professor who enjoyed publicly humiliating students who didn't have immediate answers for his detailed blackboard equations. (It always seemed deeply and satisfyingly ironic to me that I successfully tutored hundreds of hours of math to similarly anxious students during my teaching career.) Some students thrive on challenging, competitive interactions with their teachers, but I learned best on my own or in one-to-one mentoring situations where I had quiet, direct contact with the mentor and plenty of time to mull things over. I was a basic self-starting autodidact. I needed a lot of time to deeply understand and process ideas or projects, and the fast pace of college research and deadlines turned me into an anxiety-ridden procrastinator.

Moreover, I was undone by the time-consuming technology of the 1960s—manual typewriters and carbon paper copies—as well as detail and organizational work, such as that required in science labs. When faced with detail work I became obsessive and perfectionist, traits that further slowed the completion of projects. I was open to subjects that were dismissed in the traditional academic circles of the time, such as alternative medicine, nutrition as a contributor to mental functioning, Eastern spiritual traditions, *esoterica* of all kinds, modern music, and art. For me it seemed that subjective values and experiences played a significant role in defining what reality is, and I found shallow the suggestion that subjectivity was merely another name for narcissism. I reacted defensively if challenged in what I perceived as an unkind or cold manner and lost my complicated train of thought if interrupted or asked to respond quickly and systematically to questions.

Later, as the mother of four bright, physically active, outspoken, argumentative children, I experienced this uneasy feeling about the educational process again as a parent. Each of my children seemed to have distinct learning preferences and energies. One had an intellectual, scholarly bent, and was happy reading a book or working alone at his computer. Another was gifted with visual-spatial, problem-solving aptitudes, was physically active, and liked working with his hands. The third had an introspective, philosophical spirit focused on values, which he applied through interests in physical fitness and activities such as organic gardening. And the last possessed a deep appreciation for aesthetics and culture, which manifested in a love of handling beautiful objects and a concern for preserving them in museums. Two of them seemed to fit into the expected sedentary, reading-based academic life more easily than the other two. At the end of each school year I found myself designing playful rituals and projects for my burned-out kids and those of my neighbors to help them clear any negative feelings they might be harboring about the just-past academic year and to get their chair-bound bodies and imaginations moving freely: having them build a round bonfire pit using a string compass to mark a geometric circumference; laying the circumference out with the best stones they could find; burning piles of dittoed worksheets;

sending little good-wish notes for the next year up in smoke; roasting marshmallows and encouraging summer activities—camp, publishing a newspaper, playing ball on our hayfield with the neighbor kids, making video movies, and reading. Why was going to school with their friends socially okay, but often academically tedious (with some notable exceptions), and so lacking in *joie de vivre* and love of learning for these children? School also seemed to be pretty good at providing basic skills acquisition and practice, but the truly invigorating learning happened during free play time.

Early on in my home and academic tutoring career, I had also noticed that when I asked kids why they thought they were having trouble with a subject, their answers were typically: the teacher doesn't like me (most frequent response); the teacher doesn't teach right, I don't get it; the teacher is disorganized; I don't understand the book, it's hard for me to read; the teacher doesn't make it interesting, it's boring (most frequently used descriptive word); there's too much noise and disruption in class, I can't learn anything there; the teacher is always yelling at me to sit still and stop talking, but I don't talk *that* much. Whenever I spoke with their teachers I often heard the same complaints in reverse. Without either subscribing to the mutual negative projections or dismissing youthful attempts to articulate self-awareness through these projections, I began to hear a story about personal preferences, communication gaps, misunderstandings, incorrect assumptions, defensive postures, irritations and, yes, bias and prejudice.

My search for answers, sparked by my own self-reflection and by the concern I had that my children and my tutees would continue to develop uniquely, zestfully, and at their own pace, began in the late 1960s. The social revolution that shook the United States during the '60s and '70s brought me into contact with a body of literature that addressed a variety of contemporary issues: feminist consciousness raising in particular, and gender relations in general; educational theory that encompassed ideas about personality development, learning styles and sensory processing; existentialist and postmodern philosophies and their applications in semiotics and theories of language; environmental concerns and their connections to human health; Native American and Celtic culture; poetry, music, art and movement as soulful activities; and most important for me, works on Jungian and transpersonal depth psychology.

My reading led me to one painful moment of awareness after another that Western cultural assumptions, based on the Cartesian separation of mind (spirit) and matter (body), the mechanistic world-view of Newtonian physics, the corporate model that emerged during the Industrial Revolution and their embodiment in our institutions, such as our educational system, were outdated and hugely exclusionary. The mechanistic, consumerist emphasis of our society produced many practical solutions to the logistics of living and career ambition, but devalued soul and meaning and promoted feelings of isolation and alienation among some students. The purpose of education seemed to be the attainment of careers with the highest possible incomes, rather than the fostering of passionate individual interests and vocations or the development of vital, capacious people who felt connected to the world in which they lived.

I needed an intellectual structure inclusive and neutral enough to help me do several things: help me with my ongoing challenge to structure and synthesize the scattered pieces of information I was gathering; get me to take a long pause before passing judgments on behaviors or motivations; teach me to say "I haven't a clue as to what's going on here, but I have a concern." A structure that would help me look for what was typical and normal in children, rather than for pathologies—which can be a challenge in special education, with its cadre of "identified" kids.

Furthermore, I wanted a structure that extended beyond myself and included the entire educational community, that would help me develop creative, individualized lesson plans and assessment models; that would provide a foundation for working collaboratively with other educators; and that would help us reflect in a deeper way, without releasing psychic contents more appropriate to the clinical psychologist's domain. We would rather rejoice in the differences among people, than merely tolerate them through high-minded but inadequate models of equity and justice, and we all wish to see kids as embodied spirits, and not as damaged objects in need of remediation. My intuition was telling me that capable kids were dropping through the cracks at school at least partly because of a reflexive rejection or exclusion of who they were.

It was the depth psychology of Carl Gustav Jung, which I discovered during college in the campus bookstore, rather than in any psychology course I ever took, that became fundamental to my thinking about human development and what constituted effective education. Later on Jung's ideas would become enriched by the contributions of pedagogical and developmental theorists such as Howard Gardner, Carol Gilligan, Elizabeth Murphy, Reuven Feuerstein, and George

Leonard; the philosophical essays on education by Alfred North Whitehead and Paolo Freire; and the sociological/therapeutic approaches of James Garbarino and Stephen Frankl. And, of course, it was the synthesis of these studies along with the experiences of my own teaching career that helped me develop my point of view. I think all these approaches are interrelated and contain en-spiriting potentials for changing the way our classrooms operate, but also require patience and an appreciation for complexity that is sometimes hard to articulate.

So let's start with Jung and see where we go.

Although the twenty volumes of Carl Jung's *Collected Works* range over a wide variety of psychological topics, the one called *Psychological Types* has proved enduringly helpful to me for observing how students and teachers adapt and function in the school environment. Furthermore, it has provided me with intellectual grist for how we might alter those environments to maximize and use the diverse ways in which individuals function to the benefit of both the individual and the school community. Jung's work on psychological types emerged from his efforts to understand and reconcile the incompatible therapeutic models of Freud and Adler (Bennet, p. 47). Clinically, Jung used it to help people understand their relationships better (unhappy marriage partners, or warring parents and children). Because schooling could be described as a process of acquiring content in a relational setting, it occurred to me that Jungian typology might have applications for the classroom and for collegial cooperation. In no way was the theory of types meant to be a reductive "pigeonhole" system, but rather an open-minded way of looking at behaviors in a context of inborn, adaptive, developmental psychological predispositions, working themselves out in the vicissitudes of individual experience.

Jung's concept of the psyche posits a dynamic system in which a person's conscious adaptation is compensated and balanced by the unconscious situation. His thinking about the psyche was influenced by Hegel's dialectic and by Newton's third law of motion, which posited that for any action there is an equal and opposite reaction. In other words, the psyche seeks homeostasis in a never-ceasing dynamic give and take between what is consciously accessible to it and what is not. The payoff for this psychic clash of polar opposites is the differentiated (specialized) consciousness that characterizes modern people. In other words, as primitive societies evolved into modern ones, people began to take up specialized occupations and interests that brought conscious attention to particular ways of functioning. The blacksmith needed different skills from the tailor or dressmaker; the lawyer from the musician; the teacher from the farmer. To me, consciousness has to do with what we know about ourselves (I am female; I grew up in a small town in an extended family; I got my driver's license when I was twenty-four), the ways in which we identify ourselves and the roles we play (I am a daughter, a sister, a wife, a mother, a grandmother, a teacher), the social adaptations we are skillful in using to conform (or not!) to our culture's expectations (I am friendly and helpful), and the assumptions and beliefs we have about how the world works (people are basically good, will behave as they are treated, and humans are an evolving species). In addition, *consciousness* is not just a matter of how much we think we know or the career skills that we have developed; there is also knowledge gained through sensory, intuitive, and feeling factors that rise into and fall from consciousness as situations demand. Unconsciousness is the term we use to denote what we do not recognize about ourselves and includes material that has been forgotten, repressed, and denied because it is inadmissible and/or "bad" (the Freudian position); ways of functioning at which we are not so skillful (a person's feeling life may be more developed and accessible than their logical capacities); potentials we are not using in addition to inadmissible contents (the Jungian perspective). This unacknowledged side always reminds me of Peter Pan, that eternally boyish figure who had Wendy sew his shadow (I've always thought this was perhaps the shadow of his unexperienced, unconscious maturity) to his feet. It is important to emphasize this aspect of unconsciousness: although we are each consciously well-developed in unique, specialized ways, unconscious aspects of our psyche do not just disappear and leave us alone. Like Peter's shadow, they trail us around and exert their influence in the form of verbal slips of the tongue, projections (both positive and negative) onto other people, bursts of irrational temper, stridently expressed opinions, misunderstandings, and rigid defenses. They are truly blind spots because they are polar opposites to what we believe about ourselves.

For example, females of my generation were traditionally expected to be compliant, deferential, and nice. While I was growing up, one often heard comments such as "Susie is so warm and loving; she doesn't have a mean bone in her body." Well, Susie's conscious attitude may be open-hearted and friendly, but she does indeed have an unconscious mean bone. If it remains unconscious, if she consistently represses feelings of independence and anger, she may allow herself to become swamped by the needs of others, a martyr, a victim. If she does not acknowledge her anger when, for example, someone takes undue advantage of her kindness, the anger will nevertheless sneak out like mean little licks of fire: she might "forget" an important appointment with the offending person; she might make cutting, sarcastic comments framed as humor; she might "accidentally" damage something that belongs to the person; she might have occasional, disconcerting bursts of temper that are "not like her." By becoming more assertive (making the opposite of what she thinks she is more conscious), and taking care of her own needs (in my day, called selfishness), Susie can take the mean out of the bone. Conversely, males were (and still mostly are) expected to be aggressively macho and decisive, and to not express "girly" vulnerable feelings. If those feelings remain unconscious, men may project them onto women as weaknesses and become abusive in some way, or they may project them positively and set women up on idealized pedestals. Both are uncomfortable and restrictive positions and hinder the individual's growth.

Keeping in mind Jung's view of the psyche, we can then see how each person's preferred ways of perceiving and evaluating information (just like all our other conscious adaptations and roles) have compensatory, unadapted counterparts in the shadow zone. Someone else may have just the opposite way of functioning and the opposite unconscious situation; neither way is right or wrong, just different. However, these differences are always bumping up against each other with sometimes extremely unhappy results and the ramifications of typological differences in our work as teachers are critical and will be discussed at greater length in Chapter 5.

Speculations about individual differences in psychological type had a great deal of historical precedence when Jung began to develop his theory using functional definitions (how people gather information and make decisions based on that information) for mental processes and language more suited to the modern age. These precedents suggest that even in ancient times people recognized inborn temperament and character similarities and differences. For example, the ancient Greeks developed ideas about four bodily "humors" that influenced temperament; the Chinese and Native Americans devised sophisticated medicine wheels based on the four elements and four directions; astrology provided an early, systematic interpretation of personality based on where our stars were in the twelve houses of the zodiac at the time of our birth, which is also an arrangement of a multiple of four; Ayurvedic tradition theorizes three energic states that when in balance lead to a fourth state of harmonious equilibrium. In the early twentieth century Eduard Spranger, a contemporary of Jung, developed a typology based on four values rather than four cognitive functions. As a psychologist/philosopher, Spranger was most interested in the connection between personality and ethics. These values—ethical/religious, theoretical/scientific, aesthetic/artistic, and economic/commercial—seem to correspond to certain of Jung's functional types. Spranger's typology provides a convenient additional framework for teaching typology because it helps to group Jung's functional types according to their possible motivational energies. Ernst Kretschmer was another turn-of-the-century temperament theorist who proposed two basic human character types, the schizothymic (corresponding to Jung's intuitive function) and the cyclothymic (corresponding to Jung's sensation function). For Kretschmer, the schizothymic temperaments discriminate into either the Appolonian, motivated by a search for spirituality, or the Promethean, motivated by the search for power through science, while the cyclothymic temperaments discriminate into the Dionysian, motivated by joyousness and action, or the Epimethean, motivated by duty and the desire for social status. I have attempted to draw the conceptual frameworks of these three modern temperament theorists together in a comprehensive chart at the end of the chapter. The strengths of Jung's typology are both its usefulness in anticipating situational behaviors and the neutrality of its language of mental functions, whereas the ethical and character descriptions of Spranger and Kretschmer are more susceptible to bias, especially regarding notions of gender differences in the Victorian social context in which these theories emerged. The strength of the Spranger and Kretschmer configurations is their applicability to issues of motivation and objectives.

Likewise, Jung proposed a four-part scheme, saying that we each have one conscious, differentiated, preferred, and well-adapted *psychological function*, by which we either perceive or evaluate our environment. Three others remain more or less inaccessible (unconscious). As well as these four functions, Jung identified two *attitudes* that describe the first, most basic difference between people, the one he observed with regard to Freud and Adler.

He called these two attitudes *extraversion* and *introversion*. They are recognizable even in the temperaments of newborns and it is now generally accepted that they are to some extent biologically/genetically determined. These two terms are commonly, but mistakenly, interpreted to mean "outgoing" and "shy." Jung's definitions are more specific.

Extraversion and introversion denote the direction in which an individual's interest, attention, or libido (life energy, in Jungian terms) flows. Although all of us, to some extent, use both extraverted and introverted adaptations in daily life, one orientation is usually preferred over the other. For the extravert, interest flows from the subject (self) outward on to objects (other people, events, concrete things). Jung writes:

> When orientation by the object predominates in such a way that decisions and actions are determined not by subjective views, but by the objective conditions, we speak of an extraverted attitude. When this is habitual, we speak of an extraverted type. If a man thinks, feels, acts and actually lives in a way that is directly correlated with the objective conditions and their demands, he is extraverted. . . . Consequently, he never expects to find any absolute factors in his own inner life. . . . objective happenings have an almost inexhaustible fascination for him, so that ordinarily he never looks for anything else.... the moral laws governing his actions coincide with the demands of society, that is, with the prevailing moral standpoint. (pp. 333–34)

Extraverted people tend to be "quick on the uptake," with rapid responses to external situations. They are energized by the demands of the outer world and become bored and lethargic when circumstances force them to be alone and/or introspective for extended periods. Extraverted children like to talk their thoughts out and are the kids who eagerly shout answers out in class without raising their hands or waiting their turns. These kids do not mind being interrupted—they will happily veer off into a new discussion as their ideas flow rapidly. Extraverts usually keep their telephones close at hand as a hedge against "alone time"!

For the introvert, however, the direction of interest is inward and any action that results from the perception and evaluation of an object is mediated by a subjective viewpoint. What results are responses that do not always fit the objective situation, but which rely on how the sensory data impact the subject. Hence introverts often have highly individual but very coherent intellectual and value systems that do not always follow the prevailing social standpoint. Furthermore, the intensity of the object's impact on the subject may be so great that the introverted person can appear withdrawn, reserved, or shy in order to deal with it. Introverts tend to avoid crowds, or remain at the periphery, and become uncomfortable with too much action or clutter around them. These conditions can be exhausting, and introverts need regular times to "recharge their batteries" before rejoining the extraverted fray. Introverts appear slow as they need to go deep with their evaluative processes and often seem "a little off the beat," needing extra time to formulate their responses. Until they have worked their ideas out inwardly, they will usually not wish to contribute to discussions. If this inward processing is interrupted before it is completed, they become frustrated and will often just "clam up."

Western cultural bias favors extraversion, probably due to the Cartesian, Newtonian, and corporate models that dominate our culture and demand "objectivity." Jung admonishes us that:

> the subjective factor has all the value of a co-determinant of the world we live in, a factor that can on no account be left out of our calculations. It is another universal law, and whoever bases himself on it has a foundation as secure, as permanent, and as valid as the man who relies on the object. (p. 375)

As far as the four functions are concerned, Jung called the two information-gathering (perceiving) ones *sensation* and *intuition*. Because these two functions gather data, but do not evaluate them in any way, he called them irrational. Sensation collects data through the five senses we are familiar with and through at least two more (as practiced by physical and occupational therapists): the vestibular (sense of balance and spatial orientation), and the proprioceptive (sense of gravity and skeletal compression). Sensation types focus on the details of objects and events, especially those of material reality in the here and now. As Elizabeth Murphy writes, sensation types "build conclusions based on the sequential organization of this information" (p. 31). Ideas, theories, and symbolism are usually of lesser interest to them. Sensation type children tend to be orderly and organized; they usually work steadily until they complete an assignment; they keep track of their pencils, papers, and assignments; and like to answer questions requiring knowledge of details and specifics.

Intuition appears to gather information through the enigmatic "sixth sense," which may be a separate sense in itself or which may use the seven senses (that is, seeing, hearing, touching, smelling, tasting, experiencing gravity, and balancing) in some other way. At any rate, intuition takes data and immediately casts them into patterns, seeing the world holistically and diffusely, rather like an Impressionist painting. It instantaneously builds details into a Big Picture. A Jungian analyst friend of mine used to say that intuitives "live close to the Unconscious," spotting trends, connections, potentials, and possibilities about people and situations that have not yet come into the collective consciousness. Intuitives are comfortable in the world of theory, speculation, and imagery, often making creative connections among apparently unrelated ideas. Hence the intuitive temperament focuses on the future, but envisions the future as bridged to, or patterned by, the past.

Thinking and feeling, in Jung's arrangement, are the two evaluative, assessing, or judging functions, and because they are called upon to process information or make decisions about data, he called them rational. But feelings and emotions are commonly considered to be the opposite of rational! Often misunderstood, Jung's definition of the feeling *function* is specific and has no more to do with emotion or affect than the other functions, as we have discussed at length in our chapter on the rationality of the feeling life. We can be in emotional states while expressing ourselves in any of the functions. Rather, well-discriminated feeling judges through the heart in just as matter-of-fact a way as thinking judges through the head. Feeling tells us whether we like or dislike something; it underlies the values, morals, ethics, and aesthetics of a culture and is personal/relational in nature. Feeling types value harmony in social situations and are often good hosts who like to bring compatible people together. In my seminars they are natural mediators of heated discussions, often bringing participants to mutually agreeable resolutions.

Thinking discriminates data by organizing them into a sort of mental filing cabinet, sorting out and discarding irrelevancies. It evaluates perceptions impersonally, analytically, and logically. Thinking types often appear to be cool and unmoved by relational needs. They are valued in professions such as the law, accounting, or research, where careful analysis and application are required. Just as feeling, in the Jungian sense, does not mean emotional, thinking does not mean smart. Intelligence resides in both these functions.

One of my favorite teaching stories illustrates a thinking/feeling polarity difference between student and teacher. It concerns Jack, an extremely mathematically gifted five-year-old with whom I worked for two years in a gifted-talented program. One bright autumn day there was a fire drill at school and we had to go outdoors. Canada geese were flying in V-formation overhead, and I directed Jack's attention to them, saying, "Aren't they beautiful? See how their blue and green feathers flash in the sun!" Jack looked at me and inquired in a no-nonsense voice, "How many are there?"

Although people have and use all of these psychological/mental capacities over the course of a lifetime, one attitude and one function emerge and discriminate in a more complex, adapted, conscious manner than the others. Preferences are probably biologically based and are further influenced by the environment in which an individual develops, in a nature/nurture dance. Jung called these preferences the superior attitude and function.

Furthermore, Jung thought that a secondary, less well-developed function serves as a back-up support to the superior function. He called this the auxiliary function. Of the remaining two functions, one (called the tertiary function) is somewhat available to consciousness through effort, and the other remains mostly unconscious, as a psychic blind spot, and can sometimes display itself in primitive, compulsive, rigid, emotion-laden manifestations. Considered from a more positive angle, this unconscious function can be described as a highly permeable membrane that allows untapped possibilities to "leak" through. Jung saw a developmental aspect to the functions that occurred over the course of a lifetime. As small children experiment with them, one function begins to consciously discriminate; by the teens and twenties a fairly conscious auxiliary function emerges; the tertiary function, if courted and worked on, adds new energy to the personality during middle age, while the inferior function becomes the permeable membrane to the unconscious in later life. To recapitulate: one function is consciously used and the other three shade off into increasing states of inaccessibility.

One analytical aside here: It seems that the tertiary and inferior functions are implicated in what is called the midlife crisis. Jung was not as interested in childhood development as he was in the developmental aspects of middle and old age. One thing he noticed in his adult patients was the wearing out, the exhaustion of, the major function by one's thirties and forties and a yearning for new vitality that seems to arise with the cultivation of that semi-unconscious third function and the dealing with problems associated with the unconscious inferior function. This work is often central to a Jungian analysis, and is done in a safe therapeutic environment in order to contain the fragility and unadapted manifestations of these functions. If this movement is not contained, it often erupts compulsively and disturbs the person's ordinary life. The most common example, the one we make jokes about, is the middle-aged professional man who has traded on his intellect all his life, who then suddenly runs off with a young, inappropriate woman in order to access his inferior feeling function. It is important to remember that as teachers we are often heading toward such middle-age shifts when our young students are just beginning to consolidate their primary functions. That they do so successfully is crucial to healthy ego development in early life; that we do so successfully is critical for the emergence of what Jung called the Self (a larger, more inclusive center of the personality than the ego) in middle and old age. And that we examine and overcome our weaknesses is equally as important to our developing more integrated and balanced personalities, as well as becoming more nonjudgmental, inclusive teachers.

Each member of a pair of functions (perceiving/irrational and evaluating/rational) is a polar opposite of the other in how it operates. They are *not* points on a spectrum. In other words, when a person is collecting data in sensation mode, the opposite pole (intuitive mode) is unavailable. Likewise, one cannot be evaluating or making decisions out of the thinking and feeling modes simultaneously. Figure 4–1 is a schematic rendering of these oppositions.

Taking this schematic rendering to its next step, we can see that if we place the superior function at north on the vertical axis, the inferior function will be its polar opposite at south. It follows that the auxiliary and tertiary functions fall at the poles of the horizontal axis and the function opposite the auxiliary will be the third or tertiary function. If, in the Figure 4–1 schematic, intuition is the superior function, either thinking or feeling will be auxiliary, either thinking or feeling will be tertiary, and sensation will be inferior. The four rotations of this schematic, placing the superior function at north and the inferior function at south, would play out as shown on Figure 4–2.

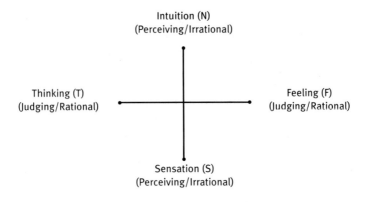

Figure 4–1

Figure 4–2

The schematic representation also shows us that if the superior function is one of the perceiving functions, the auxiliary will be an evaluating one and vice versa. Naming the preferred attitude and the superior and auxiliary functions gives us a Jungian type descriptor. For example, a person could be Extraverted Sensation Feeling or Introverted Thinking Intuitive. The shorthand for recording the types assigns letters for each attitude and function: E for extraversion; I for introversion; S for sensation; N for intuition; T for thinking and F for feeling. (Since both introversion and intuition begin with I, N was the letter selected for intuition in order to avoid confusion.) Thus, the Extraverted Sensation Feeling type can be noted in shorthand as ESF and the Introverted Thinking Intuitive as ITN. Looking again at the axis diagram above, one can see that the polar opposites of these two types would be INT and EFS. Continuing in this manner until each type and its opposite are listed, sixteen basic types emerge (see Figure 4–3).

Jungian typology has been made accessible to lay people through the popular books of David Keirsey: *Please Understand Me*, co-authored with Marilyn Bates, and *Portraits of Temperament. Please*

INF	ENF
INT	ENT
IFN	EFN
ITN	ETN
ISF	ESF
IST	EST
IFS	EFS
ITS	ETS

Figure 4–3

Understand Me contains a quick, forced-choice temperament-sorter that I had my students take in order to get an informal read on their types. I used the book as a text in my graduate practicum course and often assigned it when giving workshops on temperament/typology or teaching teacher-training classes, as it also contains excellent descriptors for each type. Many readers are probably also familiar with the work of Isabel Briggs Myers. The Myers-Briggs Type Indicator (MBTI) is widely used by corporate personnel departments when hiring employees for particular jobs demanding specialized skills, and by schools as part of the application process. Of particular interest to teachers is Elizabeth Murphy's *The Developing Child*, which describes how typology plays itself out in the classroom and gives suggestions for individualizing instruction.

Where Keirsey appears to part company with Jung is over the issue of the goals of typology/temperament. Jung sees the ultimate goal of human development as Individuation, a lifelong process that invites the exploration and integration of those elements of ourselves that are shadowy, neglected, repressed, or denied. Some of those elements involve our difficulties with the tertiary and inferior functions, as mentioned above. Jung posited that by doing this work, an enlargement of personality takes place such that ego-centered consciousness gradually gives way to a new center of the personality that he called the Self. I think this expanded, more "whole" consciousness corresponds somewhat to our idea of Personal Awareness. Moreover, in his clinical practice, typology helped Jung predict the actions people were likely to take in various situations, based on their habitual modes of adaptation, or their types. Keirsey seems to see this integration as reductive instead of augmentative. Rather, he prefers the term *temperament*, a way of adapting that becomes more and more discriminated over a lifetime, each temperament having its own goal, not necessarily that of Individuation, which motivates behavior. This seems the more reductive process to me. Although my personal bias is toward the overarching goal of Individuation in the Jungian sense, Keirsey's arrangement of similar types into temperament clusters based on their goals is germane to understanding ego development in early life and is extremely helpful to us as practitioners for expanding our awareness of the young people we teach. Jung's typology, on the other hand, leads to a greater depth in thinking about the implications of development over a lifetime and of life as a vital and changing process. Jung's *Psychological Types* was published in German in 1921, and by 1923 an English edition was available in the United States. Two American women, a mother and daughter with no connection to the European psychoanalytic community, no training as psychoanalysts, and no credentials in psychological test development, happened to read the book. Jungian typology provided the basis for a twenty-year collaborative study for Isabel Briggs Myers and her mother Katharine Briggs. What led Katharine Briggs to her intensive study of Jung was an interest in observing the natural, healthy personality differences among people, especially as they concerned how individuals habitually related to their external environments, and how it was that some people achieved excellence in their outer lives. Briggs and Myers' focus eventually led to the addition of a second pair of attitudinal polarities to the Jungian ones of Extraversion and Introversion. They called this pair of attitudes Perceiving (P) and Judging (J). Isabel Briggs Myers' interest deepened further during World War II, when she worked to place people in war-effort jobs most suited to their temperaments, where they could serve most efficiently and productively in times of crisis. During the war she began to develop test items and collect data from various sample groups, such as nursing and medical students. By 1956, in collaboration with the Educational Testing Service, Isabel Briggs Myers published the first Myers-Briggs Type Inventory (MBTI). Until 1975 the MBTI was used only as a research instrument. In that year it was published by Consulting Psychologists Press and became available to psychologists. As of this writing, the MBTI manual is now in its third edition (1998), with revised item selection and scoring methods, standardized on a U.S. population sample. The formerly gender-weighted thinking/feeling axis has been altered to reflect a gender-neutral polarity. At the present time the MBTI is considered one of the "Big 5" psychological-testing instruments, and many psychologists consider it more helpful in assessing people's strengths and potential for success than IQ tests. Its main drawbacks are its specificity to career development and its focus on the extraverted orientation. Some critics think that certain types are overrepresented in certain professions due to the wide use of the MBTI as a placement tool. In other words, the MBTI might justifiably be seen as a pigeonholing instrument in its application to the workforce. This criticism should guide us as teachers to not make the same reductive mistake, but rather to use it as a tool to increase our attentiveness to students and how they function best.

As noted above, the Myers-Briggs addition to the Jungian type descriptors was the Perceiving/Judging attitudinal polarity. Both mother and daughter were interested in how individuals extraverted their energy into the outer world of working life. They noticed that some people preferred to complete tasks and experienced a sense of satisfaction when closure was the result of their efforts. Others seemed to prefer the ongoing process of their efforts and tended to shift their interest to new projects when the old ones neared completion. Myers and Briggs called the former attitude Judging (J) and the latter Perceiving (P).

You will recall that the two judging functions are thinking and feeling, and the two perceiving ones are intuition and sensation. The "P" or "J" at the end of an MBTI type description indicates the function that is *extraverted* by the individual, while the "E" or "I" at the beginning tells whether the superior function is *extraverted* or *introverted*. Thus, Myers and Briggs refined and simplified the Jungian type descriptors by eliminating the need to reverse the superior/auxiliary function designations in the sixteen-type listing. For example, if one person's Jungian type is INF and another's is IFN, they nevertheless share similar characteristics. The first person will be more perceiving because of her superior intuitive function; the second more judging due to superior feeling. However, if one condenses the two descriptors, putting the perceiving function first and the judging function second (INF), and using the designations P (perceiving) or J (judging) at the end (INFP or INFJ), we can still tell which function is superior and which is auxiliary and maintain the subtle descriptive difference. As a result of this addition to the type theory, Myers and Briggs were able to simplify and standardize a four-letter descriptor for each of the sixteen types, while still conveying the Jungian notion of superior and auxiliary functions. In their scheme, the four pairs of polarities were listed by their letter designations in the following order: the E/I attitude first; the perceiving preference second, the preferred judging function third, and the P/J attitude last. For example, a person could be ESTJ or INFP (Extraverted Sensation Thinking with Judging Attitude, or Introverted Intuitive Feeling with Perceiving Attitude). Myers and Briggs' theoretical contribution was spotting and codifying this implied subtlety in the Jungian construct: extraverts *extravert* their superior function while introverts *extravert* their auxiliary functions. For anyone interested in pursuing the theoretical aspects of the MBTI, Naomi Quenk presents a clear, concise outline in her book *Essentials of Myers-Briggs Type Indicator Assessment*. The MBTI four-letter system, like the Jungian three-letter one, consolidates into sixteen type codes. In Figure 4–4, I arrange them in the Keirsey clusters, with each member of a cluster sharing a developmental/motivational goal.

In the following comprehensive chart (Figure 4–5), I have attempted to draw together the salient features of Jung, Spranger, Kretschmer (as outlined in Keirsey), and the MBTI to show how Jung's superior/auxiliary functions fit with Keirsey's clusters of similar temperaments,

ISTP	ISTJ
ISFP	ISFJ
ESTP	ESTJ
ESFP	ESFJ
Goal: Liberation; Freedom	*Goal:* Responsibility

INTJ	INFJ
INTP	INFP
ENTJ	ENFJ
ENTP	ENFP
Goal: Scientific; Precision; Understanding how the world works	*Goal:* Meaningfulness; Becoming

Figure 4–4

according to the temperament goals. I have also included statistical data showing percentages of occurrence of the various types in the United States as well as the goal descriptors for each of the temperament clusters. It is a chart densely packed with information, but if readers feel inclined to study it a bit at a time, it will provide a broad overview of modern type/temperament theory as well as suggesting correspondences to the work of present-day learning preference theorists like Howard Gardner and to right brain/left brain learning theory.

Readers will also begin to notice subtle oppositions, beyond the obvious polarities, that cause interpersonal problems among the various clusters: vertical, diagonal, and horizontal. For example, horizontally, the NT and NF types share a similar capacity for intuition and often meet comfortably on that basis; however, the NTs find the NFs lack of precision bothersome, and the NFs find the NTs focus on precision at the expense of messier existential and relational factors too limited in scope. Many of my teacher-training students have objected initially to studying type theory, because it appears too complex and not relevant to classroom practice; many of them have told me years later that some knowledge of typology did help them observe students more keenly and neutrally; several have even developed teaching materials based on temperament that they use in their classrooms and in giving workshops of their own. I personally enjoy studying and writing about theoretical, speculative material. I like to know what makes people tick, so I offer the insights of Dr. Jung and the people who have added to his theory with the hope that it may save you some unnecessary wrangling with students and colleagues in your professional practice. Other ethical and pedagogical ramifications of type theory, based on my teaching experience, will be discussed in Chapter 5.

SP
(Cyclothymic) (Dionysian)

Jung	MBTI	% 1998 U.S. pop. sample
ITS	ISTP	5.4
IFS	ISFP	8.8
EST	ESTP	4.3
ESF	ESFP	8.5
		27.0 total

GOAL: Artistry, freedom, liberation, action

Good-natured, artistic (esp. crafts and production art). Hands-on workers. Risk-takers. No-nonsense facts-and-figures approach to problem solving. May sidestep codes, regulations in favor of pragmatism. Entrepreneurs. Little use for theories, abstract ideas. Good social talkers. May be delayed readers because not interested in symbolic systems.

NT
(Schizothymic) (Promethean)

Jung	MBTI	% 1998 U.S. pop. sample
ENT	ENTP	3.2
INT	INTJ	2.1
ETN	ENTJ	1.8
ITN	INTP	3.3
		10.4 total

GOAL: Scientific, precision, understanding how the world works

Analytic, curious, efficient, inventive, logical, nonsensual, impersonal, independent, theoretical, scientific, precise, exacting, intellectual, reflective. Value abstract thinking—do not value mundane details of daily life. Extroverted types rise to high positions in all organizational settings because provide conceptual structures. Force of outside authority or experts carries little weight.

Figure 4–5. Cross-referencing Jung, Spranger, Kretschmer, and the MBTI.

SJ
(Cyclothymic) (Epimethean)

Jung	MBTI	% 1998 U.S. pop. sample
IST	ISTJ	11.6
ETS	ESTJ	8.7
ISF	ISFJ	13.8
EFS	ESFJ	12.3
		46.4 total

GOAL: Economic stability, duty, responsibility, usefulness

Dependable, factual, painstaking, reliable, serious, patient, maintainers of society's traditions and institutions. Hard-working, long-range planners. Stable, loyal, thorough, consistent. Pragmatic — not interested in imaginative, symbolic activites.

NF
(Schizothymic) (Appolonian)

Jung	MBTI	% 1998 U.S. pop. sample
ENF	ENFP	8.1
INF	INEJ	1.5
EFN	ENFJ	2.5
IFN	INFP	4.4
		16.5 total

GOAL: Spirituality, search for meaning and purpose, becoming

Enthusiastic, humane, sensitive, perceptive, empathic, insightful, imaginative, creative. Good communication skills. Strongly religious, spiritual or philosophical. Life events are experienced as full of significance — thus perceived by others as hyperalert and oversensitive. Often charming, charismatic, inspirational. Fact, details, logic are stressful. Usually have a diversity of interests which presents as a short attention span to others.

MAY NOT BE A
VISIONARY, BUT HE KNOWS HOW TO
GET
THINGS
DONE.
        BOOM

AT THE   IS A
CENTER

CHAPTER FIVE

Know Thyself
Part II

Whenever I gave a seminar on temperament/typology to graduate interns in special education or to colleagues at the agency where I worked, I included an outline called "Speculations" in my packet of materials. After presenting an overview of the theoretical aspects of typology and collating the results of the temperament sorter they had taken, I asked the participants to explore some possible implications of the theory for teachers as listed on the "Speculations" page. Because we were accustomed to working on multidisciplinary teams intervening on behalf of developmentally delayed infants, toddlers, and preschool-aged children, we were already in the habit of observing, discussing and evaluating the developmental process as nonjudgmentally as possible. We routinely thought about ways that we could systematically alter approaches that were not working and reorganize the classroom environment to better serve the kids. As one colleague remarked, "There is no blame in special education." In other words we try, as much as possible, to tame our egos in order to accommodate the diversity in our students, their families, and our own professional teams.

UNDERSTANDING ONE ANOTHER

The first implicit and pragmatic extension of temperament/typology theory is a plea for mutual, nonjudgmental understanding. In their book *Please Understand Me*, David Keirsey and Marilyn Bates have popularized this aspect of temperament theory by providing systematic, lucid descriptions of each type that illustrate why the various types might clash. And if that is all a reader gets out of it, that is a lot: being able to acknowledge the possibility that, if a child in your classroom or a teaching colleague is driving you nuts, it may not be because she or he is diabolical or stupid, but because she or he is just not doing things your way. How many times have I heard an obviously well-grounded and organized extraverted-sensation-type teacher label a dreamy, imaginative, introverted-intuitive kid as a "flake" who needs to "buckle down" and "get real"? The same teacher may jump to the conclusion that a reserved child is "depressed" or "sad." Conversely, I have also heard the impatience in the voices of creative, spontaneous, process-oriented teachers when they refer to their detail and goal-directed students as "ordinary," "conforming," and "bean-counters." Whenever we demean or dismiss a child's preferred way of functioning, even with ruefully humorous comments, we cause an invisible wound to her spirit and to our own. We are dismissing the most natural, normal essence of who that child is, labeling her strengths as weaknesses, and dismissing her best adaptations as worthless. Even if we never say the words aloud, our body language, our eyes, our classroom activities, and our expectations tell her so. At the same time we are dismissing the opportunities that our "different" students offer us to become more conscious of, and potentially strengthened in, our own less-used functions. If we continue to teach, year after year, from our own best adapted modalities we run the risk not only of pressuring the children we teach into warped versions of themselves, but also of presiding over tepid classrooms and facing early burn-out.

Although I think the implications of typology/temperament are ethically and developmentally more wide-ranging than he seems to, David Keirsey makes an excellent point about the importance of satisfying and consolidating the goals of each of the temperament clusters around strong, flexible egos in early life. (Refer to chart at the end of Chapter 4). For educators, that means accommodating each child's temperament strengths while providing kind, scaffolded, support for weaknesses. It means modifying our teaching styles and methods of evaluation to access and strengthen a child's functional, attitudinal. and sensory preferences (see Gardner; Murphy).

We will all tend to teach and evaluate our students out of our own most conscious, preferred way of functioning. If we are successful (that is, most of the children in our class are passing state examinations, learning to read, using math concepts, and, most important, are well-behaved and diligent), we will probably conclude that our way of going about things is pretty good for everyone. The bell curve will look just as it is supposed to: a few kids will be performing poorly; most will be bunched up in a broad average range, and a few kids will be performing outstanding work. And yet, sometimes, particular children who are not "doing well" in our subject thrive under the tutelage of a colleague and occupy a better dot on the learning curve in his or her class. What is making the difference? Why is the child motivated in one class and not in another? Is it merely a preference for one class subject over another? Or is it possible for a student to be competent in most areas, given support and respect for his preferred ways of gathering and processing information? Certainly I found the latter to be true in my tutoring experience, where I could get to know a child well on a one-to-one basis and organize myself to teach to his or her strengths, even if they weren't my own. Arthur tells me that over time he became quite flexible about systematically rotating various types of classroom activities on a weekly or thematic basis at the high-school level to suit different learning modalities, which was satisfactory for all constituents: he moved desks to create small groups or discussion circles; he had the students role-play historic people or events; he gave classroom writing assignments; he allowed students to present their learning artistically; he provided worksheet questions for practice; and he organized hands-on projects. Remember—the operative words here are over time; you do not need to do all of this on your first day of teaching.

At this point in any given seminar presentation, participants begin to murmur "hmm," and make comments such as, "I think I see why my roommate takes care of all our bills and I take care of getting our study group together." They start telling me about their students and how certain behaviors confuse or irritate them while others seem more desirable. They express a greater willingness to regard others from a more neutral standpoint, giving them the benefit of the doubt that they might indeed be normal, albeit different. I call this more open attitude the First Great Pause: the conscious intention to back off from premature judgments that identify a child with her behaviors and to observe, observe, observe; the willingness to make an attempt at greater understanding of the Other; the sincere effort to refrain from imposing one's preferred ways of going about things as the *only* ways to create a classroom where all students can successfully learn.

THE E/I SPLIT

Perhaps the first and easiest difference for us to observe in our students and to use as an example is the extraverted/introverted attitudinal polarity that Jung identified as underlying the Freud/Adler split. That this attitudinal difference could actually drive two psychologically sophisticated colleagues apart attests to the difficulties it can present to classroom teachers. This is also the polarity that interested Myers and Briggs with regard to how people extravert their energy into the outer, objective world. Remembering Jung's admonition that these polar opposites are codeterminant and equally valid from a psychological point of view, we can begin to see more clearly the American bias in favor of extraversion.

See if there is a ring of familiarity in the following evaluation or report card comments (I understand that most report cards are scanned from byte-like comments these days—these examples might reflect your initial reflections about a student): "Jane is a quiet, reserved child who prefers to work by herself and who doesn't participate much in class discussions. Therefore, it is sometimes difficult to evaluate her immediate comprehension of the material even though her written work has been satisfactory. Socially she does not seem to make friends easily and usually prefers activities that involve just one or two other children. Jane also needs to finish her work faster in order to keep up with the other children. I am hoping that next term she will raise her hand more and participate in class discussions."

Contrast the comments on Jane with these, about her classmate Joey: "Joey is a sociable, outgoing boy who makes friends easily and who is a natural leader. He always has his hand in the air and loves to participate in class discussions. He finishes his work quickly and accurately and is a joy to have in class."

Although stated in somewhat nonjudgmental, but behavioral, language as teachers try to do, one can clearly hear a note of disapproval in the report about introverted Jane. The implication is that something is slightly "wrong" with her, that she doesn't conform to the extraverted, outgoing, friendly demeanors that are considered healthy in American children. Both reports use *"is"* language, which equates the child with his or her behaviors: Joey *is* sociable; Jane needs to finish her work faster (which implies Jane is too slow).

As we begin to develop an appreciation for the energy rhythms of the E/I polarity, the most basic of human attitudinal differences, several changes in our practice can occur. First, we can assess which attitude is more comfortable for us and thus spot where our personal preference may be coming into conflict with a student's. In the Jane/Joey examples, the teacher's bias was chosen to fit the cultural bias in favor of extraversion, but it is important to recognize that the bias could be exactly opposite. I have always found it easier, for example, to teach students on a one-to-one basis than in a group. As an introvert, I like the extended time frames of tutoring, which provide opportunities to go more deeply into lessons. Wiggly, physically active kids who are always "out there" can strain my patient endurance. The mere thought of teaching twenty-five to thirty children in a public school classroom, in five or six classes per day, not to mention the endless after-school phone calls, e-mails, paper corrections, hastily kept accountability records, study-hall duty, and extracurricular responsibilities is overwhelming to me. My reports on Jane and Joey might have sounded quite different: "Joey can be disruptive to the class at times when he calls out answers and talks out of turn to his neighbors." "Jane is a quiet, well-behaved girl who focuses on her work and who produces thorough, well-thought-out assignments. I enjoy having her in my class.

Next, we can easily modify our classroom environments and activities to accommodate the E/I rhythms. Such modifications might include seating arrangements where introverted children are placed at the edges of the room, slightly "out of the crowd," thus lowering the energy level of their immediate surroundings and making it easier for them to participate in class. Highly extraverted children might sit in the middle, but near the teacher, who could develop a scheme of gestural cues to help them wait their turn. Quiet activity areas might be established where small groups could work together or individuals could work alone. Likewise, areas could be set up for noisier, large-group, hands-on activities, such as block-building in a hallway or painting a cooperative wall mural.

Finally, we can begin to eliminate "is" language from our reports and frame them in more neutral, existential, descriptive, and situational terms: "Jane seems to enjoy working quietly and independently in the activity area I have set up in the back of the room. Her carefully completed assignments and projects demonstrate her ability to think through complex ideas. Her friend, Mary, also enjoys working in the quiet area and the two girls seem to have formed a mutually supportive small group. Although in the past Jane seldom volunteered contributions to class discussions, her perceptive answers on our weekly take-home quizzes show that she understands the concepts we are studying. Jane is raising her hand more lately; it seems as if these independent opportunities for thinking through the material before class may be helping Jane articulate her ideas within the group. Whenever Jane contributes to the class discussion, her comments are pertinent."

"Joey seems thoroughly at home in our class literature circles, which we are using to encourage interest in reading and to explore more deeply the themes in our book selections. The open-ended, informal discussions in these groups allow the children to participate without raising hands and waiting to answer as in formal classroom participation. It has been gratifying to see how quickly Joey has learned to demonstrate his reading comprehension through the respectful, interactive discussion that this type of informal group encourages with peers. Moreover, the organization of his rapid verbal responses within the group seems to be carrying over into his written work. Lately the work he does during quiet desk time has become more extended and detailed."

ANOTHER MINORITY IN THE CLASSROOM

The concluding chart in Chapter 4 shows the percentage of certain types in the U.S. population. Wherever there is an IS or ES combination, the rate of occurrence is generally higher than the opposite IN or EN combinations. I have already discussed the bias toward extraversion in the United States, but there also appears to be a preference—at least in terms of representation in the population—for sensation over intuition in the S/N polarity. Though in no way statistically valid, the informal data I have collected over a twelve-year period, from teacher-training groups of about twelve students each, tend to parallel the MBTI survey distributions for sensation and intuition. It would therefore follow that intuitive types constitute a minority of both teachers and students in American public school classrooms.

Although female students have predominated in each group, I have taught mixed classes where the male students represented at least half of the intuitive types, thus belying the idea that intuition is stereotypically peculiar to females. This observation highlights a gender issue that further complicates the minority status of intuition in the classroom and will be discussed later in the chapter.

If my small, anecdotal data samples are more or less representative, they suggest that the teaching profession, especially in the fields of special and elementary education, is overrepresented by extraverted sensation types (usually accompanied by feeling and a judging attitude, that is, ESFJ types or, secondarily, ISFJ types). Whenever I asked my teacher trainees to write short papers on the values they held most dear and would attempt to convey during their teaching careers, the SJs invariably discussed "organization," "responsibility," "structured environments," "a good work ethic," "consistent, clear rules," "attending to task and following through," "being fair," and "setting and meeting predetermined goals." The SPs also tell me about "common sense," "being flexible and adaptable within practical situations," and about the "value of hands-on projects."

The extraverted sensation types tended to use quick, concise, visual organizers, such as little charts, outlines, lists or bulleted facts in their written presentations, often identifying a wide range of categories. The introverted sensation types usually answered questions with the same sort of pragmatic organization as their extraverted peers, but tended to use more examples and details within a narrower range of categories. They were also apt to turn their papers in late. Sending them via e-mail at the eleventh hour helped them meet deadlines.

The sensation type students with a judging attitude preference seemed to come to conclusions easily and rapidly, while the ones with a perceiving preference did not like to take such definite stands and preferred their ongoing practicum work with students over written assignments; they usually handed in papers very late! Sensation types, if asked to write a 1-1/2 to 2 page paper, typically handed in exactly 1-1/2 to 2 pages, and liked seminar formats that told them exactly what was expected of them. It also follows from the statistical data that American classrooms are overrepresented by sensation type students. Happily, they and their teachers will mesh, temperamentally speaking, in the type of classroom activities that they prefer, and it is they who probably puff up that bell curve.

But what happens to the intuitive types—the polar opposites of the sensation types—in these circumstances? One way of looking at the problem is by analogy to the experiences of ethnic minorities as they face the challenges of becoming accepted into the dominant cultural context which promotes assumptions that their culture (by analogy: temperament/type) is somehow inferior and short of the mark. Ethnic minorities are also perceived as exotic, not quite natural, inscrutable, and therefore, ultimately unassimilable: a terrible catch-22. The exoticism might be regarded as attractive, alluring, engaging, interesting, but not really acceptable. Some coping strategies one notices in underrepresented temperament types resemble those demonstrated by ethnic minorities in the process of assimilation: hyper-opportunism, which involves taking the measure of the system and "working" it; wary, defensive, hyper-alertness; and withdrawal, which presents as a somnolent, spacey inattentiveness.

In such a situation there is huge pressure to assimilate, to fit in with the crowd. Just as the ethnic minority may try to suppress any extrinsic differentiating characteristics of language, appearance, and dress, so the intuitive temperament/type minority, especially when they are children seeking approval at home and in school, try hard to learn how to gather and process information through the sensation mode, usually accompanied by extraverted feeling and judging—which is a wearying, often anxious task. However, like skin color, eye shape, or hair texture, temperament is intrinsic and immutable, no matter how much psychological plastic surgery, bleach, or straightener is applied.

Over the past twenty-five years I have noticed a variety of ways in which intuitive children negotiate acceptance into their predominantly sensation type classroom environment. One strategy may predominate, but often they are mixed and used as the situation demands. Intuitive children often perform assignments rotely and quickly in order to conform to expectations, then go off to spend their free time pursuing their interests independently (the hyper-opportunistic orientation with a tendency toward auto-didacticism); or they become obsessive about details, agonizing over minutiae and turning in six pages for every two required (the hyper-alert adaptation); or they exist in a dreamy haze (especially the introverted types) and are often perceived as eccentric, "arty," or idealistic. I suspect that the haze provides a shield behind which they can withdraw and tune out the world; in this manner they use a sort of passive refusal to adapt to sensation expectations and to test whether and how these expectations will be enforced.

The first adaptation can lead to a sort of fuzzy, nonrigorous grasp of subject area content in the collectively approved curricula, unless the content is of particular interest. After-school activities often provide more outlets for imaginative, creative endeavors. I recall one extremely bright, intuitive student who purposely kept his GPA around 87, a decently acceptable level, which he could manage with minimal effort, but which held him back from acceptance into the more intensive academic tracks. Outside of school he focused a gifted and creative intellect on writing projects: movie reviews; movie scripts; a self-published newspaper featuring a whimsically hilarious sports reporter; poetry and short stories. He made movies, perfected his hoop shots, slept, and dreamed. In this manner my young friend was able to keep his creative intuition and sense of humor intact and go on to a satisfying career as a writer. But his educational experience didn't have much to do with formal schooling or relationships with teachers who greatly inspired him, at least through high school. Highly inventive people like Steven Spielberg routinely report this sort of relationship to formal education and often appear to be nonconforming and anti-authoritarian. For teachers who are focused on behavior management and collective responses to learning, these characteristics will seem aggressive and invite power struggles.

A more goal-oriented girl whom I tutored is representative of the second type of adaptation. She stood at the top of her class by maintaining vigilance over the details of her subject areas. A schoolteacher mother provided her with excellent modeling and support for organizational skills. With an almost rapturous interest she pursued the theoretical aspects of biology/genetics in her regular classes, but also took advantage of college enrichment courses and summer programs. Always wryly humorous about her hyper-vigilant perfectionism, this young woman, whose intuition was backed up by thinking, found support for her interests in high school courses paired with related outside enrichment. She sailed through college and graduate work, which challenged her creative individuality.

Friends of mine who are college professors, many of them intuitive thinking types, tell of similar encounters. The "spacey" intuitive types are the bane of a sensation teacher's existence. They lose their books and papers. They are usually unclear about daily assignments and often hand in homework late or not at all. Their lockers are in shambles. They often appear to have little use for conventional authority and are apparently marching to a different drum. The most-often heard remark about these students is "He is not living up to his potential" (that is, sensation expectations). To their sensation counterparts, making contact with them sometimes feels like Earth trying to call Major Tom.

In all these cases, the vigilance required for an intuitive to manage sensory reality in all its detail and practicality is either tiring, boring, or compulsive. Although intuition paired with thinking has a natural tendency toward competence, understanding of how systems work, and rigorous scientific enquiry, kids with this temperament may be regarded as a bit nerdy and excluded from in-group social activities. However, if intellectually motivated, they may also be regarded as "brains" and sought out to help with homework or to be the star of the debate team. Often impatient to leave high school behind, they may find their metier in college and graduate school, frequently entering the teaching ranks at the university level where, paradoxically, the intuitive type is overrepresented in the profession. They are also highly sought after as the idea, planning, and systems people in corporate think tanks or policy-making organizations, often rising through the ranks to positions of high authority and prestige.

The intuitive feeling types are a different story. The aims of their interests are relational rather than logical patterns: relations to themselves, to others, to the world, and even to the cosmos. They often "know" things about people or about the significance that events will have for the lives of themselves and others. Usually they cannot describe logical steps toward acquiring or encompassing their big-picture knowledge (as the NTs can, through their thinking functions), or explain it very well to others. For instance, when I have tutored NF teenagers, they often have a great deal of trouble organizing the steps of solutions to math equations or geometric proofs, but often "just know" the answers because they grasp the problems holistically, not sequentially. Using standard formats for outlining class lectures or ideas for compositions is painful for them, but the use of free-form outlines such as "spiders," helps them group ideas into a kind of immediate organic coherence. For math work I often had them turn the paper ninety degrees and use the vertical lines as guides to help keep numbers lined up or draw schematic images of word problems.

If NFs are introverted, their relational interests go inside and manifest as ongoing self-reflections that border on the mystical at times. If extraverted, they sometimes join the ranks of Tarot card readers, astrologers, and psychics. Frequently regarded as eccentric or "kooky" by their more facts- and figures-oriented SJ opposites, or their competence-oriented NT confreres, the exhausting level of hyper-vigilance they must maintain can drive NF types away from schooling altogether. Several extremely bright, intuitive, creative NF friends I made in college withdrew at the end of their first year. All expressed a concern that the analytical (NT) and applied analytical (SJ) emphasis of college work was blocking their creative, imaginative energies. If they do pursue a more conventional education, it is usually in service to people; they make excellent, empathic psychologists, for example. When one young man in my teacher-training course noticed that the Keirsian goals of the NF type are "becoming," and "finding meaning and significance in everything," he exclaimed, "Yes! That's exactly why I want to become a teacher; I want to help kids with their *becoming*." Because parents, teachers, and colleagues often do not understand the NF type, these greatly relational people often express feelings of isolation and loneliness.

What do I look for if I'm trying to spot an intuitive person, without having a test-based knowledge of his or her temperament? A slightly unfocused look about the eyes, a wide-eyed gaze that seems to take in the big picture rather than the details. An intuitive/feeling (NF) type may be identified by a tendency to dress in slightly costumey clothing (an Aussie hat with a feather stuck in the brim, a knee-length belted sweater over black velvet tights, dangly earrings, beaded vests, crystal necklaces, string bracelets, clothing with unusual colors or textures), a slight rhythmic difference (once, while watching a chorus line of eight-year-olds in a dance production, I observed one little girl on the end who was continually a half-step behind her peers), a charismatic presence coupled with an acute sensitivity to the needs of others. In educational settings, the rhythmic difference may manifest in schooling that does not follow the common sequence or career track. NF's often return to school for undergraduate college degrees at later ages or follow graduate programs with independent studies in subjects such as comparative religions, depth psychology, or the arts. Intuitive thinkers (NTs) may collect degrees; for example, several NT lawyers I know are also doctors of medicine or have MBAs. In both cases there is a highly developed sense of originality, individual effort, and ethics with scant regard for "experts" and "authorities." The need for discovery through personal experience predominates. In any case, a curriculum that has a place for independent projects or, at the college level, for interdepartmental majors appeals to intuitive types.

Intuitive people often have a flair for imaginative adventure: if introverted, in a fantastic inner life; if extraverted, in the outer world. Years ago I accompanied an extremely charismatic, extraverted intuitive woman and five little preadolescent boys as she talked our way on to a riot-squad bus in Paris. The gendarmes, completely charmed, apparently forgot about Algerian terrorists and student protestors for a half-hour while the boys tried on their helmets and plexiglass shields and claimed the bus as their play space. She knew exactly what those boys would like and procured it for them.

These personal experiences and observations may give you some clues about teaching intuitive children. Observant and kind sensation teachers can assist them by devising plans for helping them gather, organize, and manage materials while honoring, instead of criticizing, their temperament difference. Teachers can provide opportunities for imaginative projects that demonstrate acquisition of content, such as role playing historical figures or presenting thematic art projects.

One intuitive teacher I knew taught high school history using historical novels as text. Because intuitives like symbols and imagery, a math teacher I knew used such imagistic teaching tools as mandala drawings and labyrinths to teach the geometry of circles. Intuitive kids also like to brainstorm ("how many things can you do with a brick?"). When academic projects are set in an imaginative or overarching theoretical framework, intuitive children become more enthusiastic about and willing to rehearse the facts and details they need to achieve mastery. As Alfred North Whitehead observed, "Without generality [the strength of the intuitive] there is no reasoning, without concreteness [the strength of the sensation type] there is no importance" (brackets are mine; *The Aims of Education*, p. 53). What magic can be wrought in the classroom when both strengths are honored and used!

Elizabeth Murphy reminds us that type should never become a dodge for avoiding educational success. She says, "If an assignment is well designed and has a clear instructional goal, then all students should be expected to meet it. The way a teacher helps students reach a goal may differ according to the different personality types of the children, but the expectation for students to meet the goal should not" (p. 87). This statement is all well and good as long as the teacher is aware of, acknowledges, and values the frequently marginalized intuitive minority, which often has no use for predetermined instructional goals. This became apparent to me in one of my graduate seminars when a book I used for additional reading laid out an analogy for good teaching. It proposed that a successful educational process resembled a train on track to various stations in a cross-country journey until it arrived on the opposite coast. I asked my students whether or not they agreed with this analogy and had them write a short in-class essay giving their reasons. I wrote along with them. When we shared our writings, the sensation type students agreed that the analogy was a good one; they liked the idea of having clear, sequential goals and a predetermined outcome. The two intuitive students I had that year hesitated and both wrote something about how they might like to get off the train and look around. I let myself really go in my essay: Yuck!!! A train??? On *tracks*??? Nothing doing!!! I wanted to travel by bicycle—maybe I wanted to stop in Omaha rather than Chicago; maybe I wanted to pop a wheelie, get on a plane and fly to Rio; maybe I'd like to double back and see someplace twice. Murphy's book contains many useful teaching and assessment strategies, including examples of such basics as how to frame test or homework questions to accommodate these typological differences.

Murphy also reminds us that although some functions are preferred and much better adapted, all the functions and attitudes are used some of the time by all individuals. She notes that classroom environments should contain areas or centers constructed to reflect the characteristics of each type. A child is then free on a daily basis to choose the function-related activity that corresponds to subject area interest or fluctuating interest or energy levels. Such areas and activities are usually simple to accomplish, do not require extra funding or supplies, and can be implemented at both the elementary and secondary levels. At the elementary level such areas might include research centers containing reference books or computers where children can work alone or in groups; "creativity centers" with dress-up clothes where students can act out imaginative texts such as fairy tales, adventure stories, or biographies; hands-on centers containing art materials, building blocks, or math manipulatives; skill practice centers containing math fact worksheets and writing practice booklets. Well-planned areas like these can be found, but mostly at the pre-school and elementary levels; they can be implemented in later grades as well. Although high school students usually have access to school-wide centers such as a computer room or the library, and can take electives such as industrial arts or music, Arthur tells me that as he gained teaching experience he could easily and rapidly create classroom centers as needed: desks could be shifted into small groupings for collaborative work; the four corners of the room could become one-desk quiet areas for working on individual projects; having a large table at the back of the room accommodated hands-on activities; a large pad of newsprint on an easel allowed his students to question each other and rehearse course content facts. Arthur also says that teachers can use daily lesson planning to consciously construct and rotate weekly activities to suit the various temperaments. Because high school teachers often do not have rooms of their own and have to share space with colleagues, a rolling cart or large canvas bags pre-packed with type-related materials are helpful in creating extemporaneous centers for carefully constructed lessons.

THE SHADOW KNOWS

For those of you old enough to remember the Shadow radio character, you will recall the maniacal cackle of laughter at the end of the introduction. When I heard it as a child, it hinted at dark secrets, which the title character knew and I did not. There was a psychological truth to that cackle that I became more aware of as an adult. Although Arthur discussed the shadow problem with regard to behavior in general in Chapter 2, Jungian theory proposes a shadow inherent in the typological functions that underlies some specific difficulties with clashing temperaments. That is, if one attitude and function are preferred and well adapted, and one function is auxiliary and reasonably available, what happens to the others? In Jungian terms, they would be unconscious and compensatory to the conscious standpoint. They would be unavailable to consciousness and would underlie a psychological blind spot over which one wouldn't have much control. They might pop up at unexpected times and their emergence might look maladapted, affect-laden, or compulsive. I remember a very one-sided, highly introverted intuitive woman I met on a trip to Europe. Her extraversion and sensation were so undifferentiated that going to the grocery store was a major problem; she couldn't organize a grocery list and was nearly agoraphobic about being among other shoppers. If required to attend a cocktail party because of her husband's business, her behavior was quite primitive for an intelligent, sensitive woman. She would accost strangers, pull out cigarettes, and start puffing clouds of smoke into their faces, hike her dress up over her knees with uncharacteristic abandon, and converse about minute personal details in a loud voice. She seemed unable to control herself in anxious social situations, and it took days to recover from the exhaustion and embarrassment she felt afterward. In these situations, she was literally not herself; instead she was "beside herself," in the shadow zone.

Because these more unadapted functions and attitudes can cause such a painful level of discomfort, the defense mechanism of projection may be used to get rid of the distress by placing the responsibility for it on someone else. When a sensation type teacher pejoratively refers to an intuitive child as "flaky," for example, he speaks more about his own uncomfortable relationship to creative intuition than he does to the child's actual character or abilities; the teacher projects his inferior function onto the child who has the intuitive "hook" for the projection, then dismisses the natural way that child gathers and processes information as inferior. That certainly solves the teacher's ego defense problem, but it causes great stress for the student, who perceives it as a basic rejection of his being. Worse is the possible projection scenario where J (a preference for closure and completion) type teachers project their difficulty with P (a preference for process and open-endedness) characteristics on to their NP and SP students, labeling them "attention deficit disordered," or "ADD/ADHD," and recommending drug treatment. It is possible that many of these P behaviors are representative of type, not pathological, and that suitable instructional techniques might be better treatments than Ritalin.

Since most people go into teaching because they are motivated to help their students learn, reflecting on the type shadow problem is essential to developing suitable lessons. The first paper I assign my graduate students after I have outlined type/temperament theory is to write a two-page paper describing someone who drives them nuts, who irritates the hell out of them, giving specific details or illustrations about the traits they can't stand. A nervous titter usually runs through the class. Already they suspect that something may be going on beneath the surface of their familiar way of operating that may be hindering tolerant or—if "tolerant" is not their treasured value—constructive or productive interactions with others. When I hand the papers back, I ask the class to compare their peeves to the perceptive/evaluative preferences of their own type and to the preferences of their opposite type. For some students there is a little epiphany as they "get it": maybe they are most at sword's point with people who are functioning in a polar opposite manner. Moreover, their conviction that there is something inherently wrong with the other person is fairly intractable. As the weeks go by and they comment on the behaviors of children or colleagues, I still hear the quick-to-judgment labeling, such as, "she doesn't like/want to learn"; "he is disrespectful and antsy"; "she is off in a cloud (or naïve, or disorganized)"; and so on.

One extraverted sensation/feeling graduate student in my class wrote about her frustration with the academic expectations that an introverted intuitive/thinking professor held for her work. She said that no matter how hard she studied, she simply could not get a good grade on his systematic, theoretically based, scientifically rigorous tests. Conversely, this professor dismissed her as "uninspired academically," and "a very average student." Yet in evaluating her practicum work with children and her seminar performance, I gave her top marks for her ability to construct fresh, original activities around the strengths of her students and for her easy acceptance of individual differences. Among her colleagues, she was always at the center of cooperative efforts. Whenever strongly expressed opposing viewpoints arose in class, she was able to restate arguments in ways that led to more inclusive understanding of the subjects under discussion. Her insights were sometimes sublime regarding relational and personal issues. These strengths will probably be central to her development as an effective teacher—someone who should not be dismissed so lightly by more theoretically inclined teachers who wield great power over GPAs, professional recommendations, and a student's sense of worth. This example points up the historical and extreme bias in the intellectual development of Western culture over the past 400 years, that thinking is superior to feeling as an evaluative function. Thinking types with just average intellect are often judged as superior in evaluating perceptions than feeling types are; the ability to make rational, logical, objective, "scientific" evaluations is considered the greater skill. Both Whitehead and Jung deplored the devaluation of the feeling function in our culture and wrote volumes about the necessity to reintegrate it as a balanced partner to thinking. Both also recognized the correlated gender devaluation of females (who are culturally expected to "carry" the projected inferior feeling function) that occurred as a result of this bias.

The judgment by the professor of the student is possibly an emotional one based on his own discomfort with his inferior feeling function. The shadow becomes especially problematic where a type polarity is accompanied by a built-in power differential: "me teacher, you student." In these situations, whether at school or in the family with a powerful opposite-type parent, a child will give up his ontological impulse to know and love his own being in the service of a second impulse to fit in, to be productive or significant in terms of what the family or school or society deems important. Lifelong, unsuccessful, unhappy attempts to perform against one's most natural gifts can result. The ensuing frustration and anger can also lead to shadowy self-destructive actions and uncivil classrooms, as we pointed out in our chapters on behavior.

Conversely, the teacher's power advantage blocks his own possibilities for self-reflection. In the end it diminishes the teacher's as well as the student's spirit, and eventual burnout is almost guaranteed. Clashes between the faculty thinkers and student feelers are common at the university level where the feelers project "coldness," "dryness," "all head, no heart" on their professors, while the teachers counter-project "fuzzy-thinking," "mushy," "emotional" on to their students.

Combating the shadow means coming to know it as a repository of potential energy. It means withdrawing projections, best identified when we make judgmental statements about others. One of my good friends, a high school language teacher and a sensation/feeling/judging type, recently took a sabbatical. It was so much fun to witness her growth as she engaged in foreign travel, made a film about her experiences, and developed fresh curriculum ideas that she wrote up in manual form. Fearful at first of taking on her creative intuitive side and feeling unsure about her intellectual capacity, she nevertheless persisted, and made a significant contribution to her school as well as to her own self-understanding. If beginning teachers can learn to become alert to and then witness the shadowy projections of their inferior functions and attitudes, then withdraw and take personal responsibility for them, then explore their untapped potential, they will be on their way, just as my friend is, to fearless teaching.

LABELS AND THE SP TEMPERAMENT

While we discussed labeling in Chapter 2 from the point of view of behavioral control, labeling could also be viewed as a subset of the shadow problem itself. The use of labels in the educational field—particularly special education—has become so widespread and so pathologically associated that the subject begs an additional discussion. While it may be true that there is a valid range of disabilities with characteristic presentations that need to be diagnosed and treated—I am thinking of Down syndrome, autistic spectrum disorders, cerebral palsy—there are also inherent shadow problems related to labeling. The psychodynamic danger (which has primarily interested Marcia) occurs when labels become receptacles for our own unconscious weaknesses and inferiority, such as the possibility of confusing type with "disorder" discussed in the previous section. This confusion may reflect a shadow in the system due at least in part to typological oppositions and their projections on to behaviors, rather than to actual disabilities.

The philosophical danger (which intrigues Art) results in the encapsulation of projection. It is the role of psychology to identify and treat real problems; it is the role of philosophy to create credible categories of experience. When categories become reified (made to seem actual), they threaten to make the applied experience of educators static, and upon being applied they follow behind students like a ball and chain for the duration of their schooling.

I believe the P/J (perceiving/judging) attitudinal opposition, especially as seen in the SP/SJ (sensation/perceiving and sensation/judging) split of the Keirsey configuration may play a significant role in identifying some children as attention deficit disordered, a label that has become an educational dumping ground. You will recall that the goal of the SPs (sensation/perceiving) involves liberation, freedom from restriction, pushing limits, achieving short-term outcomes within process; that of the SJ (sensation/judging) type involves responsibility, organization, conserving social values, and setting and completing long-term, preconceived goals. If, as outlined in the section on classroom minorities, SJ teachers who are in the majority find SP children disruptive, antsy, and inattentive, there might be an unnecessary quick-fix rush to the Ritalin bottle rather than educational solutions based on instructional models appropriate to the SP type. Perhaps the most interesting discussion of the P/J attitudinal polarity that I have come across is in Thom Hartmann's book *Attention Deficit Disorder: A Different Perception*. Hartmann's typology distinguishes between "hunter/gatherers" and "farmers." Hunter/gatherers rely on natural adaptive traits important in primal societies: They constantly scan and monitor their environments for danger or opportunities to find or hunt for food. The ability to scan the environment quickly and perceive minute changes represents an exquisite form of attentiveness. Hunter/gatherers are able to sustain intense bursts of energy in order to hotly pursue a goal, then just as quickly disengage their focus and energy when the hunt is over; they are highly independent and flexible and can easily initiate or change strategies on a moment's notice; they are bored by routine tasks, but like taking risks that get results; they are concrete thinkers and are often impatient with the theoretical, symbolic, or abstract. They are often late readers for whom the written symbols of language are irrelevant. They usually have remarkable visual-spatial aptitudes combined with superb hand-eye coordination. They may also have hyper-acute vision and spend a good deal of time using these gifts to practice and perfect their skills.

The obituaries of the late Ted Williams intrigued me with respect to Hartmann's descriptions of the hunter/gatherer type: throughout his remarkable career as one of baseball's greatest hitters he displayed many of the characteristics associated with that temperament. Hunter/gatherer types also forego manners and social amenities when something needs to be accomplished urgently, like the stereotypically gruff, demanding surgeon in an operating room. It seems to me that Hartmann's descriptors parallel those of the SP temperament in the MBTI.

When I taught children who displayed these characteristics, I tried to keep the lessons short and fast-paced. To encourage reading acquisition and comprehension, I often devised hands-on projects that required reading directions. Sports magazines, comic books, and short news articles were kept on the shelves. I experimented with print/ground color combinations to maximize visual/spatial competence and with activities that involved the body to enhance fact memorization (for example, spelling words), using textured letter shapes (sandpaper, velour) for fingertip tracing. Often brief cross-body warm-up exercises, such as tapping opposite hand-to-knee seemed to help SP students focus on and organize their work.

Hartmann's farmer types emerged historically with the beginning of settled agricultural communities. They rapidly multiplied in number and came to provide a different set of skills for the human community. They are not easily distracted and can carry through long-range projects without immediate goal-achievement gratification. They pay attention to details in a way that helps them to follow through on off-season tasks (for example, repairing equipment during the winter months in preparation for next year's planting). Farmer types are not easily bored, are usually active in the community, and are not natural risk-takers because farming does not involve much immediate danger. Because farming produces food for the community much more efficiently than hunting, farmer adaptations gradually overcame and replaced hunter skills in perceived value. Hartmann quotes anthropological evidence that suggests that "over the past 8,000 years on every continent and among every people, hunter/gatherers have been wiped out, displaced, slaughtered, exterminated and oppressed.... Today fewer than 2 percent of the world's human population are genetically pure hunter/gatherer peoples and only a remnant of them is found in our gene pool" (p. xxxviii).

Looked at from the point of view of our predominantly SJ cultural perspective regarding "attentiveness," SP skills appear to be pathological or disordered. Judgmental assessments include such terms as "disorganized," "disruptive and impulsive," "impatient," "poor social skills," "probable reading disabilities," "difficulty following directions," "poor sense of the consequences or their actions," and "daydreamer."

One of my most instructive encounters with a child whom I now suspect was a burgeoning SP type occurred in the pre-school where I did part of my special education internship. Alfie was a nearly five-year-old boy who displayed some behaviors that were no doubt related to difficulties in his early home environment. However, his experience in school provides an example of how encouraging natural preferences can sometimes help moderate other difficult behaviors.

Alfie

Alfie had a favorite tricycle in the cavernous motor room where we spent part of every morning. Each day he beelined his way to that trike, hopped on, and peddled as fast as he could toward the opposite wall amidst the horrified shrieks of his transfixed teachers and therapists. I used to watch in awe—I had raised a child with similar skills and determination—as he slammed on the brakes within an inch or two of the wall and skidded to a halt. It seemed dispiriting to me that the usual consequence was to take the trike away from him as a hedge against trips to the emergency room and lawsuits. Combined with the ongoing general effort to obtain Alfie's compliance in the classroom, this trike deprivation seemed like cruel and unusual punishment to me. Finally, one of the speech therapists suggested making reversible red and green stop/go signs glued onto sticks. Teachers stationed at intervals around the room then invited Alfie to play a stop-and-go game with them, which capitalized on his excellent visual/spatial and kinesthetic skills while rendering his Evel Knievel rides less hair-raising for his teachers. This game had some worthwhile secondary outcomes: Alfie learned to recognize the words on the color-coded signs and soon developed a repertoire of practical sight words gleaned from other signs around the building, such as Exit, Kitchen, and Boys and Girls. He also became more aware of safety issues at street crossings.

In general I have found that keeping SP children as physically liberated and exuberant as possible actually helps them acquire academic skills. I would hazard a guess that the brain chemistries of these children are genetically different from those of their SJ peers. The kind of risk-taking, split-second decisions they thrive on probably parallels extremely rapid-fire synaptic responses. If this is the case, then suppressing that energy level in a normal SP type child probably does actual neuronal damage as well as guarantees disruptive behavior. There will be three or four of these kids in any given class of twenty students. Instead of regarding them as disruptive and opting for a pathologizing label, these children deserve to be taught using instructional strategies tailored to their type. Their energies need to be channeled rather than suppressed, and as educators we need to delay judgment in order to more accurately discriminate the roles that type and pathology are playing in a child's behavioral expressions. SP children are at risk for reading disabilities and for dropping out of school; in the worst cases the anger and frustration they feel can erupt into behaviors that land them in legal trouble. Given proper support SPs can grow into virtuoso musicians if interested in music, gifted professional athletes if good at sports, military leaders if thrilled by strategy and combat, and talented teachers if they love doing hands-on projects with kids.

Of all the temperament types the SPs have engaged my empathy and concern to the greatest degree. Because their behaviors are so negatively judged, my heart always goes out to them even if they are giving me a headache. Whenever I see my own SP son back a huge wagonload of hay into a barn, with only inches to spare on either side of the door, or watch him craft an elegant piece of furniture, I think of Alfie, I smile, and I hope with all my heart that he too has found an inspiriting outlet for his own genius.

TYPE AND GENDER

When the MBTI was last revised in 1998 (Form M), a stratified random sampling of the U.S. population was also taken. U.S. census results were used to correct for the over-representation of Caucasian females and under-representation of African American males in the sample, thus ensuring the high level of reliability that this sample is considered to have. Although other samples had been taken prior to 1998, they were usually drawn from specialized groups such as "medical personnel," "high school students," or "teacher candidates." The overrepresentation of certain types within the specialized groups thus skewed the results and led to misconceptions regarding actual national type distributions. Some of these misconceptions involved distributions along gender lines.

For an example, let's return for a moment to consideration of the E/I dichotomy. Prior to the 1998 sample it was thought that significantly more women preferred extraversion, while more men preferred the introverted attitude. Other samples had also suggested that the extraverted attitude largely predominated in the United States. The 1998 survey indicated that not only was the gender difference in the two attitudes not very significant, but that the numbers of people preferring each attitude occur at about equal rates. However, Naomi Quenk, one of the revisers of the MBTI, reminds us that "Even though the national representative sample indicates about an equal frequency of people reporting a preference for Extraversion and those preferring Introversion, our culture in general clearly favors extraverted qualities over introverted ones" (p. 75). Then why the preference for extravert-ed qualities? One highly speculative conjecture I ask my graduate stu-dents to consider regards the pool of elementary and middle school teacher candidates that I have been keeping informal surveys on for several years. The extraverted attitude consistently predominates in this specialized group comprised mostly of women. Historically speaking, might the bias toward extraversion be a pedagogical prefer-ence with extraverted attitudinal expectations placed on kids early in life due to overrepresentation of that attitude in the teaching force? We are all familiar with the directives to share; get along with others in a friendly, outgoing way; be objective; do your work quickly and accurately; play team sports and get involved with lots of extracurricu-lar activities; raise your hand and participate in class discussions if you expect a good grade.

The only consistently gender-related functional opposition revealed both by the 1998 sample and previous surveys is on the Thinking/Feeling scale. Women show a 75 percent feeling to 25 per-cent thinking preference, while men exhibit a 57 percent thinking to 43 percent feeling distribution. The trouble begins when type and gen-der become confused. Our cultural bias demands that in order to be "masculine" a man ought to be a hardheaded thinker while to be truly "feminine" a woman must be big-hearted and relational. If the gen-ders deviate from these expectations, harsh, negative judgments with enormous pressure to conform may result, as well as limited access to socially sanctioned roles. Besides being labeled unfeminine, a female thinking type is often regarded as "cold" or "pedantic," while her male counterpart will be perceived as having a "steel-trap mind" and being an "original thinker." The fear of being regarded as unfeminine and therefore undesirable might be one force that drives talented thinking type women away from the study of science and mathematics, and may underlie the phenomenon called math anxiety that we see in (mostly) female students.

I still chuckle whenever I think of two girls whom I tutored in math many years ago. They were both obviously capable students, but were struggling with trigonometry and intermediate algebra. My first job seemed to be to calm them down, and then to assess and fill in some missing links in their comprehension of the math sequence (which was more closely linked to recent curricular changes than to their abilities). Both girls handily passed their math finals; one went on to become chief CPA at a good-sized corporation and the other an outstanding student at Harvard.

The vilification of Hillary Clinton (considered a brilliant lawyer in a profession that attracts thinking types) in the press and by her political detractors is an example of the attacks that can be launched against thinking type women who are in the public eye. Critical comments about her looks, clothing, age, and marital problems, which would rarely be noted about her male colleagues, routinely come up in conversations about her. She was roundly criticized for her hard-headed, independent handling of the health care issue and, indeed, had she displayed a more feeling attitude toward participants in the political haggling, she might have prevailed. And do readers remember the flap she caused with her cookie-baking comment? Because she is culturally expected to demonstrate mostly relational attitudes, but often does not, a lot of people dislike her. Conversely, if she regularly displayed relational tendencies, she would be considered "soft," the classic catch-22 in which women are often trapped. It takes enormous self-confidence and a thick skin for a woman to weather the kind of demeaning, and sometimes vicious, projections that have been visited on Hillary, and to continue to pursue a traditionally male career in the public sector.

Conversely, the societal judgments on feeling type men can be equally detrimental to their gender identity. Frequently heard jibes against such men are "wussy," "sissy" "pussy-whipped"—terms that are just as sexually loaded as those used against women. If these men are intuitive as well, the whammy is doubled, as intuition is also strongly linked to societal expectations of females, "women's intuition" being the truism. (Remember: the national sample shows no correlation to gender on the Sensation/Intuition scale). The doors to masculine power and entitlement are often jammed shut to men who display feeling characteristics.

Over the years I have noticed some strategies that the young men and women in my classes use to cope with these gender/type confusions. If the men are intuitive feeling types, they may cultivate a sort of hyper-manly Hemingway-esque image to disguise the functions that render them culturally vulnerable. For instance, one intuitive feeling man I know has developed a second career out of heli-skiing on the world's highest mountains. Others chop wood, lead outdoor camping expeditions, run marathons, and lift weights. They often display a love of "gear," such as tents, stopwatches, campfire food, hiking boots, or bicycles.

Another coping strategy (often used both at home and in school) is to fall back on one of the more acceptable, but less-adapted, functions.

My observation is that many intuitive feeling men work hard at adapting through either the auxiliary or tertiary functions (sensation or thinking). These less natural preferences can present as somewhat rigid and compulsive. They obsess about details, work harder than they need to accomplish fairly straightforward tasks, and criticize others whom they perceive as slackers or incompetents. Their descriptions of these "slackers" often sound like portraits of people who demonstrate the very qualities these intuitive feeling men are trying to disguise in themselves.

In the past twenty-five to thirty years many popular books have been written about men's difficulty with expressing their feelings or emotions. Men now routinely attend weekend workshops that help them "find their feminine sides," which I think compounds the difficulty by suggesting that "feminine" and "feeling" somehow still go together in the culturally expected way. Such workshops may function as pressure releases, but until feeling is universally regarded as a natural, valuable masculine characteristic as well as a feminine one, the gender expectations won't change much.

In my seminars, sensation thinking type women appear to cope by deferring to the men during class and seeking me out privately afterward to discuss their ideas. They seem to have cultivated a sort of passive or faux introversion as a shield when they are around men, but will engage more openly in all-female groups, thus providing some anecdotal evidence for the findings of Carol Gilligan in her research at the Emma Willard School. The attitudes of the very few intuitive thinking type women I have encountered in my teacher training experience sometimes present as ironic or slightly supercilious. A young, extraverted, intuitive thinking woman once handed me a journal assignment that was written near the beginning of her notebook. She had neglected to remove the Alf cartoons and critical comments about the class, which she scribbled on the last few pages. These pages happened to flip open first when I read the assignment. Our thinking/feeling opposition was apparent whenever she challenged me in class; her theoretical and logical grasp was more precise than mine, while the relational arguments I was making ran straight up against her blind spot. The theory interested her, but its ethical implications with relation to the primacy of the feeling function bored her. I wrote a note to her under one of the cartoons saying that I understood how she felt; the class had bored me, too, as the students had not gotten my point—perhaps we could find a more straightforward way to deal with misunderstandings, especially since avoiding misunderstandings was the reason we were considering type theory in the first place. Her criticisms led me to try to structure my talks more precisely and her red-faced embarrassment at having her cartoon trove discovered led her to a more inclusive consideration of the topic. I came to like and respect this student as the year went on, because her forthright, intelligent questions and observations raised the intellectual caliber of the class.

TYPE AND EVOLUTION

A friend of mine, who was also interested in temperament theory, told me he thought the function types developed to serve some evolutionary, survival purpose. I often ask my teacher-training groups to recall what they know about aboriginal cultures and brainstorm what the survival value of each of the four temperament clusters might have been to early humans. Ideas about SP survival skills include protection of the tribe by warriors and provision of food by hunters; SJs might have been responsible for daily, long-range tasks such as preparation and storage of food and maintenance of shelter and clothing; NTs would probably have filled chieftain roles, planning strategy and policy for tribal military engagements, settling disputes, and negotiating tribal alliances. The survival value of each of these types seems straightforward, but students seem to have more difficulty generating ideas about the NF types. Although many of them quickly conclude that in ancient times these people were probably tribal shamans, priests, or medicine people, they find it difficult to assign an evolutionary or survival value to them. The closest they can get is to "healing"; only if they are NF types themselves can they articulate ideas about "having a vision for the tribe," "seeing in advance where the tribe is going, what is in store for it in the future," or "envisioning what the tribe will become."

When I ask them to jump ahead in time and speculate on the roles the various types play in contemporary society, they see the SPs as, for example, engineers, professional athletes, military people with skills for flying jet aircraft, or rock and virtuoso musicians. They see SJs as maintaining conservative, traditional social values, and executing the day-to-day responsibilities of life. SJs, they offer, may enter professions such as medicine and accounting, where a grasp of details is paramount.

In today's world, NTs are valued for their creative competence in research and development areas, university teaching, and in all places where "think tanks" flourish. They are the people who develop

encompassing theoretical structures, which overarch practical applications in business and technology.

In her Cognitive Profile descriptions, Dr. Lois Breur Krause says
that NFs are creative learners who often "lack aptitude for both logic
and memorization. Most at home in the abstract, the NF represents
the greatest risk for noncompletion of the educational process. The
NF learns best through metaphor, building new learning on a structure of comparison with some other known concept, no matter how
far afield" (see www.cognitiveprofile.com). I think of this as "learning
by analogy." NFs bring seemingly random and unrelated bits of information together in unique and inventive ways. Often treated derisively
and dismissed as overly "idealistic," "fuzzy," "speculative," "having
unwarranted assumptions about nature and society," or "kooky," their
insights and contributions frequently go unrecognized. Alienated and
discouraged, they may just drop out.

Krause goes on to say that "NFs are perhaps the world's greatest
resource of new technologies and ideas. Unfortunately too many of
them do not succeed in school to get to the point of contributing to
the extent of their potential." What a shame, for it would seem that
the evolutionary value of the NF type is the wide, inclusive net she or
he casts. NFs are not bothered by ambiguity or bewildered by myriad
facts. Each piece of information is regarded as important and beloved
because it is part of the great "Cosmic Weave of Meaning." Logic and
analysis simply do not cut it for NFs as the most valued means of evaluation; to the NF they make reductive, exclusionary, linear judgments.
The developmental process of the NF type over a lifetime is circular
and increasingly capacious. Using their ability to connect disparate
elements, they serve the community by containing its vastness and
diversity. Hence, when gifted, their contributions are often central in
defining great cultural paradigm shifts. Alfred Einstein's scientific
imagination would be an example of profoundly gifted NF creativity. I
offer this extended observation of the NF type, because along with the
SPs they are the most vulnerable kids in any classroom. They will
exhibit extreme sensitivities and get their feelings hurt easily, especially if introverted. If thwarted in their creative desires to freely explore
and experiment with classroom materials and activities, they can lose
their intellectual edge.

Both authors of this book, as you have probably guessed by now, are
introverted NF types who look back on their experience of public
school and university education as one of confoundment. This con-

foundment propelled us into the teaching profession with a passion-ate intention to wait upon, to attend, and to cast protective nets around the souls of kids as best we could, which often translated as doing for others what was not done for us. Temperament theory has provided us with a flexible means for precise response to the actual condition of each student, and we offer it to our readers as one possible means for cultivating an attitude of attentiveness.

CHAPTER SIX

Philosophy 101, Kindergarten Through Graduate School

Recently, as town historian, I was asked to create a presentation on the history of our town for all the second graders. I brought in numerous nineteenth-century farm artifacts, such as a two-handled plow, a flail, a double oxbow, and a broad axe. Early in the discussion, I asked the students how old they thought our town was. Every hand shot into the air with fervent flapping. "Six thousand years, Mr. Willis," one boy shouted. "A zillion," another countered. "When the Indians left," offered another student in the back of the room. After hearing at least thirty ideas on the matter, I was about to proceed with showing the flail, when I noticed the frantic wave of a bright-eyed little girl. "Yes," I said, "What do you think?" "When God was created!" she proclaimed triumphantly. And before I could respond, her teacher hissed, "Shhh—Susie, don't try to be so cute!" As Susie wilted, so I wilted, even as I rejoiced in her unwitting audacity to be in possession of such an idea.

Of the fifty-five students in the room, each and every one instantly had an idea about the age of our town. Seven-year-olds aren't the only ones full of ideas. From our earliest years to the ends of our lives, ideas dance in our heads as one of the primary means of teaching everyone around us . . . and ourselves. As Alfred North Whitehead wrote, "We do not initiate thought by an effort of self-consciousness. We find ourselves thinking, just as we find ourselves breathing and enjoying the sunset" (*Adventures of Ideas*, p. 47). Whitehead further observed that "Most of us believe that there is a spontaneity of thought which lies beyond routine. Otherwise the moral claim for freedom of thought is without meaning" (p. 47).

Many of us remember the all-night bull sessions in college, in secondary school, in elementary school, at camp, or at a favorite rendezvous where we spun out of our imagination our latest notions of what constituted what. We argued and dazzled each other with the glitter of ideational bits and pieces to be revisited over and over again. Early on, we threatened one another with some higher authority— often Mom and Dad, or a respected teacher—to act as a final arbiter of our formulations. In these alchemical sessions, we explored imagination as we wove the eccentricities of our separate selves into the fabric of tradition. We were as apt to applaud the daring, nonconforming notions as we were to hoot down the errant. We seemed to understand that Truth is only the faintest apprehension of a much larger Reality, beyond our understanding. We could fall silent at such moments and drift into thought or change the subject.

PHILOSOPHICAL SPECULATION

These images that present themselves to us are as readily translated into words as they are into shapes and sounds. These images tell us what we are experiencing and what we are likely to experience. They are the memories of ourselves. To bring ideas into full play within and between individuals is the very crux of teaching. We love the bright, open wonder in the eyes of little children. Why then wouldn't we love the selfsame wonder in the eyes of adolescents, of young adults, of old adults, or the wonder in our own eyes? Why, after kindergarten, do we suddenly feel the powerful impulse-to-ideation as a threat to education? Why do we seem to relegate the philosophy in ourselves to some private place, or to some postdoctoral doggerel? Do we really believe that only little children can be divinely inspired, while the rest of us become properly dead from the neck up in the service of vocation? Why do we blush or turn apologetic, or become taciturn and dismissive, when ideas turn speculative and explorative and wide-ranging? Why do we say, "I have no time for that, it's not very practical," or "sorry, that was omitted from my education"—the latter comment being the more credible? Why, in other words, do we abandon one of the most compelling and interesting elements in learning, namely philosophy? Kids love it, we once loved it, and it has a thousand applications.

WHAT DO I DO WITH PHILOSOPHY?

A few years ago, a group of us hosted a cocktail party to celebrate the visit of a former French foreign-exchange student, Bert and his fiancée. Bert was successfully launched on a promising career as a well-prepared civil engineer and taking aim at the position of CEO in a multinational corporation. At one point in the evening, I asked, "Bert, are you glad you majored in engineering?" fully expecting rapid affirmation. "Ah, no, not at all," he replied. "I wish I had majored in philosophy. My company wants people of broad, problem-solving abilities—and I am having to learn this now." Several other businessmen at this soirée concurred that top management requires the broad range of exposure to ideas that only a philosophy background would provide. Narrow-gauged training is no longer apropos in a multinational and cybernetic world. Even global business, it would seem, is recognizing a larger context for philosophy than was practiced in our educational definitions of vocational training.

For a teacher, philosophy has at least three salient functions. First, when students express an idea, they manifest precisely how their understanding associates itself. The great Israeli psychologist Reuven Feuerstein used clustering of ideas as his primary indicator of how a student thinks about something, how she or he connects these ideas, and as a further means of enhancing these associations in richness and amplifying variety. In Israel, at least, he further used ideation to change professional notions about what constitutes a valid cognitive stage by expanding and refining many of the diagnostic categories applied by professionals, such as Down syndrome and attention deficit disorder. He declared his fundamental motive was predicated by the dilemma of Israel itself: Israel could not afford any throwaway children; each life was precious and useful; Israel had a relatively small population, surrounded by enemies. Of course, no teacher or administrator would ever admit to thinking of children as "disposable," but, in fact, the size of our classes and the manner in which we teach largely prevent the attention to how each student formulates ideas that would assist the expanding and vital association of each precious child. Instead of using Feuerstein's *instrumental enrichment*, we use formulaic curricula and testing to determine the actual thinking of each child, which is about as accurate as Ptolemy's maps—rigorous analysis based on gossamer. To the degree that your witnessing capacity copes with your student load, try to find out just how each one of your students thinks. Devise your own means and methods for doing this. In considering these means and methods, refer to Marcia's analysis of typology and the ramifications emerging from typology in Chapters 4 and 5.

As the second salience in the use of philosophy, your students will become entranced by the content of your subject matter if it is couched in the framework of their ideas: encourage argument, enjoy disputation, make room to hear your students out, allow yourself to be impressed by their ideas, and become a dialectician in their space no matter how unmediated or unformulated their thoughts. Human beings are contentious—the trick is not sullen or masterful control of a class, but rather exercising a methodological attitude that offers flight to the expression and exchange of the actual notions of your students. This is not solipsism or narcissism; rather, it is involvement and crossover into your subject field.

I always built debate into my courses. The method I used in my social studies classes went something like this: a stated question, for example, "Is the underlying universal reality one of change or permanence?" Two groups formed around the opposing views, rehearsing and coordinating their arguments. These two groups then debated each other, as a student judge and I kept score and acted as referees. Each group opened with their assumptions stated as clearly and concisely as possible. This was followed by point-for-point argumentation, wherein each group was compelled to repeat the argument of the other side and then answer it ad rem (directly to that point). *Argumentum ad hominem* (aspersions cast against the character of the other team or team members) caused the loss of points, and points were accrued for the quality and inclusiveness of responses to each argument. When a given idea had been exhausted, I would guide my students toward an examination of how that idea presented itself in a particular historical framework: did thinkers of the time espouse one side of the argument over the other? If so, did that bias manifest in the politics, art, commerce, or science of the times? This method worked well to cross-pollinate the big picture with the detailed, structured arguments. This example would be as germane in a physics class as in a social studies class, an English class, or a class in probability and statistics. Each subject would have a different take on this question as it brought the contents of its discipline to bear. For example, a physics teacher might ask, "How does classical Newtonian physics (permanent mechanical relationships) interface with quantum mechanics (ephemeral, statistical relationships)?"

P. W. Atkins explores the chemical elements in his book, *Periodic Kingdom*, in a philosophic sojourn through the mental land of chemistry, with ideas immediately accessible to most. In what sense are our thoughts to be found in the Periodic Terrain? In *River Out of Eden*, Richard Dawkins employs the metaphor of a digital river to explicate Darwin's view of life. We can ask the question: which does each of us strive to be—an ancestor or a descendant? In other words, what is more important to us, passing on our genes or personal survival?

At the beginning of the year, the enthusiasm for these debates verged on delirium, but as the school year wore on, mediation and depth gave the debates a calmer tone and the majority of young people astonished themselves with their ability to conceive and articulate concepts not consciously perceived before. In short, students came to love their own minds and the excitement of their own reach.

For my world history classes, I found the more general and classical questions to be better for brainstorming and debates:

- How can there be one, yet many? (framed, perhaps, by the ideas of Greek pre-Socratic thought *viz*, Empedocles vs. Heraclitus).
- Is reality grounded on change or permanence? (*viz*, Heraclitus vs. Parmenides).
- Is man by nature evil or good? (*viz*, Hobbes vs. Rousseau).

You can also select a compelling circumstance, the starker the better: For example, in the "Melian Debate" by Thucydides in *The History of the Peloponnesian War*, should the citizens of Melos surrender in the face of the superior forces of Athens, or hold out and face annihilation? As students discover the range and complexity of each argument, they also discover that their ideas meet, rearrange, and become coextensive with the concepts of the ages. They begin to define for themselves their take on current events as they see into the universality of human dilemmas. They become able to step outside the fads and fashions of their cohort and inside their greater selves, in which a higher mind and a core soul are waiting to be activated and awakened.

At various times, with a few colleagues, we would hold philosophy club sessions, sometimes after school hours, sometimes during lunch. There was always a philosophy leader (student or teacher) who acted as convener and expediter. Discussants would raise their hands to be recognized, speak to the point of the previous commentary, and then yield to the next discussant. The philosophy leader's job was to maintain a dialectical and respectful atmosphere, while at the same time cultivating the passion and impetus of the ongoing discussion. Sometimes the exchange of ideas took the form of informal debate, sometimes a sharing, and sometimes an information session, or a combination of all three. Over the years these philosophy sessions successfully ran a balance between emotional and logical expression. Topics usually altered between the specific and the abstract, for example, toxic spills followed by the nature of time. Students enjoyed this expansion and contraction of topics. The size of the gatherings, ranging between five and one hundred, never seemed to affect the quality of exchange. I found that when young people are keenly interested in both the process of learning and the subject of discovery, they conspire together to make the whole thing work despite the number of individuals gathered in one place and other disconcerting variables of temperament and timing. My experience was that because of the zeal with which the majority of students embraced both abstract and concrete ideas, nearly everyone in the class was swept up in the enthusiasm, regardless of initial interest. With reasonably sensitive leadership, they were very nearly self-regulating.

When students feel their knowing to be merging with their analysis, they are powerfully inclined to cooperate with each other, openly and eagerly. It is only when the formation of thinking is predicated in the absence of feeling that we suffer boredom and alienation. We need to feel what we think. The experience of palpation (the intimacy of touch), auscultation (focused hearing), quale (the perception of a quality, such as "red," separate from objects having the quality) and dehiscence (the contents of pods bursting open), in the language of Maurice Merleau-Ponty, are necessary if our feeling is going to join our thinking. In other words, we must touch, hear, universally identify, and open to the ideas present in ourselves and in those around us. The teacher must witness and nurture these emerging ideas in her students. Teaching and preaching in this sense are enemies and opposites. To get the point across is not the point. Lying in wait for the teachable moment, so that you might pounce, is surely healthy in predator-prey relationship, but defeats the use of philosophy. "Gotcha" is relevant to the power trip, but not to synthesis. Early in my career, I delighted in leading students into logical traps, until one day a particularly energetic, young lad screamed at me, "Aren't you ever wrong?" It was just then that I realized I was using philosophy for my own edification rather than as a means for extending the souls of students into their own minds. I abruptly broke off my intellectual brinkmanship. My attitude became shaped by increasing astonishment over the ideational exuberance of young folks and the access they had to the thoughts embraced by subject disciplines.

This leads to a third use of philosophy: *ideas from which subjects emerge*. For many years, I have advocated that teachers introduce their course of instruction with the large and interrogative ideas that preface their academic scripts, thus providing considerable impetus for the *dead* data that invariably follow. With such an introduction, students can find the aesthetic connectives that will allow them to take ownership of the curricular subject. During this phase of the course, errors, mistakes, opinions, judgments, projections of values, and beliefs and temperament are grist for the conceptual mill. Wrongness and rightness are of lesser importance than exploration verging on familiarity, recognition, and connection. As a teacher, make it possible for kids to swarm all over your subject. Let them learn to inhabit and become native to their subject. Let them learn to like your subject and you right from the start, not by making it easy, but by making it available to their minds, linked and linking to the ideas already in their heads.

Flip through any textbook for high school students and exercise books for elementary school students, and you will find virtually no foundation in philosophy. What you will find are taxonomic increments laid out according to certain assumptions (explicit or implicit) the author holds about cognitive development. In the introduction, if there is one, you might even receive a certain rationale and justification for the mastery of said subject. Before, amidst, and after the formulation of the subject material, you will see little of the fundamental ideas that presume and comprise the discipline. References to key concepts, crucial events, and foundation rules dance upon the surface of the subject, more as warnings and admonitions than as groundwork made manifest. Most of our texts lead us detail by detail back to those unspoken assumptions, rather than presenting us with the philosophical integrity of the subject matter right from the outset of instruction. Marcia notes that whenever she introduced an algebra or geometry course to a tutee, she would recap the historical setting in which the mathematics arose to address the particular aesthetic, scientific, spiritual, and pragmatic urges of the culture in question. For example, students were usually quite intrigued by discussions and hands-on activities that elucidated how the ancient Egyptians triangulated the bases of the pyramids, the burial sites of their god-kings. Understanding the mechanics of the math seemed to be easier for her students once they made the connection to the culture and its foundational (pun intended) ideas.

The mystery of the discipline is there—in abundance—along with illustrative figures to aid you on your excursion, but where is this trip going and how did it begin, and why do we think we need to take it? Do we take it on authority? Because it is required? Because we will surely use it someday in our careers? Because not to take it will lead to our annihilation? How come "being good" and learning this subject seem synonymous? Is virtue conformity? When my father was in a particularly irritated mood, he used to say, "If you don't know, I can't tell you," by which I think he meant, "If you have not experienced such and such, then by virtue of the nearly infinite number of variables involved, it is impossible to speak to your unconnectedness." This, in a nutshell, is what these textbooks and exercise books seem to be saying to us. But by some act of perfidious natural selection, many of us can proceed through formulae without any requirements for meaning, without seeing any larger and supporting framework. Some of us can simply thrive on a treadmill without any notion of the big picture. We do well with rote learning, with concatenations of busy synapses launching variations of the cat's cradle. We copy out of our sequencing faculties what is required and are properly rewarded with stars, exclamations, smiley faces, and numerical bits verging on 100. A few of us are so blessed as to provide ourselves with discovering—all on our own—just what ideas produced this discipline and because of our knowing, we can predict what the books and what the teacher will say next. But at least a third or a sizable number of us are lost to the mystery of the discipline, and we experience no excursion at all. We are lost. Authority, requirement, our future, and annihilation seem ominously related and just around the corner.

Ideas are a major means of accommodating your students to their own native capacity to touch subject to object, and object to subject; to match their notions to unfolding concepts; to suggest designs within themselves that can link designs within the discipline; and to give foundations for explaining later experience.

PARBOIL IN DEPTH

Rather than a philosophical and meditative people, we Americans are a busy, pragmatic lot. We would be more likely to say: "Now that you have said it, what are you going to *do* about it?" rather than: "Now that you have done that, what are you going to say about it?" Busily self-calming, deeply invested in personality formation, we delight in neologisms, our patois, and our trickster selves. Jackassing and media entertainment are a way of life in the United States. The problem for us and for our children is that this brand of dynamic is allowed to percolate to the depths of our beings. We are consistently off-center and distracted. We seek equanimity and calm in the behavior of the *cool*. But feigning coolness in the practiced modulations of the voice and body muscles has put the cart before the horse for our children. Activity of all sorts is read as perturbation and disquiet of the soul. The young seek risky sensation as an antidote to insecurity, as a way of coping and embracing parboil, the mindless chatter of activity that Theodore Roethke called "the kingdom of bang and blab." (*The Lost Son*, p. 51). As one advertisement has it: "This is life—deal with it," as the actor trashes the environment with his four-wheel-drive sport utility vehicle, signifying salvation through adrenalin. But we know better later on in life that adrenaline is not the only answer, as we seek out the various palliatives offered by the East and other exotic climes: T'ai

Chi, martial arts, sweat lodges, meditation techniques, and holistic medicines.

But the association of activity with disquietude, of learning with core disruption, is no small matter to many of our children, as is evident in our policies of pathologizing disquietude with such labels as ADD/ADHD and tranquilizing them with drugs such as Ritalin and Prozac. Chemical intervention merely stimulates the in-depth security in their own natures that children seek. There is an inverse relationship between the dynamism of the activity of learning and the perturbation at the core of being—the greater the calm at center, the more desirable will be the commotion at the surface. We want novelty, variegation, and movement when we are at peace within. When we are disturbed within, we turn away from our growth, especially when it is fed to us through institutions by mandate. Alfie Kohn, in his brilliant book, *Punished by Rewards* not only warns us away from rat and pigeon psychology (extrinsic rewards and punishments), but also illuminates the intention of this chapter:

> Children are more likely to grow into caring people if they know they themselves are cared about. A warm, nurturing environment is the *sine qua non* of positive development. (It also turns out to be useful for the more limited goal of getting children to do what we ask.) If children feel safe, they can take risks, ask questions, make mistakes, learn to trust, share their feelings, and grow. If they are taken seriously, they can respect others. (p. 239)

And one of the central means of caring for children is to listen and respond to *what they say and how they say it*. This is what a philosophical approach—a thinking approach to the actual ideas that children have already formed or will form in response to their experiences—can do: It can respond directly to what is said and how it is said, without the distractions of praise and blame. When one knows one is being listened to and addressed, one experiences at once a peace at the center and a excitement at the surface. It is a parboil where it belongs: in ego consciousness and in the coloration of personality, rather than an invasion into the serenity of the soul. And conversely, for the teacher, the attitude of *intending* to listen and respond to the actual student continuously yields an enormous intrinsic reward—for it is impossible to dislike anyone truly perceived. The act of brushing aside one's own projections, one's own labels, one's own prognostications, and all other defense measures one has adopted for personal damage control, and becoming attentive to the ideational expression of others, yields the sight of the *other*, who is mysterious, fresh, vital, quite amazing. It is what prompted Aeschylus to exclaim, "Seeing, he saw," and what made Socrates feel the ultimate accomplishment in being able to say, "I know nothing." This is the experience of open nonjudgment and the separation of being from behavior. And it is not only impossible to dislike someone we have perceived directly, it is also impossible—more importantly—to *fear* him or her. You may be shocked, forewarned, or experience some other variant of negative impression over behavior, but hereafter you cannot fear or hate this person. The parboil will remain on the surface of personality if we trust and seek the real person in the student. And one of the best ways to do this is to engage your ideas with those of your students in a dialectical relationship.

DIALECTIC (A FEW CHOICES FROM GADAMER, GARDNER, GASSET, AND WIGGENS)

> The movement of understanding is constantly from the whole to the part and back to the whole. Our task is to extend in concentric circles the unity of the understood meaning. The harmony of all the details with the whole is the criterion of correct understanding. The failure to achieve this harmony means that understanding has failed. (Hans Georg Gadamer, cited in Ken Wilbur, *The Eye of Spirit*, p. 96)

A questioning mind—the exercise of philosophy—is appropriate for all students, at all wakeful ages. Grant Wiggens writes, "We should assess students' intellectual honesty and other habits of mind. The cheerful admission of ignorance . . . not just intellectual honesty but absence of self-deception. It is not so much error as blind spots in our knowledge that can breed ignorance" (p. 9).

Wiggens reinforces the major thrust of this chapter:

> A vital aim of education is to have students understand the limits and boundaries of ideas, theories, and systems. Students can be helped to see the limits of ideas by talking about the history of the subject. The practical consequences of our failure to reveal to students the history of important ideas and assess the understanding of that history is twofold: for one, students easily end up assuming that axioms, laws, postulates, theories, and systems are immutable—even though common sense and history say otherwise . . . the second . . . is that it does lasting harm to intellectual courage in all but our feistiest students. One of the reasons for the intellectual poverty in this country is that most students become convinced either that they are incapable of being intellectual or that they are uninterested in being intellectual, thinking that it involves only the arcane expertise of a narrowly framed and inert subject. (p. 8)

I would suggest that starting as early as the sixth grade, every course be taught starting with a history of the subject and its concepts, and taught in a manner that gives constant feedback to both students and teacher.

Howard Gardner thinks of intelligence as a potential that can be cultivated in the right environment, with right activities. He feels the key is to personalize the teaching that goes on in the classroom. And one central activity that is natural to students is the exercise of ideas connected meaningfully to them. Wiggens warns of "an unfortunate habit" of engendering and initiating a belief: "Too many people believe incorrectly that students must gain control of common knowledge (and that they cannot be philosophical as a result). . . . Students should question as they go, else their critical judgment and imagination atrophy" (pp. 43–44).

Ortega y Gassett further observed that "so many things fail to interest us, simply because they don't find in us enough surfaces on which to live, and what we have to do is increase the number of planes in our mind, so that a much larger number of themes can find a plane in it at the same time" (Warshall, p. 13). This creation of surfaces in the mind is the very process of exchange between learners, wherein trying new things, being willing to make mistakes, accepting feedback, and exercising intellectual honesty comprise an attitude readily apparent in the teacher.

CATEGORIES OF THINKING

In seeking a framework in which to bring students' ideas about the nature of things into full play, the young teacher might be well served in adopting the widest possible categories of experience, such as in Samuel Alexander's treatise *Space, Time, and Deity*. Time would refer to whatever ideas students have formed regarding change: change of seasons, growing from young to old, the life span of mayflies, bees, giraffes, human beings, or tortoises, from the briefest to the longest lasting. Time would refer to the dynamics of transition from the past to the present: What about us is drawn from the heritage of bygone eras, and what, if anything, are we adding? What role does mutation indicate for any given occasion? How does DNA/RNA manage change, and how do these changes differ from species-wide experiences? What did Heraclitus mean when he said "Into the same river you cannot step twice?" What does eternity have to do with time? Students will have, each and every one, their own unique take on the nature of time, upon which teachers, no matter their discipline or the ages of their students, can build and expand.

Space would refer to how things are positioned and connected in extension and in relationship to each other: the spatial relationships of termite mounds, birds' nests, rivers and lakes and oceans, human cities, solar systems, and galaxies. What do the four forces of physics have to do with spatial relationships: the weak force, the strong force, gravity, and the magnetic field? What is tiny? What is immense? Is there any limit to being small or being big? What do we mean when we say, "Birds of a feather flock together?" What is a dimension? Two dimensions? Three dimensions, or more? What does infinity have to do with space? With finity? Here again, each student will have her or his own notions about space, reflecting how they individually associate the vast array of cultural thought regarding space.

Deity in Alexander's treatise would refer to the values we imagine each process and form have beyond the mere realization of fact: Can chipmunks think? Do fish feel? What would be the ideal house to live in? Is war necessary? And *ad infinitum*. Deity here is used as the direction energy takes or might take or should take into the future from its present process and position. Any educational institution that omits these considerations and judgments, omits thoughts about the future, about what is possible, about what is desirable, about what would be ideal, is sterile and null. Every age asks of its young to leave the earth or the culture a little better place than they found it. What a "better place" might be in the ideal world is left to youth's imaginations and to the philosophical spins they formulate and put into practice.

"OPEN IDEAS, OPENLY ARRIVED AT"

The habit of philosophical openness in a school allows young people to readily translate the tractless and powerful images formed in their feeling life, pressed out of Awareness, into the concrete symbols of their thinking life. Language, mathematical notation, and other significations, such as musical signs, are more readily linked to the sweep of imagination if the attitude of philosophical openness is cultivated. It is like reaching out and touching the inexpressible—and then talking about it. It is bringing together the intellectual and the artistic, the logical and the aesthetic. It allows us to "go out to meet what we see." And, of course, the better we can do this—that is, putting powerful images into practical symbols—the greater our academic success. Can you put a hunch into a graph? Can you write a clear analysis of an outrage? Can you speak calmly and forcefully in the face of anger? Do your articulated ideas accurately represent your feelings? Your emotions? Your impressions? In an open philosophical learning environment, most students have an excellent chance of answering in the affirmative. It is always such a turn-on for students when they realize that they know much more than they can think, and are aware of so much more than they know, and yet can talk about it.

Above all, philosophy calls from students ideas that are both fresh and renewed in the practice of thought. As Whitehead so cogently described it, "The use of philosophy is to maintain an active novelty of fundamental ideas illuminating the social system. It reverses the slow descent of accepted thought towards the inactive commonplace" (*Modes of Thought*, p. 174). And, as if anticipating our next chapter, Whitehead shines light on the interplay of understanding with feeling: "Philosophy is akin to poetry, and both of them seek to explain that cultural good sense which we term civilization. In each case there is reference to form beyond the direct meaning of words. Poetry allies itself to meter, philosophy to mathematic pattern" (p. 174). Practicing philosophy with students, as in cultivating the arts in them, opens access for them into their own Awareness.

As our friend Dick Searles, a retired high school English and drama teacher, informed us, "Drama and fiction are rampant with philosophical notions that yield endless debate. In order to get my students thinking about character motivation and analysis, I used to take two characters (say Huck Finn and Hamlet) from widely different literary genres and periods and talk about the same philosophical concepts with regard to each of them: how has the idea of the hero evolved from classical to modern times? How do narrative (chronological statements, such as 'the king died and then the queen died') versus exposition (statements involving cause and effect, as in 'the king died and then the queen died of guilt') appear in each work? One might approach these questions as narrative devices, but literary techniques are inseparable from philosophical ideas, ideas about justice versus mercy or divine providence versus actual human fears, to give examples."

In this chapter we have considered the actual ideas that students engender about what is real, and in the next we discuss how students experience that reality through the faculty of the feeling life, the medium of the arts.

IF YOU CAN

IMAGINE IT

" ART IS A HUMAN ACTIVITY
HAVING FOR ITS PURPOSE
THE TRANSMISSION
TO OTHERS OF THE HIGHEST
AND BEST FEELINGS TO
WHICH MEN HAVE RISEN."
~ LEO TOLSTOY

CHAPTER SEVEN

The Rationality of the Feeling Life

FEELINGS AND EMOTIONS

Feeling and emotion are often treated as synonymous in our culture, but they are entirely separate activities in the self. Our sense of this difference is well located in the French words *sensibilité* for feeling and emotion for emotion. Emotion is the interpretation that the behaving Personality makes of both our feeling and our thinking life. A feeling could lead to a sad judgment, a happy judgment, an exclusionary/inclusionary judgment, a bored judgment, *ad vivum*. Likewise, thinking could lead us to a sad judgment, a happy judgment, an exclusionary/inclusionary judgment, a bored judgment, *ad vivum*, from which emotion is then formed to express or not to express within the behavior that Personality interprets. Emotion is the display of a biochemical/neurological response to feeling and thinking, as Personality reads that feeling or that thinking.

Sensibilité, on the other hand, indicates a full, active engagement and response, often compassionate in nature, to the life surrounding us and might be conceived of as the gestural movements within us. Feeling flares out in expanding arrays like cuttlefish, which change their color and shape in response to the oceanic environment in which they swim. Likewise, it is through Feeling that we bring our human sensory existence into contact with Personal Awareness, continually altering our responses in the direction of greater accuracy with respect to the environment of that most inclusive aspect of ourselves. Unfortunately, psychologists have defined Personal Awareness as the "Unconscious" and many philosophers have judged Feeling to be merely proto-thought. Neither of these definitions could be further from the truth. As will be discussed in Chapter 9, our Personal Awareness is the most capacious arena within and outside ourselves and constitutes our sense of connection with all things. Personal Awareness is, if anything, supra-conscious. Likewise, Feeling is the agent that translates our Personal Awareness into a large, imagistically patterned, personally meaningful knowledge base, which Understanding then delineates into discrete pieces of information to be transmitted by persuasive language, mathematical equations, and scientific theory. Feeling should neither be confused with the processes of analytical thought, nor diminished in significance by the criteria of analysis. In other words, Feeling is not taxonomic or categorical. Thus, when the conduit of Feeling is wide open, it feeds a constant stream of multi-contextual perceptions, experiences, and historical legacy into the realm of Understanding. In this manner Feeling helps Understanding remain flexible and open to new information, rather than settling into ossified structures and categories, which do not serve anyone's growth and development. One may think of Feeling as the meaningful, existential, continuously expanding and contracting content of our lives and of Thinking as the structuring of that content. This meaningful content is what the French refer to as *sensibilité*. This chapter concerns itself not with the emotional life that was implicitly discussed in Chapter 2 on behavior, nor with the compulsive reduction of the feeling life to the analytical processes regarded as rational by our culture, but rather with the nature and rationality of this *sensibilité*.

HOW WE FIND IT

As teachers we can help our students find meaning using a variety of approaches. One approach is suggested by Maurice Tuchman in his essay, "Hidden Meaning in Abstract Art," where he cites Marsden Hartley's notion of five underlying Feeling modes or themes, which inform an expansive *sensibilité*. The themes that manifest in the creative work of our students give us a "hook" for what is meaningful to them at any given time. Indeed, it is through the arts and liberal arts that the Feeling life expresses itself most abundantly. Tuchman calls these modes Cosmic Imagery, Vibration, Synesthesia, Duality and Correspondence, and Sacred Geometry (pp. 118–22). A cursory examination of the range and focus of these modes of Feeling reveals their characteristic tidal nature, as feelings sweep forward and backward between Awareness and Understanding, in a kind of flotilla function in ourselves. In *Modes of Thought*, Alfred North Whitehead puts it this way: "Feeling is the agent which reduces the universe to its perspective for fact" (p. 10). "Perspective for fact" is like standing on a mountain, looking in every direction, and being able to see how all the things within view fit together. Feeling is the very experience of this viewing, the experience of the rich detail and complex patterns spread out before us. Feeling gives us that "aha!" sense of fullness, majesty, life-in-motion, and design. In four lines of her poem "Renascence," Edna St. Vincent Millay captures the essence of this Feeling-fullness:

> The world stands out on either side
> No wider than the heart is wide
> Above the world is stretched the sky
> No higher than the soul is high (p. 11)

Tuchman's modes of feeling describe possible curricular trajectories that play themselves out in increasing explorations of our Personal Awareness.

Cosmic Imagery

In the art of adults and children we find cosmic imagery in abundance: Vincent Van Gogh's painting "Starry Night"; Marc Chagall's stained-glass depictions of the interconnectedness of sea, earth, and heavens; the extemporaneous crayon drawings of children, filled with house and family, smiling sun, blue sky, rainbows, butterflies, moon, stars, and green grass. All express a feeling for the mysterious immensity, the eternal grandness of the universe in which we live as it connects to and radiantly infuses the details of our worldly experience. A small child recently painted Marcia a picture, slapping on large vertical, cascading dabs of blue, red, and purple sparkle paint. "Look at this!" he cried. "It's a waterfall! Isn't it *beautiful*?" Having grown up near Niagara Falls, Marcia could relate to the sense of grandeur his picture evoked.

By eliciting this sense of wonder, math and science teachers, as well as art teachers, can make content meaningful for students. For example, whenever Marcia home-tutored housebound students in geometry, she always introduced the subject with pictures and discussions of how ancient Greek and Egyptian structures, such as the pyramids, were built on foundations of sacred geometry. She encouraged her students to talk about the perfection of the circle as a geometric figure and to draw circular mandalas, in which diameters, radii, and centers emerged as natural parts of their artistic expressions. In this way the subsequent introduction of theorems and formulas—the nuts and bolts of the subject—never lost contact with the underlying meaning. Invariably, students would become more excited and curious about the details of the course as the feeling-for-grandeur inspired their thinking.

Vibration

Vibration is the very action of Feeling. Probably experienced most consciously in the arts that involve music and movement, it is palpable. In this mode we experience our cycles and seasons, and matter and energy seem as one in their oscillating dance. Vibration affects our sensibilities in many forms: for example, through music, from Camille Saint-Saens' violin concerto *Havanaise* to the keening over death in a tribal enclave. In the classroom, "vibes" tell a student "the teacher likes me" or "the teacher doesn't like me." Teenagers plug their headsets into iPods for stimulation; tribal drummers beat repetitive rhythms that bring dancers into a purposeful vortex of energy to guarantee rain or good crops; toddlers shriek and make themselves ecstatically dizzy playing circle games. Asian cultures have given us the concepts of chi, chakra, and kundalini energy. Vibration occurs when something is happening, both externally and internally. Tuchman quotes the painter Kandinsky: "Words, musical tones and colors possess the psychical power of calling forth soul vibration . . . they create identical vibrations, ultimately bringing about the attainment of knowledge" (p. 35).

We see the vibration mode used in the classroom to stimulate attentiveness in children most often at the pre- or early school levels: movement songs and activities before beginning a lesson; stretching exercises; beanbag tosses; marching, galloping, and skipping. In later grades, the uses of vibration in the academic curriculum are negligible and are usually relegated to music instruction or after-school sports. Both Marcia and I have experimented with finger labyrinths, playing complex background music (especially Baroque music) during seatwork, and drumming and tonal exercises. These types of vibrational exercises can help children calm down, speed up, or concentrate, all depending on the desired environment for a particular activity.

Synesthesia

Synesthesia is the feeling mode that takes the diverse elements of our seven senses (that is, seeing, hearing, touching, smelling, tasting, experiencing gravity, and balancing) and weaves them into fresh, new, harmonious patterns. Children can use poetry to register and connect the disparities: we can smell blue, taste C sharp, paint T'ai Chi movements, or balance on a printed word. Kids use pretend-play and puppets to work out and bring to repose social confusions: relationships with siblings and friends. going on a long trip, or taking care of pets. Synesthesia is somewhat operative at the high school level in debates, historical reenactments, the creation of original metaphors in poetry writing, or in a drawing-as-essay. It seems to both of us that synesthesia is a play-based modality where the feeling life brings in the toys and the thinking life builds the toy room. Tuchman quotes the poet Baudelaire: "I want to illuminate things with my mind and to project their reflections upon other minds" (p. 32).

Duality and Correspondence

Duality separates us from our sense of connection; that is, if my mind is separate from my body, how do the two act together? How do they relate and connect? Correspondence tells the tale of how one domain fits with another. One illustration of this connection came recently, while I was watching a PBS program on sacred places. I heard a nun say, "We are spiritual beings on a human journey, not human beings on a spiritual journey." She was commenting on how she perceived humanness and spirit to be linked. Sensibility perceives this human journey as one of separation, a feeling of having lost paradise, or of a quest for identity. We feel separate from our source in the "click" of becoming human beings, feel we have come from wholeness into the world of duality and division, which often causes us to feel grief at our core. We then begin to cover over this grief with a less-acute sadness, and then overlay the sadness with anger, sarcasm, and restless humor. Who am I? How do I relate to others? How do I deal with having been ejected from Eden? We feel pulled in two directions while holding on to both. We feel a desire for revenge, for meaning, or for connection. We experience tides of hope lifting us toward Eden, toward oneness, and then the receding tide carrying us into pain and incongruity. In her book, *The Life of Poetry*, Muriel Rukeyser writes:

> The fear that cuts off poetry is profound: it plunges us deep, far back to the edge of childhood. Beyond that it does not go.
> Little children do not have this fear, they trust their emotions.
> But on the threshold of adolescence the walls are built

> Against the assault of puberty, and in those silvery delicate seasons when all feeling casts about for confirmation. Then, for the first time, you wonder, "What should I be feeling," instead of "What do I feel?" (p. 15)

We search for correspondences, for links between all those polarities tearing us apart and making us sick. Tuchman notes: "Richard Wagner was among the originators of the idea of correspondences, and was the most articulate advocate of the *gesamtkunstwerk* (total work of art)" (p. 32). This quest for wholeness or unity is the human journey of sensibility. So many students over the years have asked me, "Why do I have to study this?" or "Why do I have to do that?" "Where is it going to take me?" They want to be on a trip that is felt as a direct correspondence between their feelings and the thoughts brought about by the subject matter. The journey must provide them with the conviction of relevance. Most teachers answer this question by giving career advice, which begs the question, instead of helping the students to join their feelings to the analysis. For example, every year students asked, "Why do we have to study the Middle Ages—that was a long time ago—what does it have to do with us now?" Put on the spot, I would respond, "Okay, that's a fair question. Let's do a little exercise. Take out a sheet of paper and, in fifteen minutes, answer the following three questions: 1. Who is the most powerful individual in your life? 2. How has this individual affected you in your everyday life? 3. What arrangements do you make with this individual in order to coexist?"

The discussion that usually followed clearly indicated to the students that the power arrangements of the Middle Ages and their present-day situations involved problems that are ever-present. The discussion was intense and animated and no one cared whether the subject at hand would get them a job or help them figure discounts at the mall.

Sacred Geometry

Geometry concerned me throughout most of my teaching years in the forms of the architecture in which I taught. What are schools made of? How are they shaped? In the classroom, how are kids arranged, in rows, in circles, or in clusters? A school is a container of people, so we might ask if there is any given place sacred for students and for teachers in a school. Halls of ivy? And gothic mystery? We witness sacred geometry everywhere in the world and through the lenses of history and anthropology—mandalas (as in rose windows), labyrinths (as in Chartres Cathedral), Navajo sand paintings, the golden rectangle of

Hellenic buildings, and volcano-shaped gathering places in Polynesia, to name a few. Tuchman cites Ralph Waldo Emerson's reference to "Saint Augustine's cardinal mystical concept of God as 'a circle whose center was everywhere and its circumference nowhere' " (p. 42). Our feeling life tells us that if we can get kids into a *perceived* sacred place, then their feeling life can revive and even flourish. Sacred places may even be found in beat-up Russian classrooms or in Melanie's house. The Greeks called such a place a *temenos*: the safe container where the rites of passage of the feeling life could take place. As such, *temenos* in educational terms is not necessarily an actual ideal place, but rather a classroom attitude that brings to any given space a feeling of Awareness, a certain sense of "presence in the midst." Our interior feeling for great richness is invested in whatever space this experience takes place.

Tuchman summarizes what has become for us the primary task of the feeling life by quoting Emerson yet again: "Natural fact is a symbol of some spiritual fact. Every appearance in nature corresponds to some state of mind" (p. 42). And it is the state of this mind through which the rationality of the feeling life journeys. From the perspective of Carl Jung, feeling is a rational judging function that emanates from the heart of our mind rather than from the head of our mind. Feeling "goes out to meet" what we perceive; feeling is the mind making connections, relationships, perspectives, like a welcoming host who wishes to harmonize and motivate human gatherings.

The problem for American education is that by investing so heavily in Personality Formation and subsequent emotional well-being in the form of "self-esteem," we have largely sidestepped the deeper and more compelling themes of the actual functioning of the feeling life as outlined above. Our selves yearn to be related to as Thinking/Feeling and Sensing/Intuiting human beings, and not so much as accomplished actors wowing an audience. It is temporarily pleasing to impress others, but it is vastly more satisfying to be appreciated for one's "actual occasion." Popularity is amusing, but cannot substitute for real concourse with one's fellow human beings. Moreover, Feeling operates as a bridge between Awareness of the "infinitude of facts" (Whitehead, *Adventures of Ideas*, p. 231) and the interpreting intellect, by providing a perspective in which to make sense of facts.

Feeling translates pieces of the big picture in terms that Thinking can absorb and organize; emotion acts out that absorption internally and externally. This last step in the process, when Personality translates Feeling and Thinking into emotional terms, should not serve as the basis for our developmental psychology. White teeth and a big smile are nice; clear and expanded hearts and minds are nicer.

HOW ARE THINGS GOING?

Our assessing, evaluative life comes as much from the domain of Feeling as from Thinking. We might be told "go with your feelings," and admonished to stop projecting our feelings on others. And our students are constantly sharing their feelings with each other in accepting or rejecting any given state of affairs. Notions, thoughts, and ideas are free wheeling and woven into the fabric of the feeling life. If this is stating the obvious, my entire teaching career was composed of school experiences organized around the presumption of an altogether different centrality: the "dum-de-dum" of academe, or "we pour, you open, and you contain what we pour." This centrality said, "We are here to train you, shape you, lead you out, guide you toward becoming efficient, accepting, nonfelonious members of society." This centrality said, "We are a loosely hierarchical, capitalist system that prizes problem solving within an industrial cybernetic continuum, beyond which we are concerned with neither your thoughts nor your feelings." Yet another presumption of this centrality is: "Greed, or the desire to acquire power, prestige, and property, is the dominant, guiding, and key motive in human nature; all other motives are to be bent in service to the civilized practices of competition and acquisitive initiative." Feelings and thoughts, aesthetics and examined life, are subordinate functions to this way of defining productive life. There is no ambiguity here. Teachers are to produce the greatest number of winners and the least number of losers in a strictly defined framework of legal and conceptual development. Marcia tells the story of home-tutoring a teenager out of school for a prolonged absence due to a serious accident. In an effort to establish a three-way positive learning environment for her anxious student, Marcia approached one of his teachers to tell her of the boy's struggle with pain and his fear that he would be held back because of the length of the absence. Before she could finish the sentence, the teacher said, "I don't want to hear anything about him. I'm not interested in his personal problems. Just have him get the work done and if he can't, he'll have to take the course again." There weren't going to be any losers in her classroom; nor was she about to use this opportunity to discover how the child's experience might alter her attitude toward her particular course content in creative ways.

Neither this book, nor this chapter, is a treatise on alternative economies. Nor are we concerned with school reform. What does concern us is the present system and how to help teachers develop *attitudes* more congruent with possible students and actual conditions. Each student, as we have said, possesses a feeling life, a life that actively and passively monitors the acceptability of inner and outer events. The Feeling function questions reality: Is this good or bad? Is this beautiful or ugly? Is this pleasant or painful? Is this safe or fraught with risk? Does the teacher like me or is she just pretending to like me? When this vast array of perfectly reasonable questions is at any particular point dismissed as unimportant, then we humans usually blossom forth with emotional expressions that range from simple to highly complex. Energy is delivered everywhere within our being— sensations ignite, thoughts burgeon, and intuitions globalize our emotions. We ignore, control, and bypass our students' feelings to our mutual disadvantage.

Like hydrogen in the universe, feeling is the most abundant element in the self. As Whitehead observes, "Feeling has the merit of preserving this double significance of subjective form and the apprehension of an object" (*Adventures* p. 233). In terms of education, this statement means that Feeling is so pervasive because it connects the student's own imaginative world with the subject matter at hand. Plato identified feeling-form combined with knowledge as virtue. Feeling combines with the other faculties—thinking, sensation and intuition—so as to motivate the self toward consciousness of connection and inclusiveness. This satisfaction or dissatisfaction with the movement of ourselves toward fullness and wholeness answers the question: "How are things going with me? With others?" Feeling tells us whether or not things under consideration are connected to us, the felt relation of things, things experienced, things touched. Feelings answer the query: "Do the data presented there satisfy my (self) formation?" Feeling also brings to rest or repose the very creative process in which we seek this satisfaction of relatedness. In addition, feeling powerfully registers our alignment with historically/culturally agreed-upon beliefs and motives and the laws and principles, which emerge from them—it is our inward current linking us to time. A historical example of how feeling works is suggested in the notations and mechanical drawings of Leonardo DaVinci. He first imagined (had a feeling for) the principles of flight, then developed the mechanical applications to bring it about. In other words, he connected an object of intellectual interest with a feeling for that object in order to bring about practical applications. A direct example from Marcia's experience with small children involves her grandson Noah. Not long ago Marcia observed him running and leaping along the length of her new couch, then jumping off the end of it. Just in the nick of time she stopped herself from scolding him and instead focused on his obvious joy in running, leaping, and jumping. Seeing Noah in this condition,

Marcia neutrally asked him what he was doing. Noah replied that he was "being a cheetah." "How come you are being a cheetah?" she asked, quite intrigued by his willingness to stop leaping and answer questions. " 'Cause, Grandma, then I can tell what a cheetah feels like. Cheetahs sure like to run very, very fast and leap on their prey." Even if there is not a budding biologist here, at four years of age Noah has certainly made the critical connection between his current passionate interest in animals and his feeling for them, which is profoundly experiential and kinesthetic. This "feeling-for" provides an obvious motivation to learn by constantly feeding and embellishing the interest. Noah has begun to take animal books and National Geographic children's videos out of the public library and already has an extensive knowledge of habitats, species similarities, paw prints, distinguishing markings, and the like. Had Marcia immediately dismissed his imaginative play in favor of her couch (a ritual response), this urge toward connection might have been damaged. It was easy enough to negotiate a few simple rules for future couch-leaping after Marcia's interested questions validated Noah's feeling-based discoveries.

We have known many colleagues who have objected to our emphasis on the primacy of the faculty of feeling and who have insisted that a classroom is a series of subliminally negotiated compromises, which inevitably simmers down into some sort of collective norm anyway—so why the fuss? We would answer: this compromise reduces learning and teaching to the lowest (least conscious, least exciting) results possible and produces a negative experience for all concerned. Chronic defensive postures on the parts of both teachers and students rarely lead to anything but chronic wariness. And wariness, by itself, is a distraction. A good, healthy fear might be appropriate to cellular survival, but does it serve our quest for connection, wholeness and the rich food for thought that nourishes intellectual growth and creativity? If one's feeling life is immature or shallow, then thinking will be shallow. This kind of thinking may have some breadth as it configures taxonomies and categories, but it will eventually run out of depth if not continually refreshed by feeling, like the fairy-tale magic pitcher that never empties.

In the words of Ron Miller: "Children do not simply learn through their mind, but through their feelings and concerns, their imaginations and their bodies. To focus solely on rational intellect, economic achievement, competition and the uncomplaining performance of social roles is lopsided . . ." (p. 219).

As a teacher, you gradually need to observe how your students answer the question, "How are things going? so that you might encourage each to satisfy her or his self-formation. Goethe noted that, "A teacher who can arouse a feeling for one single good action, for one single good poem, accomplishes more than he who fills our memory with rows on rows of natural objects, classified with name and form." (Bartlett, p. 379) Indeed, it is feeling that not only drives what is best in us, but also decides what *best* is.

ART AS A MAJOR EXPRESSION OF THE FEELING LIFE

A few years ago, I gave an essay question to my tenth-grade global studies class that read, in part: "Define feudalism and explain how each of its constituent elements relate to each other." One student, Lucas, asked if I would permit him to answer the question with a drawing. "Go for it," I responded. After an hour of intense work, Lucas produced a remarkable picture of a feudal manor surrounded by peasant hamlets, filled with little people garbed for their appropriate roles. To the consternation of a few of my colleagues, I assessed his knowledge of feudalism as excellent. Heretofore his grade record in history ranged from failure to just passing. His fellow students lingered by his desk at the end of class and expressed praise for his work. His visual essay hung on my office wall along with many other pieces of art-in-intellect, which I frequently used as illustrative visuals when teaching the material in subsequent years.

After this incident, I made it a regular option to respond to essay questions in forms of art: scenario or dramatic presentations, poetry, music, sculpture, dance, or mime. Of course, some responses required a "take home" time frame. My attitude in assessment became one of encouraging each student to find out not only their own very best means of expression, but to explore subjects in depth. Cheating was never an issue for me—if kids got pulled into the subject through the talent of their own particular temperament, then so much the better. I would also read out essay questions a day or so in advance of test taking, so that students could rehearse their responses and be that much more absorbed in the knowledge implicit in the essay.

Over the years, as children attended to the themes and particulars of a given lesson, I watched them literally doodle toward judgment as the body tried to conform to the learning at hand. Like daydreams, doodles reflect whatever connection and disconnection is transpiring as academe chugs on. Taken further, doodles can transform into scenarios or dramatic arts and capture mood, climate, mentality of characters, dimensions, and proportions set in perspective by feeling and interpreted through thought. Music—by inscribing melody, key, rhythm, and dissonance—is a sounding in and out of the feeling life and gives form to the action of the soul. Perhaps nothing so permeates the rationality of feeling as does music, free as it is of the liturgy of words. Dance and mime are the very embodiment of the feeling life and enfranchise the formation of emotions in congruence with perception and judgment. The very notion of a student dancing or acting his way through an essay will seem absurd to most Americans, and in most schools ridicule would certainly attend such efforts. In America, it is more likely that the stand-up class comic and his mobile face will be better received.

However, both Marcia and I have seen the intellectual growth that results from tapping into this sort of expression. In an after-school literacy mentoring program for fourth-grade poor readers that Marcia supervised, there was an active, highly distracted young boy—let's call him Ben. Although Ben was known in his school as a budding actor and singer, he could not stay focused on the texts he was reading for social studies, he talked and interrupted constantly, and his reading comprehension was at a first-grade level. The student teacher who was working with him felt impatient and frustrated; she often referred to Ben as hyperactive, ADD, ADHD. Marcia noticed that as they worked together at a desk, the student teacher constantly tapped her foot and changed position; physically she appeared as "itchy" as Ben. Marcia passed this observation along to the student teacher and suggested that she and Ben go out in the hall and try acting out Revolutionary War scenarios as they did shared reading. It was a year-long process, but it paid off handsomely for Ben. Joined by another student and teacher part way through the semester, the two boys and their mentors made the hall their stage. They soon began to read back and forth to each other as they acted out the characters in their books, thus demonstrating their increasing fluency and comprehension. For his final presentation for parents, Ben sang a solo of "Erie Canal," with the lyrics from one of the illustrated books that the students had read that year. The whole class benefited from the periodic skits that Ben and his cohorts performed to bring the literature to life. Ben's mentor found that the physical engagement with the content eased her impatience and helped her focus on her teaching.

Poetry, both as a reflection of the process of imagining and as the outward expression of understanding, acts as an enlargement or a magnifying glass for the feeling life and seems to say, along with all forms of art, "I have a concern." Sculpture lends tactility, space, shape, and movement to understanding. So whenever your school district and your department decide to do away with the arts, we strongly advise you to integrate the image-making abilities of your students into your curriculum as you practice all facets of it. The arts act as conduits from Awareness to Knowing to Understanding, to taking action, which then circulates back through the foundation of consciousness itself, the process of which is called meaning. As you facilitate their feeling life, you aid and abet students' intellectual growth, for it is feeling that gives meaning and vitality to intellect. Furthermore, you become, in their minds, directly associated with that which is meaningful, and once that occurs, teacher and student are bound together in a vibrant, co-creative learning process.

If students are denied meaning, then they are denied ownership of the vessel in which they are moving along. Students must be able to *occupy* the ship and sail it—not lie down in it like slaves. And to occupy themselves, they must be able to find their feelings and thoughts onboard. They must be able to both think and feel their good fortune to be aboard such a connecting ship.

When I began teaching poetry about midway in my career, I asked my first class, "Would you prefer to study the great poets, or combine the study of great poets with your own poetic attempts, or simply make the course an experience in poetry writing?" To my surprise and initial disapproval, they overwhelmingly decided to make it a course in their own poetic life. I asked myself, how could they reject the great tradition, where they would find forms to emulate and thus be enriched by the expressions of titans? Didn't they understand that our uniqueness is only enhanced by the influence of the best and the brightest? It slowly dawned on me that their choice was based on their hunger to find out precisely how they individually and collectively felt on any given occasion. Academics are so much a piling on of *arbitrary* disciplines that one seldom, if ever, has an opportunity to discover one's own *inner* discipline. Of course, cynics (80 percent of our colleagues in education) will say that I had been gulled by the students, that students will always prefer the utterances of their own untutored egos to the necessary rigor of understanding the "highly accomplished." Be on guard against such self-appointed realism, both in yourself and in those around you. The test of the viability of an interpretation of student life should be, does your choice of attitude expand or contract the lives of your students? Does it lead to chronic wariness or does it lead to meaning? And your intention to use the arts in expressing your subject matter has little or nothing to do with mingling psychology and art, and everything to do with mingling learning with the feeling life, *dum vivimus, vivimus* (while we live, let us live).

As a teacher, your good fortune will be to cultivate a large appetite in yourself for all the art forms, so that you will be able to recognize and serve the sensibilities of your students. Integrating the feeling life into your curriculum will help students claim ownership over your material. They will learn how to translate their presentiments into the subject matter and translate the subject matter into their presentiments, as Ben did in the example above. "I don't get it, Mr. Willis!" can be met with accurate perceptions of how each student's feeling life is arranged and by aligning this arrangement with creative expression. Translation by means of artistic expression makes real what is taught and includes at least two dimensions: what is real for the student and the authentic presence of the teacher.

I had a student (we shall call him Fred) who was in the habit of spitting on the desks of students whom he thought were unsympathetic to him. When I confronted him on this obnoxious behavior, he replied, "I have nothing in common with any of them—they're creeps!" "What is it that you are interested in, Fred?" I asked, wanting to know what he would want someone to have in common with him. "Only one damn thing," he said. "Yes? And that is . . . ?" I again inquired. "Trains—anything to do with trains," he finally acknowledged. While I confessed that I knew little about the world of trains, I was interested in learning about them and would enjoy being his train student. For the next several months, Fred did indeed introduce me into the mysteries of the rails—schedules, types, histories, and much more. My genuine interest allowed me to translate his feeling for trains into the subject matter of global studies. His drawings and models, as well as other work, brought him to interface with much of what trains connect with, and hence, led to the possibility of intellectual transformation.

Talent is often ascribed to the arts, and "brains" to academics, as if talent were an unreflecting automaton that took care of itself, whereas "brains" needed careful and expert nurturing. In fact, talent is the means through which the actions of thought formulate meaning. Unfortunately, you will be teaching for the most part under circumstances that deny the humanities full play, and instead measure academic achievement within strictly controlled definitions determined by administrators influenced by psychometricians, behaviorists, cognitive psychologists, and politicians. Happily, your use of the arts to facilitate student learning will bode well, even for these pundits. Your results, by their lights, will be salutary.

THE ELEMENTS OF INTELLIGENCE AS THEY PLAY OUT IN THE FEELING LIFE

As with Marsden Hartley's five aesthetic themes discussed above, there is another way of looking into the feeling life of students that I used throughout my teaching career. I formulated descriptions of and looked for four *energies* in assessing intelligence, not as categorical absolutes, but as a means of discovering the thrust that propelled each student into learning and helping me discover what they still needed to cultivate. I called these energies sense (analytical reasoning), sensibility (aesthetics), guts (tenacity), and humor (the capacity for detachment). Not to be confused with words that describe functions of temperament, these energies or thrusts of intelligence concern the ability to acquire and retain knowledge, and to understand from the experience of that knowledge. While the phrase "intelligence of sensibility" overlaps with vocabulary used to describe the feeling function, they are to be distinguished from one another. The former designates the impetus or energy that it takes to know and understand, while the latter refers to a functional way of evaluating data. Marcia and I spent six weeks one summer working out how each function of temperament might appear if propelled by one or the other of these energies of intelligence. In this chapter we are concerned with describing how the feeling function would look when propelled by each of the energies of intelligence. Our purpose is to provide beginning teachers with another modality for assessing the strength of the Feeling life in their students. Here enumerated and discussed are these energies as they play out in our feeling judgments.

1. For the energy of sense (the thrust of analytic logic), as it plays out through feeling, the question is always, "Is the feeling logically congruent with experience? Is the feeling in line with what we know as true?" In early March 1972, I awoke abruptly and sat up with a start. I was filled with a feeling of absolute menace taking place downstairs. Yet I could detect no reason for this heightened state of alertness. After about thirty seconds of analyzing my feelings, I decided there must be an intruder below. I grabbed a baseball bat and went downstairs, fully expecting a furtive form somewhere below. And there, beyond the kitchen in an open storage room, I saw the wall glowing. Only then did my mind acknowledge a house fire. As yet there was no pervasive smoke or flames as the fire moved between plasterboard and clapboard. I called the fire department and luckily saved the house. There is always a lapse of time as sensibility and sense work out a likely scenario. The truthfulness of feeling must meet

the truth of analysis. In my house fire, my analysis fell briefly short of the truth. It was a menace, but not of the kind I had first thought.

Students consistently experience this lapse as they seek to corroborate the two poles. A strong impression, but what does it mean? If lapses are too protracted, if negotiations between feeling and thinking go badly, blocks can occur. "Why do you use such big words, Mr. Willis?" "Yeah, I get it, but I don't understand it." "I'll never remember that!" Any analysis of temperament must take into account this dynamic interplay between the feeling impression and the conceptual determination. "Sorry, Mr. Willis, I just couldn't think. I knew it, but I just couldn't think it." Skeptics, often correctly, assume a ruse, but as often as a bogus excuse arose, there was a legitimate confusion between a pervasive feeling and an attending logic. In fact, sometimes the ruse was the "objectification" of the disconnection. Also common are students who blame themselves for poor preparation when a crossover between experience and analysis never occurred in the first place. A blank can occur where a student's mind should have been. Feeling must work with thinking and thinking with feeling.

2. The energy of sensibility, or the operation of feeling, is where the feeling thrust meets the feeling function, in a sense heightening or doubling the modality. Sensibility asks, does my feeling approve with this action, does it sit well? Feeling itself frequently carries the day as "it feels just right" or "it doesn't feel right." If the feeling consents or does not consent, so the rest of you might find a way in or a way out. Scientists and theoretical mathematicians want to sense an idea to be whole and beautiful before they give it their imprimatur. Although nature, it is feelingly assumed, is intact and whole, in the majority of American schools people find themselves placed unnaturally, in classrooms of twenty or more, competitively unequal, losing more than winning, less rather than more, on the short end of a sticklike system that rewards top grades, top looks, and top personality.

As Marcia discusses in Chapters 4 and 5, we approve of students who learn compliantly by traditional methods, but we are not so fond of those who learn best through their moving bodies or aesthetically. How will you, the teacher, accommodate them? Sensibility establishes value, and if a student undervalues himself and his surroundings, how can teachers persuade him or her otherwise? In my view, if your attitude is to choose the methods or teaching that "just feels right" for your students, you will help to make subsequent events "sit well" more often than not. Secondly, if you take to heart Thomas Moore's attitude in *Care of the Soul*—wherein feelings are not to be regarded as signifiers of pathology or ruses to be brought to consciousness so that they might evaporate, but rather as accurate indicators of the frequently frustrated and actual experiences of the students—then you will be honoring them in ways that affirm their real learning situations. You will be a realist without being a cynic, caring without being romantic. Thirdly, by being willing to orient the students' individual expressions around their points of strength in the humanities, you will be giving their boats a shove from the shore. Their passions will find an expression in your course.

3. The energy of guts, or the operation of tenacity—the question here is: Will the feeling endure in the face of opposition and change? Will the student be able to stay the course? Or will feeling be swallowed up in the chronic embarrassment American culture exhibits toward feelings that are exposed—not to be confused with our behavioral displays? Recall our commentary in Chapter 2 on defiance, on implacable intentionality. Will the feeling life of your students be sufficient to see them through thick and thin? Guts can eventually develop and refine into high tenacity, persistence *par excellence*. All of us rely on our feeling to carry us through mood swamps and unforeseen vagaries from without. How will students identify and strengthen their courage, if not in part from your nudges of encouragement? Good teachers all seem to embody for students the sentiment "You can do it!" A teacher needs to be tenacious enough to stand with students while their courage wavers, for as long as it takes. Kids cannot always keep the charge of their tenacity on their own, and will call or check in with you periodically years after you have had them as students. In this way they maintain the gift of their own guts. Marcia notes that in some of the schools where she has worked, primary-age children stay with the same homeroom teacher for several years, until their tenacity is well established.

4. The energy of humor, or the impulse to see content in context— does the feeling stay clear of precipitous emotion, or that disruption of feeling that is the false expression of feeling? Humor refines to detachment, which in turn perfects itself in the spaciousness of perspective. How do we stay clear of all the noise, what Theodore Roethke called "the bang and blab," that prevents us from witnessing both ourselves and others in context? It is not so much that we take ourselves too seriously, as it is that we become encapsulated in the emotions and trappings of the personality disporting itself. Anger masks sadness, which masks grief, in a culture that esteems the most superficial element of ourselves—personality—as the peak of human development.

Think of exercises that help your students stand back and see their (and your) foibles from a distance. In the classroom, I told jokes on myself, engaged in deliberate pratfalls such as banging into a desk, or acted out in Chaplinesque style a character in history. If the joke was on a student, it was highlighted with appreciation and affection: "Boy, Joe may not be able to sit still, but he can really move!" Marcia enjoyed this energy most of all when she played with infants and toddlers. She calls it "being a goof" or "Elmo humor": hiding objects up her sleeves, dressing dolls by putting shoes on their heads, putting the plastic cowboy on the horse backwards. In all cases the purpose of this humor was to show our fallibility admixed with our authenticity.

Humor is quite capable of increasing the spaciousness of feeling content so as to allow us to conduct imagination experiments based on hard data. If we trust our humor, our spatial travel, we can go anywhere and see our story spin. A little humor goes a little way, and a lot of humor goes a long way. Delight, even joy, is the very action of perspective in play. Of all the energies of intelligence that I have experienced kids loving, it is laughter they most enjoy and which most opens their minds. "Boy, I really like that teacher, Mr. Willis—she makes us laugh—she's really fun!" After all, it is a great relief to be free to think and feel without misplaced constraints. In this verse from *Songs of Innocence* by William Blake we find this humor:

> When the voices of children are heard on the green
> And laughing is heard on the hill,
> My heart is at rest within my breast
> And everything else is still. ("Nurse's Song," p. 32)

HOW DO WE SUFFER FOOLS?

Perhaps in no other profession is the daily confrontment with foolishness more commonplace than in teaching. Deficiency of mind seems to surround us at every turn—in spasms of temperament, in a cacophony of noises, in unmediated clamor and obliviousness. What is to be our attitude toward fools and foolishness? If one sees the feeling life as dumb (stupid), then fools will not be suffered. But if one sees feelings as dumb (wordless intelligence), then one is likely to suffer fools gladly. Francis of Assisi said, "Preach the Gospels at all times. Use words if necessary." The Gospels, in our context, would be the attitude that you embody, which is read by students with little attention to your words. If you suffer them gladly, so will they suffer you. If you accept their feelings as a fundamental part of their mentality, and not as a deficiency of mind, then they will respond to you in kind, trusting that you know them well. And they will be far more likely to show you the grace of a complete mind, as it arises from time to time. None of this implies a certain *behavior* on your part, but rather an *attitude* of experiencing young people in an inclusive manner. The closer you get to Henry Adams' description of the joy of Francis of Assisi, the greater your enjoyment of your students: "Francis loved them all—the brothers and the sisters—as intensely as a child loves the smell and taste of a peach, and as simply . . ." (p. 341). And it was Francis of Assisi who, when addressing the Chapter of his Order at Sancta Maria de Portinuncula in 1215, called himself "a pauper and an idiot—a great fool—in this world . . ." (p. 338). If this seems "over the top," well, then, so is teaching inclusively with feeling.

CHAPTER EIGHT

Teach Anywhere

SPACES, PLACES, PACES, AND FACES

The classroom is only one of the spaces shared by you and your students. So, teach anywhere—in the halls, in the cafeteria, on the grounds, *sotto voce* in the library, in the foyer, in the chat rooms of cyberspace, in the school theater and assembly hall, in the tempest of a field trip, on long sojourns abroad, and at home. Remember that you are the student in these places as well, learned and learning. Give your spirit all the space it desires. There is nothing that requires you to limit learning and relationships with your students to a classroom. Desks in military order, bulletin boards of "now hear this" items, blackboards smeared with dry chalk, whiteboards smudged with Sharpie ink, and square walls and ceilings on which you hang only certain things do not describe the sole locale in which to teach and learn. The Hellenic Greeks, indeed most of the tribal world, recognized that young people wiggle a lot and are driven to fidget and move around. The young body thinks well on the fly, not so well in the statuary postures of an ordered class, and especially poorly at eight in the morning when the brain is still tilting toward alpha waves. The Greeks practiced *paideia*—the feet and legs moving as the teacher remonstrates with his students in the academy. And this occurred after a morning of exuberant exercise. First the body opens out, then the mind unfolds, and, if there is a relevant activity to follow, the soul kicks in with its two cents.

Personally, I found the halls the best places to teach, because students associate breaks between classes with the freedom to socialize, grab a snack, and be one's own strutting self. In the halls, I was best able introduce ideas and observations that were initiated elsewhere and carried forward in a mood of inquiry, such as, "Well, Mark, what do you think? Was Hobbes right? Are our lives by nature, 'nasty, brutish, and short'?" "Well, Mr. Willis . . . what was his name—Rousseau?—I agree with him—we are basically good at heart." Students within ear- and eye-shot would circle around like young wolves, and off we would go. Of course, I was perpetually walking students to their next classes, with apologies for tardiness, or writing notes, or both. I spent no small amount of my most successful teaching time in a compensating or apologetic mode. The daily schedule allowed three or four minutes to move to the next class, but it is within the realm of learning to carry on the ruffling banter of dialectics in such brief periods.

My colleague Frank pointed out that contemporary education is increasingly broken into byte sizes and that one should seize "the teachable moment" when attention is present. Someday, perhaps, increased passing time between classes will be recognized as accommodating these interludes of exchange and learning. Other places also offer joyous moments. I found the thirty-minute lunchtime with students in the cafeteria a grand time to weave our stories. As you scout your preferred pedagogical terrain, try not to eliminate any promising and moving spot. Think big. I have often yearned for a second environment that would contain an open-air café where faculty and students could come together to share and learn. We implemented just such a plan at the Barlow School in Amenia, New York, in the 1970s. In planning for this, both faculty and students felt that there ought to be three centers, one for exclusively student gatherings, one for faculty only (both of which were already in place), and one inclusively for faculty and students. As we collectively built a one-floor, one-room, indoor/outdoor café, cynics warned that no one would go there because of the incipient threat each group posed to the other. In fact, it became one of the most frequented gathering places on campus. The rule was if a teacher and students wanted to hold a class there, they had to ask permission of those already there. If permission was granted, then the class began and others could join in or not as they desired. The café was a lively place, and well attended both formally and informally.

COMPARE AND CONTRAST

Few of us are so in touch with Awareness that we can travel at will, as Emily Dickinson and William Blake did, to different climes and times while sitting at their writing desks. Einstein, Schroedinger, and Pauli might be conveyed by the native curiosity of their minds outside the cultural bubble in which they were raised, but most of us need more palpable inducements. Madame Blavatsky and the Magus of Strovolos might travel anywhere on the globe without taking a step outside their national boundaries, but most of us actually must step well into other cultural contexts in order to compare and contrast the assumptions of our age. Hallucinogens might give us a notion of greater things, but they addle our brains and pose a serious threat to our neurotransmitters. Living abroad in the context of different cultures is an indispensable catalyst to our waking brain. Without travel most of us cannot find similarities and differences of sufficient impact to stir us into the journey that is coextensive with our yearning. In all my years of teaching, I did not know a single student who did not come roundly alive to her or his learning as a result of foreign travel. For this reason, I have spent no little time trying to facilitate such experiences for all my students. And aside from the hectic pace, it was as much a joy to participate vicariously in this travel with students as when kibbitzing in the halls or on the grounds.

Travel, both internally and externally, helps us to expand our notions of right and wrong, ugliness and beauty, true and false. Comparing and contrasting is the exercise of consciousness expanding itself. We must have differentiated elements to integrate: If the world were green, how would green get our attention, and would blue even affect us? In his *Letters to a Young Poet*, Rainer Maria Rilke writes:

> We are set down in life as in the element to which we best correspond, and over and above this we have through thousands of years of accommodation become so like this life, that when we hold still we are, through a happy mimicry, scarcely to be distinguished from all that surrounds us. We have no reasons to mistrust our world, for it is not against us. Has it terrors, they are our terrors; has it abysses, those abysses belong to us; are dangers at hand, we must try to love them. (p. 69)

We, as teachers, need to aid and abet our students' experience of all that surrounds them and, with Rilke, encourage them to "arrange our life according to the principle which counsels us that we must always hold to the difficult" (p. 69). In this way we shine one narrow beam of our flashlight consciousness, so that the details and patterns of our Awareness become luminous. This learning to love the difficult is a love of the suffusion of light over a multiscape, allowing the beam to widen until the light pervades the whole multiform. It is a byproduct of becoming ever more familiar with that which surrounds us, of wanting to own Terrence's great declaration: *homo sum; humani nihil a me alienum puto*—"I am a man; I consider nothing human strange to me." When your students commit one of the greatest errors against the spirit by saying, "Hey, this is weird!" take them abroad and rub their noses in weird. And if they say, "I want to see my country first," ask them why they feel the need to rub themselves in their own scent.

WITHIN ANYWHERE

If the classroom does not define the teaching environment, what does? In his exploration of the interior life of teachers, *The Courage to Teach*, Parker J. Palmer posits six spatial paradoxes, which work in conjunction with one another to produce a viable learning environment and which are dependent on attitude, rather than on actual physical space (pp. 73–83). When I first read them, I thought they provided an excellent basis for teacher *reflection*—a major concern in present-day teacher training—regarding the creation of dynamic learning environments through attitude. I recommend these paradoxes as a means to evaluate your teaching and I use them to present the following evaluation of my own experiences with attitudinal spatiality over the course of my career.

1. *"The space should be bounded and open."* I was reasonably effective in leaving students with a sense that their respective journeys bore much relevance to my own trip. But as a public school teacher and social studies department chairperson, I felt bound by New York State Regents exams to such a degree that I fashioned most bodies of data around anticipated multiple-choice and essay questions. I felt far freer to generate text more compelling to students when I taught in private schools exempt from most state standards than in public schools, where one was predominantly judged according to numerical results on Regents exams. In private schools, I taught such courses as The History of the City and Medieval Philosophy, whereas in public schools we taught within the confines of global studies and American studies, which were tacitly slanted toward an almanac mentality, circumscribed by politics, economics, and civil rights. We were constrained by the imposition of state standards regarding notions of diversity. I sought to enlarge the social studies space by creating elective courses in psychology, sociology, and anthropology, and I collaborated with two colleagues in establishing a humanities course. I give myself a B– here, because I was only partially successful in overcoming the uncompelling nature of state curriculum.

In the public school arena, I have known several colleagues who did a much better job of bounding their classroom space in district and state categories with significance, creativity, and relevance. Their compliance in no way compromised the dialogical nature of their students' journeys. Ken, an eighth-grade social studies teacher, stayed within state curricular concepts but related them to today's world, such as when he and his students studied the Age of Expansionism in the United States. He would ask his kids if they had ever been forced to do or be something that they were not at peace with. "People are like nations," he would say, as he brought events and ideas within his students' purview. "How many of you ever rebelled or took risks in asserting your interests? What might be the consequences? Why do we obey laws? How many of you have ever broken laws? What is an outlaw: someone who is antisocial? What does the Constitution have to do with you?" All this and dialogically much more was presented in the context of studying about the American Revolution. Ken would frequently bring in folk singers and storytellers, such as the time when an African American couple had all the kids crowd under one table so they could appreciate the packing of a slave ship. Ken would use role playing extensively, as when studying nineteenth-century industrialism, with students acting out factory bosses and workers. Ken's space was truly bounded in curriculum, yet open to a full spectrum of exploration.

2. *"The space should be hospitable and 'charged.'"* Students need to feel safe, need to feel trust, a place where they can be themselves, but not so complacent that they fall asleep. Nodding off and trivializing the lesson steal the "charge" from the hospitable learning environment. Teacher and students need to feel risk and difficulty simultaneous to their enjoyment of hospitality. A friendly climb up the north face of the Eiger comes to mind; or a land/sea rescue; or entertaining a somewhat daunting question, such as: "What role would you be willing to play if escaped slaves came through your neighborhood on their way to Canada in 1858—recognizing that any help would be regarded as a felony, and that any neighbors who did not like you would be sorely tempted to turn you in?" Good teachers are notorious for their repertoire of challenging spaces for students in a hospitable environment. I give myself relatively high marks on this paradox, maybe A–, a minus because every now and then I erred on the side of hospitality as one or two students fell asleep in the comfort of their condition. In this teeter-totter balance between comfort and risk, I tended to favor comfort over risk. Perhaps the loss of my friend John, a great mountain climber and teacher-colleague, who fell 4,000 feet off the Eiger just at a time when he and I were planning a college preparatory school of

mountaineering in Switzerland, sensitized me to the actual hazards of risk. In effecting this balance, become alert to your own life's conditioning experiences.

Mark rarely had the problem of comfortable nodders, and was particularly effective in creating a safe, yet charged, learning environment. In his Participation in Government course (PIG), when students were studying the rights of the accused, he would suddenly and vigorously frisk one of his students (set up in advance) while the rest of the class looked on in shock. He had planted a bag of oregano (for pot) on the student, and with much bravura, he found it and brandished it about. As his department chairperson observer, I was as much taken aback as his students and was led immediately to the question of *Miranda vs. Arizona* and *New Jersey vs. T.L.O.* Mark also ran the Mock Trial program involving PIG and Advanced Placement American History and Literature students. Juries were often composed of seventh- and eighth-grade kids, while the prosecution and defense roles were played by eleventh and twelfth graders. Using nineteenth-century business practices versus worker safety as the basis for one mock trial, Mark managed all three learning centers in a safe and highly charged educational environment: teacher-centered, as Mark played the role of the instructive judge; student-centered, as kids struggled to manage the various roles of prosecution, defense, jury, and witness; and community-centered, as everyone felt compelled to know the case.

3. *"The space should invite the voice of the individual and the voice of the group."* Here Parker Palmer certainly betrays his Quaker roots, as do I. So great is Quaker respect toward the individual as one who is able to reflect the light of the spirit that one dissenting voice can prevent the remaining collective from going forward. Making decisions by consensus has been called by Friends (Quakers) "a sense of the meeting," and truly teaches a group to listen with great care to each of its members—who perforce carry such enormous weight. And, of course, this induces each individual to be equally careful to lay aside both compliance and defiance and listen to the emerging collective voice, composed as it is in the truth of individuals. This balance and synthesis would seem to be the trickiest of aerial acts, and yet, is not so difficult if your attitude is unambiguously one of attentive respect for each of your students and of the class as a whole. You care to hear the authentic voices of your students, no matter how long it may take, and hold each in awareness, no matter how unpracticed, awkward, or eccentric their voices may be. Equally, you are impatient with, even intolerant of, mere wisecracking, bogus posturing, and other forms of

insincerity, so that your students can readily differentiate their voices from their noises. They usually know the difference quickly enough.

This is one of the main reasons why you must bring your Self into class: your voice must reflect the light of your being, foibles and all. Students will forgive your contradictions, but not your hypocrisy or your duplicity. They will accept you, "bag and baggage," as long as your real light shines through. Every so often, my patience gave way altogether and I would bellow like an angry bull at the whole class or at an individual. A student might say, "Wow, Mr. Willis, that was harsh. You hardly ever yell. You must have been in a terrible mood." One student, Joey, told me one day that when I yelled at him it was embarrassing and it hurt his ears. In my career, I remember only one young woman who was more than put off by my display of temper, and she never opened up again around me, for reasons I was unable to discover. The others simply felt badly, briefly, for me, or for themselves, or both. For this reason, I give myself a B+ for tempermental outbursts. Cathy, please forgive me—to this day, I feel bad that I intimidated you.

None of this is to imply that you assume a confessional voice. Students cannot be your therapists and such a tone diverts attention away from what we believe to be true, individually and collectively. Nor should you assume a familiarity with your students inappropriate to their age, development, and condition, the actions of which always diverge from the truth. This space is at the center of this book: the place where the I and the We and the They can meet at the crossroads of perception and judgment.

4. *"The space should honor the 'little' stories of the individual and the 'big' stories of the disciplines and traditions."* Though he does not say so, Parker Palmer is referring to the semiotics of heritage and legacy. Our little stories combine in the big stories, not in a splendid, democratic symmetry, but in the fantastic woolliness of history. Through listening to the interpretive experiences of each other, we begin to learn to listen to our archetypal and universal stories. Even at the pre-school level, we see children encouraged to bring in show-and-tell items, stand in front of the group, and tell their stories; this activity sets a foundation for increasingly sophisticated listening and telling later on. Dostoyevsky could express archetypal stories because he had witnessed and imagined so many individual narratives; he was a one-souled congregation all in himself.

Regardless of your subject matter, the story is there—in class and in history. In physics, what was Newton thinking when he invented calculus as a way to describe angular momentum? What sort of story would the student have to narrate in order to express a similar reach? Does he think Leibnitz was a parallel inventor? Why did Pascal say, "I am terrified by the eternal silence of those infinite spaces?" Do you ever feel that way? What sort of momentum did Harvey command when he wrote *On the Movement of the Heart and Blood in Animals*? The connection of the little story to the big story is so central to the student-teacher learning that we devoted a whole chapter to the use of philosophy, or ideas, in facilitating narration.

When the story becomes lopsided or one-sided, we enter extremes of narcissism on one side and *flatland* objectivism on the other. Parker Palmer notes something that I experienced years ago in teaching creative writing: "When my little story, or yours, is our only point of reference, we easily become lost in narcissism" (p. 76). Students come to believe that their personal narrative is the only truth and stands monumentally by itself because it was said or written. The errors I committed in the mutual narrational space of the creative writing class were of an overzealous emphasis on the little story at the expense of the big, and for this reason I give myself a straight B; I sometimes had to compensate by presenting students with big, grandiose stories, to get their attention off themselves and onto the world, and thus missed the dialogical, give-and-take element.

On the other hand, when the big story looms as having the only fact of existence simply because it is framed by tradition, the two spaces remain in mutual incomprehension. Many a teacher has sailed exuberantly along with the wind of the big story sweeping across his students, who are in an auto-note-taking mode, sublimely unaware that the students' fantasies, in and out of class, bear no witness to this inspirational wind. Their notes copy out the voice, but their minds, indeed their souls, are elsewhere. It is not they who are intoxicated by the rhetoric. And, somewhere down the line, *Horace's Compromise* (discussed in Theodore R. Sizer's book of the same name), the idea behind social promotion, comes into boring play.

Not so with Chris, a high school English teacher, who used big stories from the worlds of jazz, folk, and rock music, such as the voices of Louis Armstrong, Pete Seeger, James Taylor, and Pink Floyd, to accentuate themes for writing assignments. He was able consistently to engage the little stories of his students with the big stories of our culture. Once this connection between big and little stories begins to play itself out in the minds of kids, they are increasingly willing to make larger connections. Chris also used outrageous humor and antics to engage the attention of his students. One frequently heard a loud thump, a bang, or some other noise coming from his room. Like a Zen master, Chris made sure his constituents were alert, and for the most part they loved him for it, even though school administrators frowned on these practices as disruptive and insubordinate. Administrators sometimes prefer boredom to anything that startles.

5. *"The space should support solitude and surround it with the resources of the community."* Solitude here is not only personal time in which to ruminate on learning, but also an attitude of respect, even reverence, toward a student's inner life, the life of the soul. Community becomes perverse when it merely asserts the necessity of its own conventions, its own norms, its assumptive models. Both bodies—students and community—should have a dialogical relationship in which questioning is the basis of ongoing exchange. Testing ideas, expanding knowledge, enlarging arenas of interaction, constitute what Paulo Freire calls "consciousness of one's inclusiveness" (*Pedagogy of the Heart*, pp. 93–94). And this group and individual consciousness is not confined only to rationality: "This consciousness is a totality—reason, feelings, emotions, desires; my body, conscious of the world and myself, seizes the world toward which it has intention" (p. 94). Freire uses the word *gnoseologic* to indicate the mutual intention to know that is the crux of this space. Palmer adds that, "In a community that respects the mystery of the soul, we help each other remove impediments to discernment" (p.77).

Several years ago, I was a member of a fellowship at a nearby university that concerned itself with literary ideology. On the first day of our meeting, we were told by the convening professor: "Anyone here who is not a convinced theoretical Marxist and who subscribes to some metaphysical power really has no place in our deliberations (into postmodernism)." I inquired if a Judeo/Christian humanist was acceptable. He replied he didn't think so, but deferred to the group, who decided to tolerate my presence, at least for the time being. Was there any chance for a space that supports solitude and community here?

The biggest single enemy of gnoseological space is hegemonic space, a place where a uniform set of beliefs is required for membership and where excommunication is the penalty for noncompliance. Students know immediately if a certain truth is to be maintained and, that if this truth is doubted, then our inclusive right of knowing is also in doubt. Goodbye inner life; goodbye community quest.

Delusional or not, I give myself an A in this fifth inner space. I believe I have cultivated just such a dialogical atmosphere in my classes consistently over the years in an environment of quest and respect for the intention to know in both the group and in the individual.

6. *"The space should welcome both silence and speech."* Over my career, starting with a grade of C– and finishing near B+, I found this perhaps the most difficult aspect of attitude to master. Ours is a culture with a bias against silence. The adjective *awkward* might well be grafted to it. If long pauses are often required between us, if we are to have any chance at mutual perception, as discussed earlier, then our culture's attitude toward silence is a genuine handicap. If we cannot abide silences longer than fifteen seconds, we simply tumble after one another in unreflecting cant. As teachers, we need to provide our students with the strophes and rhythms of a space more accommodating to teaching and learning. Rushing and gushing and glittering and sputtering slip-slide over the persona like advertisements for anything but soul; if this flat exuberance predominates, we will not become acquainted with each other or with ourselves. We will become perfect consumers, but never learners.

Our penchant for behavioral performance, our tendency to see silence as either a vacuum or an overlay for pathology, and our equation of assertiveness with noisy aggression lead to dehumanizing outcomes. The subjectivities of *I* and *We*, of the individual's inner life and the group's connected inner lives, are discouraged and repressed. Introversion itself is held to be regrettable and only a certain kind of extraversion is sanctioned—a sort of slow coolness, as in the voice of John Wayne. Missing in our culture are the large spaces given to the subjective, both in its silent and expressive oscillations. Few can stand to be alone or be seen as being alone. And few of us enjoy expression that comes from the depths of the considered, natural response.

A few years ago, I accompanied a Russian friend to the Hermitage in Saint Petersburg. We headed for the Peter Paul Rubens room because, said Mikhail, "Rubens paints beauty at its most transcendent." While standing in the middle of this great hall, I exclaimed with no little mockery, "Ah—Rubens—he paints mountains of round pink flesh!" "Idiot!" shouted Mikhail, "What an American—so ephemeral." We went on arguing vociferously. Several guards came up and joined in the argument on both sides, as did several patrons. For ten minutes we disputed passionately in a tight circle until someone suggested we go below and have a coffee. Laughter. Pause. Enjoyment. Could such an event occur in our culture? Wouldn't we have been seized and hustled out? If one is afraid of silence, one is afraid of expression.

Carl Rogers once walked into a college class and said nothing for twenty minutes, just to confront his students with the experience of silence together. The discomfort level for these folks verged on excruciating. This fear of silence is so pervasive as to quite confound real speech. The social exclamations of America will not be easy to modify. At first, this might be a rather self-conscious and awkward process, but in time everyone will appreciate the comfort of a larger dialogical space. The fear of silence will give way to the relief of being able to reflect openly before committing to response, to know what one knows in a tentative context, to trust that people will await with graceful patience the content of our understanding. Rapid-fire quiz shows are good entertainment but do not comprise curiosity and discovery. In long, confident pauses, we see one another and hear ourselves.

Parker Palmer's six paradoxes describe not the exclusionary *either/or*, but rather the both/and approach. He opens up educational locales that can happen anywhere, as long as our attitude can contain these inquiring spaces. As he observes, "Holding the tension of paradox so that our students can learn at deeper levels is among the most difficult demands of good teaching" (p. 83). In Chapter 9 we consider how people encompass these paradoxes within the agency of Awareness, that vast, dumb sense of things, which is our most capacious and primary register of all that we can know, understand, and act upon.

CHAPTER NINE

Awareness

Evelyn Fox Keller, in her biography of Barbara McClintock, observed, "The ultimate task for both artists and scientists, is to 'ensoul' what one sees, to attribute to it the life one shares with it . . ." (p. 204). This same "feeling for the organism," this entering the content and context of that with which one is involved, as McClintock did in studying the genetic behavior of maize, is as essential for teachers in coming to know their students. It should be the goal of professional development to cultivate the faculty of Awareness in teachers, and subsequently to bring the faculties of Behaving, Understanding, and Knowing into alignment with Awareness. Anything short of this reduces our interactions with students, and our views of them, from organism to mechanism.

Keller goes on to say:

> The challenge for investigators in every field is to break free of the hidden constraints of their tacit assumptions, so they can allow the results of their experiments to speak for themselves. "I feel that much work is done because one wants to impose an answer on it," McClintock says. "They have the answer ready and they (know what they) want the material to tell them. Anything else it tells them, they don't really recognize as there, or they think it's a mistake and throw it out. . . . *If you'd only just let the material tell you.*" (p. 179)

In this book, the material is the student-as-subject as well as the subject matter of the course one teaches. And it is because we often initially fear this student-material that we present ourselves, and are projected upon in return, the way we do. It is not only the uniqueness of each student, or the unique mix of each group of students, but also the mix that each student brings within herself or himself, with which we are confronted. Will we ever be up to the task? What task? Will they reject me? Attack me? Like me? Will I know them and understand them in time? If I can't, there must be control and order and rules—no one thrives in chaos. Teaching is scary.

INTER-ACTION

Randall Jarrell, in one of his last and unpublished poems, wrote:

> Let's love each other for what we are
> Not for what we happen to become,
> Not for what we can make of ourselves.
> No one makes anything of anyone but God. (p. 491)

One presumes that Jarrell knew how difficult this love is to experience, and that he understood how removed is our sense of connection with each other.

As we present ourselves and are presented, we are experienced as a personality reflecting how we have been treated and how we have treated others in return. We are an admixture of behaviors, ranging from charming to brutal. Always we seem capricious and changeable: *caveat actor* (let the doer beware). One never knows what the spin will be. If interpreted by the appearances on our slippery surfaces, we are mutually treacherous and repelling.

As we perceive one another more deeply, at the level of Understanding, we are experienced as minds, busily analyzing our respective "take" on things as mere opinion, informed or otherwise, circumscribed by our times at best and at worst by narrow locale— our cultural-historic matrix. Other people don't fit in us and we don't fit in them. *Caveat emptor/caveat venditor* (let the buyer beware/let the seller beware). A shifty item. If read as mind, we are all pirates, guarding against theft, yet seeking to steal. Minds may be as fascinating as kaleidoscopics at times, but are fundamentally unlovable.

As we come to know each other, a greater but more precarious intimacy is realized as we begin to feel the essential soul within us and others. Sympathy and even empathy are often felt, along with offsetting wariness—born of experience—warning us about other beings, although crucially connected to us, largely unconscious of what they are about. *Cave canem* (beware of the dog)! Who goes there? We can now put ourselves in the shoes of others, but we can also imagine being stabbed as we reach to assist. We feel the thrill of disinterested love, but cannot sustain a condition of nonjudgment. Practical and intuitive evidence lets us love each other, but in such a niggling manner it is nearly impossible for our minds to embrace and our personality to apply. We become intermittently and contingently lovable—a periodic chart of acceptability.

But it is this feeling, this essential alertness that acts as a bridge between our fearful wariness and true Awareness. Feeling also serves as the major conveyor from Awareness to Understanding. When we feel *an other*, we open out enough to create the conditions for Awareness. Our feeling self moves toward actually seeing one another as "we are"; we cross a threshold beyond the simian activity of Persona, the machinations of the mind, and the somnambulist motions of the knower. Objects become subjects. We leave consciousness and enter wakefulness and move into attentiveness, the portal to Awareness. We begin to attend to those whom we see. In the manner of a high-speed camera, we register the past/future of others and the immediacy of their beings right now in the present, in the "quick, now, here, now, always." We naturally experience each other "for what we are." At the all-inclusive extent of Awareness, our perceptions become error-free, and are only error-ridden when the judgments of Feeling and Understanding reenter the room as they surely must. But these mistakes, against the background and recollection of experience in Awareness, are readily corrected and serve to expand wary consciousness toward attentive Awareness.

Our personalities become less frenetic, our minds more synthesizing and our souls more translative and capacious. It is virtually impossible to feel anything but love for those of whom we are Aware. We know each other as subjects rather than objects, as *each other* rather than *another*. Rather than mask-clad actors, circumscribing manipulators and sleepwalking travelers, we are beings at once distinctive and related in a family sharing the selfsame universe.

IN THE ROOM

> Therefore when Tao is lost, there is Goodness
> When Goodness is lost, there is Kindness
> When Kindness is lost, there is Justice
> When Justice is lost, there is ritual
> Now ritual is the husk of faith and loyalty, the beginning of confusion.
> (number 38)

The content and structure of this book are accurately reflected in these lines from the *Tao Te Ching* as we respond to the *material* in our room and in the roominess of our teaching. Interpreted from the perspective of our competitive culture, Lao Tsu's aphorism seems to present linear, hierarchical categories or stages of desired values descending from "best" to "worst." We see it as a structure which suggests a more inclusive/less inclusive set of attitudes, much like a Venn diagram composed of permeable concentric circles, ever widening out or collapsing inward when aligned and in oscillating play with each other. As in respiration, both the expanding and contracting lungs are necessary for breath cycles. With this image in mind we must ask how much of ourselves do we actually take into the classroom? Does the actor enter . . . does the actor and her mind make the introduction . . . does the actor, her sense and her sensibility walk through the door . . . does the emboldened soul, followed by her train of feeling, understanding, and acting come through the portal? Do we take into the room our grim intention to survive no matter what? Do we take into the room our desire both to survive and control, but also to produce there the conditions in which law and order can prevail? Do we bring into the room our surviving and thriving beings, our growing and open wisdom, and our hearts valuing as sacred each individual who is waiting there? Do we expect that these attentions to the uniqueness and interconnectedness of each of our students will gradually fashion their own control and order and learning?

These are crucial questions because they indicate how one will respond to the inevitability of fear when being confronted by students. Fear, or stage fright, is inevitable because students are—individually and collectively—the audience of the teacher. Teachers routinely put on four to six shows a day, and we want these productions to be successful. The new, unique, and real natures of our students judge us and respond to us, causing us to experience the anxiety of uncertainty, the fear of rejection, the fear of hubris, of exclusion, of being attacked, and so on. How do we respond to this nucleus of fear, our wariness? In nearly forty years of teaching, my observations of many of my colleagues (and myself as a young teacher) indicated that we run away from fear into the safest bastion available to us: into the realms of justice provided by our culture. We appeal to common beliefs in equity, notions of fairness, promulgated law, *commonsense* rules, *de facto* regulations and a modicum of distribution of power, prestige, and property. We say, with simulated attentiveness, "Look, we all have to live by the rules if we are to get anything done—that's just the way it is. We must all fit into a common working operation . . . and I shall insist, therefore, on your compliance." This is largely agreed upon by one's colleagues and is often called wisdom, instead of what it really is: the lowest order of moral response to fear, a disastrously inaccurate way to deal with the actual conditions of individual students and students collectively. To teach in the dim light of the justice-response-to-fear is to become consistently boring to yourself, as well as to your students. For the sake of achieving a certain evenhanded behavioral standard, your room becomes a mausoleum of sorts—a nest of models and paradigms speaking to no one's actual condition.

An even darker response to fear is the reversion to Ritual. In craving predictability and safety, those who revert to ritual freeze the spirit in fundamentalism, Puritanism, and millennialist hysteria. They appeal explicitly and implicitly to an outer "higher authority" as one would to a Caesar. "If you don't do this, there will be dire consequences! It's the way it's always been and will be." When we seek a ritual or rite we are looking for something that will deliver us from an apparent evil. We become fixed on a formula that seems to promise immediate protection, such as sending kids to the principal's office or detention room. Students sense the pathology and fear in this confusion of a spirit-dead classroom and begin jackassing and other forms of mockery in rebellion against the flight-fight-freeze impulse. It is a dead-end situation for all concerned. Ritual and Justice responses to fear are to be seen in an insistence that everyone must comply with the rules. In my second year of teaching, a student who had worked very hard and with great interest in my Comparative Politics course received a 63 on his final exam and therefore received a failing grade on his report card. "But I worked so hard, Mr. Willis!" "Yes," I responded, "but 63 is two points below passing— there is no altering that fact." I have deeply regretted that ritualistic response ever since—an implacable logic, true to nothing but itself— destructive of everything that learning is about. In seeking to safeguard standards, Ritual kills the spirit of intelligence everywhere it is applied. Ritual is our darkest means of running away from fear. The Justice response and the Ritual response share a major orientation: they both shift the attention of the teacher away from perceiving the inner workings of students toward the outer workings of the system which the students are supposed to accommodate. The institution first, the students second.

When we take our fear—our initial, justifiable wariness—as a means to wake up to our students, we naturally become alert to their many presences. When we bring our whole selves to this alertness— our feeling/thinking/behaving selves—we move toward *letting the material speak for itself* and away from self-consciousness, projection, and personal agendas. Often, by steps and increments, we become *attentive* to the students and, along with the student material, to the other subject matter with which we are engaged, the course material. There are two subjects that matter: the students and the course of study. This does not mean that one must become a master psychologist, as well as an ingenious purveyor of course material; it means that one is becoming a teacher who *attends* her students, one who is there for them, one who is absorbed in them and in the course subject. To become attentive is to register accurately each person in one's class, to see each person in her or his actual configuration. Students always know when they are attended. They know when their teacher sees them, rather than looks at them—know when they are perceived, rather than felt-judged or thought-judged. They are excited by the kinetic kindness of actual attention. They are, regardless of varieties of expression, thrilled by such perception, because it is accurate, allows for a complete human picture and can only be dynamically kind. They inevitably will try to respond in the same manner, even as they are youthfully prone to idealism and hero worship. But it is only in their thoughts of you, their beloved teacher that they are idealizing; the quality of their feelings (their knowing life) will equal your own in attentiveness—they want to know: "Who is this who is seeing me so well?" In this room, in this space, you will enjoy a degree of reciprocity that truly constitutes learning.

When we welcome wariness as the first tick of attention, instead of running from it toward the land of the well-regulated, we are on the path of professional development. We are on the path of professing the subject matter of the students and the subject matter of study, attending both individual and community knowledge and understanding. In Gao Xingjian's *Soul Mountain* (p. 481) he writes, "What is essential is whether it is perceived and not whether it exists. To exist and yet not to be perceived is the same as not to exist." When I perceive someone or something, she or he or it is in the space we both are in—we mutually exist. We are experienced as such. If we turn away toward categories and principles, we are not there. As we move from wariness to wakefulness toward attentiveness, we are moving our whole being toward mutual Awareness. We are both in the room, and that is our intention.

INTENTIONALITY

If our intention is to take fear as the means of becoming alert toward attentiveness, then in that context and movement we contain an intelligence that far exceeds our analytical consciousness. Unfortunately, this intelligence has been labeled the unconscious by psychologists such as Freud and Adler and has been represented as an organic ocean of repressed and rejected detritus from our evolutionary past that poses a serious threat to our conscious autonomy and to civilization itself. It is seen as the law of nature or of the jungle. This nomenclature and interpretation are not auspicious, because they have led to a running away from fear toward Justice and Ritual, rather than a realization of what we are calling *Personal Awareness*, which encompasses and conveys our complete beings. By intending to bring our entire subjectivity to the objectivity around us, we use fear as a catalyst to jump-start alertness, and we use alertness as a notification of our readiness to accept the evidence of our attention.

With Personal Awareness, we begin to see our students from the vantage point of a self empty of identifications, rather than from the singularity of our pointy little analytical noses. We see in flashes, in bits and pieces, an accurate viewing of the dynamics of each student. Though we cannot avoid errors due to the judgments of our various temperaments, we can, if we intend to, remember with some clarity these quick moments of Personal Awareness, and hence make the necessary corrections in retrospect. Rather than being enthralled and mugged by our biases and preferences, we are free to be astonished by the special qualities of each occasion and to temper our judgmental actions accordingly.

Marcia recalls the following story of Richard, a student she home-tutored for four months after a serious accident.

Richard

Richard was encased in a body cast and had to do most of his work lying on his back with a writing board propped on a pillow on his chest. Already held back one year in school, Richard was considered a struggling student by his teachers. His prolonged absence was further eroding his confidence in being able to keep up with classmates; the specter of another held-back year loomed.

Together we tackled algebra, and although my empathy was engaged by his physical plight, I frequently felt impatient and bored with what I judged as Richard's conceptual dullness in acquiring the content. Then one day, he threw his book at me and shouted that I was an idiot who couldn't teach anybody anything. The book, mercifully a paperback, nicked my shoulder, and his rage was disconcerting, to say the least. Feeling afraid, I could have tossed in the towel, reported his behavior to the proper authorities and refused to see him again (a Ritual/Justice response).

Instead, his challenge to my teaching methods aroused a certain defiance in return. It occurred to me that maybe Richard was right; maybe he needed to be taught in some way that I was missing, that I was paying more attention to the way I understood things than to his way of understanding. I sought out his math teacher of record, who spent an after-school period with me outlining three or four alternative ways to teach the concept in question. Gingerly, I returned to my orthopedically challenged student and ran through these math strategies. One, involving a simple visual cue, clicked immediately. Richard not only "got it," he went on to pass the course admirably.

Using the visual cue strategy with other math problems seemed to do the trick for Richard, while at the same time it expanded my math instruction bag of tricks, and taught me a lesson about the counterproductive nature of premature judgments. Richard and I developed a mutually attentive and trusting teacher-student relationship; I came to like and appreciate this young man in a way that still brings a smile to my face more than twenty years later. The remainder of his high school career was marked by increasing academic competence, and his family still keeps me apprised of his successes, one of which was to obtain a master's degree in a math-related field.

In holding ourselves empty in the light of our Personal Awareness, we experience astonishment at the vivid graphics of our students before they assume their places in the folds of our judgments and their circumstances. But our recollection of these moments brings us an acuity of memory that provides safe harbor for them, safe from the evaluating marauders in, about, and among us. Some brave souls refuse to hide behind guarantees of orderly conduct and allow themselves to become unprogrammatically Alert as they attempt to witness the peculiar and strange in its sum. If these souls hold to Alert witnessing long enough, they begin to care about that which is witnessed and they Attend to it. They start to experience an accurate picture of the strange object, rather than merely tolerating individual differences with a philanthropic attitude; the observer with an accurate kindness lets her or his imagination be informed by the conditions of others.

Students are just these others. Good teachers are those who have learned to go beyond Ritual and Justice; they allow the inevitable fear of the unknown to spur them to an accurate viewing of students. Ritual and Justice may be inherently sound as responses to fear, but they are not sound attitudes in teaching. Education requires the equanimity or calming-down process of Alertness-yielding-to-Attentiveness to prevail over commonplace rite and civilized response.

What we choose to do about these flashes, these bits and pieces, these snapshots, as powerful impressions, depends on the combination of our personal history and the degree to which our behavior, our understanding, and our knowledge can align with the experience of Awareness—the creativity permitted or prohibited by attitude. Our attitude literally dictates the quality and quantity of human activity. A classroom can be a cosmos, a club, or a cell, depending on our intentions and our attitude. If our attitude as educators is not well aligned, then the learning environment can fail at any level. A commissioner, an administrator, a professor, or a teacher can, in a completely reasonable and even charming way, be the source of destructive pedagogy and precipitate a decline in every direction. Earnest and sincere boards of education and other oversight committees are easily fooled and confounded, as often as not attributing failure to some analytical schema rather than to the inevitable source—attitudes that are pathetically incongruent to student process and reality. We can only know these processes (how each student works) and realities (the configurations of each student) if we assume an attitude of *awaiting the material telling of itself*, but not waiting for "an equality between what is thought and what comes to fill thought," as Emmanuel Levinas observed (*God, Death, and Time*, p. 141). Rather, we need to cultivate an attitude of waiting upon the unknown . . . each child constitutes an experience on one's human journey, in which the child is teaching the teacher, in which the functions of feeling and thinking cannot interfere, and in which one's soul is instructed by the context of an other. In the shadows of the still moment, the teacher is willing to see the student beyond any presupposition or the need for familiarity. We must be willing, how-ever briefly, to become starkly open to Awareness on a regular basis, as students appear to us and with us in time and place.

This attitude of intention is not one of expectations of equivalence between one's self and an other; it is not a search for compatibility and reciprocity. It is more similar to an attention to an opening between ourselves and others that is already there, beneath and greater than our consciousness, a knowing from *Personal Awareness* in which we (one's self and other selves) are concurrent. It can be likened to a *tapping* in to an opening that is already occurring and that, in the words of Emmanuel Levinas, is the operation of "the passivity of patience that awaits everything and nothing" (*God, Death, and Time*, p. 141). These motions of attention can be readily observed and experienced in firefighters rushing into a building to save those trapped within; or in a rescuer who dives in to save a drowning person. When lauded for their heroism, they invariable reply, "We just did what anyone would do in this situation." They are as much stymied by their actions as they are convinced that their attentions were fully warranted and a fore-gone conclusion. In such moments, we witness the complete align-ment of our feeling, understanding, and behaving in congruence with each other, the grace of Awareness. We are prompted to act *for* an other. In teaching, every situation in its routine banality invites a hero-ic response in relief (or salvation) from this banality, this boredom. The teacher is at once the firefighter, the policeman, and the doctor in service of those trapped within.

WAITING BEYOND GODOT

In Becket's aching, acid play *Waiting for Godot*, the actors wait for Godot, a character who may be Persona, or logos, or a companion-in-arms. Godot never shows up . . . there is a *ghastly blank* instead of a proper drinking partner. Translated into pedagogy, one awaits test results, a proper understanding of the subject matter, and a good and appropriate student response, not an empty mix on a distribution curve. We want *answers* and we want *results*. We want equivalence: input and output roughly equal. We want reciprocity.

When *Personal Awareness* declares Godot to be nonexistent, psy-chometrics defunct, we are then in a position to "await everything and nothing." We assume an attitude of attention that becomes focused on long-term process, not short-term answers and outcomes. Our interest in the processes of our students stretches beyond a demonstration of competency on the next exam, and becomes monthly, bimonthly, and annual. Our attention becomes indefinite, a lifetime away. Will your students visit you after graduation? Will your interest in them take you into a nether-future? Will your students become your teachers? God knows . . . we need them. As expressed in the introduction, we do not consider ourselves agents of grace and masters of fear. We simply believe that new teachers contain, within themselves, all the properties necessary to develop an attitude that is at once open-ended and discriminating. This intentional attitude will give the soul its savor and the mind its say.

HEADS SPIN

This changes
everything.

Whose Assessment?

What and whom are we testing? If we are essentially correct that real learning is about accessing Personal Awareness and then reading correctly the images formed by the press of that awareness on the feeling life, then is our testing an actual measure of that process? And further, does our assessment tell us anything pertinent about the translations that occur between these images and the symbols of thought used to represent them? And finally, what do our examinations tell us about how effectively behavior weaves the personality around these analytical thoughts?

Testing—the cornerstone of the No Child Left Behind Act—in its condensations of reading/writing/arithmetic into various arrays of multiple-choice, short-answer, and formulaic essays, says nothing about the overlay of a child's Awareness, little about the workings of a child's feeling life (image formation/imagination), projects a distorted picture of a child's analytical activity, and abandons a child's personality to dig itself out of the difficulty of institutional misconception. The learner, in the complete sense, has already been left behind, because the student's four faculties have not been addressed.

To the authors, it seems that society, rather than testing its children, is measuring itself within the presuppositions it carries about what constitutes the human mind. Our tests measure how well we think we are doing with regard to these presuppositions: the mind is an analytical structure that is built around verbal and mathematical symbols; this analytical property of mind brings order and control to perception in taxonomies of intelligible truths and values; the mind renders and projects these truths and values through language and mathematics; personality then carries out at various levels of competence these truths and values. Society's culminating judgment within these presuppositions is the assumption that there is no greater faculty than analytical thinking and its companion—appropriate behavior. Through our system of accountability—our quantifiable psychometrics—we are really measuring the ongoing competence of our educational institutions in enforcing and reinforcing these presuppositions.

To society's profound lack, we have learned little to nothing about our children, be they promoted or left behind. We are so intent on objectifying (making objects of, rather than subjects of), socializing, and academizing our kids around our scholastic notions, that we have become oblivious to the actual natures of our students. And in the process of objectifying kids, we ourselves become embedded in a hectic process of shrinking our own natures into procustean accountability schedules that fragment our professional lives into cubicles of nonrelationship. In a very real sense, teachers are beginning to resemble assembly-line workers in the nineteenth-century factories: they are seen as objects, not subjects; as functionaries, not craftspeople.

One aspect of this objectification of kids goes to the problem of what we call a lack of "legacy." In my thirty-nine years of teaching, I found that teachers frequently suffered inhibition when it came to discussing ideas and concepts with students and other teachers. Marcia noted this same inhibition on the part of elementary schoolteachers when she worked in a gifted-talented program with extremely precocious kids: nobody wanted them in their classes, because they were afraid they had nothing to offer such bright children. They seemed to feel that their education lacked a certain depth or quality. Rather than living and sharing their world of knowing and thinking with students, they confined their exchanges to the classroom and to the strict topics at hand, carefully planned, rehearsed, and qualified, and preferably shared with "typical" children. Teacher-training should help new teachers gain an attitude of open-hearted, open-minded give-and-take with young people and colleagues. There is little so daunting as the guarded expert ruling upon one's intelligence. Except for those designed to fit into the conventional norms of academic procedure, few benefit from this "gotcha" demeanor. A test should not measure the clanging noise that occurs when the hammer hits the anvil, but rather should measure how many sparks fly in all directions.

Tests and measurements, to contain any segment that accurately reflects the cognitive development of human beings, must include the dynamics of Personal Awareness and the shaping functions of the feeling life. Assessment should register the accessing of Personal Awareness and the subsequent formation of sensory images generated from that awareness, as well as the translations of those images into analytical symbols, and the subsequent interpretation of those symbols into intentional behavior. We advocate the replacement of the contemporary lock-step psychometrics with a completely different orientation to assessment, with which we might better comprehend all four of our human faculties. We do not intend to expand upon or modify the superb perspectives on assessment as elucidated in Grant Wiggins's *Assessing Student Performance*, Howard Gardner's *The Theory of Multiple Intelligence*, Reuven Feuerstein's *Instrumental Enrichment*, Alfie Kohn's *Punished by Rewards*, and Elizabeth Murphy's *The Developing Child*. Rather, we propose to add our own attitudinal experience of valuing students to their excellent proposals for more meaningful testing.

VALUING PERSONAL AWARENESS

We begin with a question: To what degree is the child awake to his or her own awareness, to her or his own subjective register of surroundings? And this question is asked simultaneously of the teacher because the teacher convokes the awareness of the student and its reciprocity in the teacher: "I am aware of your awareness, and you are aware of my awareness." As Paul Celan wrote, *"Ich bin du, wenn ich ich bin"*—"I am you if I am I"—as quoted by Emmanuel Levinas in *God, Death, and Time* (p. 175). We pause, together, in observing . . . what we might address, call to, wave at, recognize, see, hear, touch, taste, witness in the great and powerful vague, in the general, in the fullness of sensations. No feeling yet, because images have not formed around our awareness; no thoughts yet, because ideas have to materialize around imagination; no response yet, because behavior has yet to take its direction from thought. Measurement, on the face of it, is absurd, as we wonder what we are experiencing. But there are some queries that might be helpful:

- How do I know if a child is accessing Personal Awareness, is in that state of "I exist"? You might notice him sitting with an erect posture of complete readiness; or time and space may seem to disappear as her attention to something becomes absolute and unable to be interrupted; there might be a pregnant silence as his hands go loose, eyelids rise, and mouth drops open; there might be a tingling sensation across her shoulders and down her arms accompanied by a head shake and a little shiver.
- How long can the child be captivated by his Personal Awareness—a fraction of a second, a second, fifteen seconds, two minutes, an hour? The longer the span of time, the greater the appropriation of the experience.

- To what degree do you, the teacher, contribute to this duration? Do you interrupt or do you facilitate the pause? In what ways?
- If the child does not seem able to access her Personal Awareness, what is the nature of her obstruction? What is her temperament configuration and how does it relate to yours? Might her access look different from yours? If so, how do you propose to deal with this difference? Is the child hungry, or sleepy, or both?
- To what degree do you, the teacher, participate in encouraging the child to become awake to his own Personal Awareness or, conversely, in pushing the child to identify himself as an object, a thing, embedded in a hierarchy of authority?

VALUING FEELING

Any assessment of Feeling involves the facility with which students and teachers are able to form images that accurately reflect the magnitude and richness of Personal Awareness: these images are the products of the seven senses, that is, seeing, hearing, touching, smelling, tasting, experiencing gravity, and balancing. In a sense, these are seven dimensions because each foray of the imagination (image making) can include all seven sensations in its patterning. Images are never one-dimensional visions, but contain components of all other sensations. They hum, they spin, they dance, they are gustatory, they are pungent, and they orient themselves in the balance of kaleidoscopic presentation. It is no wonder that the classical Greeks included all sorts of movement in their *paideia* classes. Our secondary schools often require students to sit for long periods of time in sterile classrooms with poor acoustics and uncomfortable desks lined up in straight rows. This sort of arrangement restricts the feeling life in its need for a full range of sensory impressions and hence blunts image formation. Just as detrimental to the cultivation of the feeling life in our elementary schools are classrooms that are cluttered with external stimuli: teaching tools, games, projects, books, wall displays. This external visual racket often presents young children with too many choices, thus overwhelming the integration of their internal images. We want our children to create their own imaginative canvasses; sterile and/or cluttered environments may preclude this endeavor.

The ideal would be for testing to include media in which imagination can strut its stuff: poetry, graphic arts, musical performance, dancing, acting, cooking, woodworking, and other means of showing the extensions of the body as it projects its impressions of Personal Awareness. We discern a developmental spectrum that could be identified with, but not limited to, the following phases: sensuality developing into sensibility, into aesthetics, and, finally, into high aesthetics. With early Feeling, we have "actual occasions" recording themselves in us as powerful, large, but indistinct images, as when a baby plays with her feet or sucks at the breast, while staring intently at mother. In Feeling, our first sense of relationship occurs and crude correspondences present themselves. A cow is colored black and white, and Mother Goose and pat-a-cake play across our skin in relational sensations. With sensibility comes the coalescence of past/present/future, or notions of continuance, as in the creation of an elemental flow chart of stored memories. Feeling finds its own language; ideas come in a design format; art emerges in the company of personal expression as children paint suns, rainbows, butterflies, and flowers. In sensibility we have the coordination of impression with relationship, and we begin to make ethical and moral judgments. Mother could be beautiful and Father handsome, as are my friends and family. In the grip of hormones, we try to find relations in sexuality. We experience strong urges to bond with peers through shared activity. We are often struck by the beautiful aptness of our ideas and the symmetry of their application. We bring emotional significance to kissing, touching, hearing, or feeling anything. As we arrive at aesthetics, we find the extension of our feelings in systems and models and the sheer pleasure of bringing images to bear in our involvement with community. We begin to explore varying contexts and try to walk in the moccasins of others. We link immensity with the now and we feel the difference between legal justice and kindness, even if we cannot put the image into words. Sometimes we see ourselves as Don Quixote tilting at windmills: slightly pathetic, but proud of it. Community is expanding for us into actual conditions, near and far away. As high aesthetics merges with higher logic, as it is wont to do, we gain appreciation of and expression for the exquisite particulars in universal processes, and we strive to vision these phenomena better. We develop what Whitehead, in *Process and Reality*, repeatedly calls *appetition* for the potential novelty in everyone: everyone is unique, and no one is special. We identify beyond family, beyond nation, and increasingly come to see ourselves as conduits between Awareness and Understanding.

Evaluation here would seem to be a matter of discriminating the tastes, preferences and maturation of students, as indicated in their different temperaments, and of assessing the extent to which their images are crafted in the disciplines of imagination:

- Can the dancer dance, the musician play, the composer compose, the poet write and recite, the athlete perform, the artist sculpt or paint, the mathematician formulate, the historian write and recreate, the linguist converse in other tongues, the scientist hypothesize, and the social scientist observe and reflect the composite images conceived from the imprint of Awareness?
- The question here for the teacher in their valuing role is: At any given juncture, is the student approaching the legacy of Knowing such that the result will be authenticity? How may I help convey these images to thoughts?

Two academic achievers, call them Catty and Dolores, approached me in the hall after Global Studies class, eyes narrowed, frustrated and intent. "We don't think you care about us, Mr. Willis. All you ever do is pay attention to the kids who screw up. We score in the high 90s on your exams, and they get 60s and 70s. How can we take philosophical debate seriously in such a class?" I responded, "Let's take it to the class and ask if others feel the same way you do." They agreed to the inquiry. The next day, I opened class with these questions and invited Catty and Dolores to expand on their complaints, which they did with considerable forcefulness. The "screw-ups" answered something like this: "This is the first class we've been in where we're taken seriously. We never go to sleep and we don't cut class. At least somebody doesn't think we're stupid." In the true spirit of American compromise, these students moved toward an agreement that study and debate would go forward if everyone were included and nobody would be "put down." When the combined feelings of the class were freely aired, we came to a formulation that seemed to work for everyone. We found out that when we took seriously the expressions of the "screw-ups," that we could bring their impressions into congruence with those of the high achievers by translating their sensibility into discussable (note: I do not use the words *appropriate or acceptable*) form. If a "screw-up" said Machiavelli was an "idiot," we were able to agree that "pessimist" might be a more accurate word, or if J. J. Rousseau was termed a "faggot," we settled on "idealist" as a better description.

VALUING THINKING

Thinking appears to be at the apex of human activity because this faculty must translate Feeling into order and order into action. These three functions—the translation of images of Feeling into the symbols of language and notation; the analytical ordering of the symbols into intelligible factors; and the translation of factors into the actions of Behavior—represent a tremendous evolutionary advantage for our species. Presumably, while sentient life possesses access to Awareness, and most vertebrates own a fully functioning feeling life, their thinking life seems rudimentary and programmed in prediction of their actions (usually referred to as instinctual) when compared to human capabilities. Human beings can admit a vast store of images toward the realization of a multiplicity of behaviors. The extension of our faculties, which we call technology, truly leads to the opposite of instinctual behavior—an expanding consciousness. Under the right conditions, we can continuously and developmentally explore the enormity of Awareness. We spelunk, climb mountains, explore space and time, live in every kind of climate, and look within ourselves as well. It is not the thrust of this book to marvel at evolutionary development, but it is our intention to address ways in which this growth might be enhanced rather than confounded.

As indicated earlier in this chapter, our schools seem to be awash in superfluous testing, leaving a flotsam of paper trails, frustrating teachers, and essentially tasking all the joy out of learning. If we wish to determine at what level a student is processing information, it would be helpful first to demarcate a spectrum of thought in a rubric: common sense developing into concrete logic, then into symbolic logic, and finally into higher logic. Intuitively, a child is trying to identify patterns of analysis that are to be retained and integrated, or rejected. Are the larvae of all moths destructive of vegetation and the larvae of all butterflies essentially harmless to vegetation? If students are within the first stage of thought, they would probably think, "As we move down the road, the telephone poles are moving by us, and when we stop, they stop," as my oldest daughter told me triumphantly when she was three years old. Next, they might develop deductive systems that reinforce their earlier notions of happenstance: even though the ship disappeared over the horizon, did it necessarily drop off the edge of the ocean? If it walks like a duck and talks like a duck, it must be a duck. Literalism and object permanence are indicators of this process. With the arrival of concrete logic comes the requirement that known categories conform to happenstance. This is a linear rather than a kaleidoscopic process. Tinker Toys and Lego blocks give us tools to build structures, but there are no toys that concretize how the double helix of genes or the periodic chart of chemistry is formed. Social actualities tell us how things go. The bully on the playground is the power standard by which we must find our place in the hierarchy. At the level of symbolic logic, we arrive at a stage asking for more complex tools: symbolic and verbal logic, algebra, calculus, philosophy, comparative politics—and many more conceptual disciplines. Syllogism takes the place of certainty, as students move from the concrete to the "as if." The telephone poles may actually be stationary, as if we are the only ones moving. What if a duck is actually a teal? Variation becomes central. Is the world at base unchanging or constantly mutating? What level of vibration in the George Washington Bridge threatens to collapse the whole span? To what extent does a leader of a nation understand the tasks of his subordinates? Symbolic logic opens the mind to infinite linear possibilities. At the greatest extent of thought, what might be called higher logic, thinking would seem to become coextensive with the movement of images and could properly be said to be multicontextual. In the concepts proposed by Barbara McClintock and many others, one enters worlds within and outside of worlds. Those who arrive at higher logic characteristically discover new discrete phenomena, as in the theory of relativity or the rearrangement of molecules in maize chromosomes. They experience I/she-he-it/thee-you/we/they simultaneously. They integrate such specialties as the Mobius strip, chaos theory, string theory, and the theory of prehensions (Whitehead, *Process and Reality*) as explorative movements and attitudes for thoughts.

Assessing thought should reveal these levels, not in number grades of 65, 75, or 95, or in IQ ratings of 98, 105, 125, or 145, but as processes in translation of images representing subjective data: quantum mechanics has given us not only the verities of probability, but also has told us that no test can claim objectivity in the stolid sense that the observer does not influence the behavior of the observed and vice-versa. In other words, it is impossible to remove *attitude* from the testing situation. In our experience, teachers frequently insist that the student either understands or doesn't understand the data. They are impervious to the effect their attitude has on the results of their students or on what attitude the students may have toward the data. This can run the gamut from a welcoming attitude on both sides, to a feeling of being frozen up, excluded, or out of operation.

If testing is to better represent the current state of student thinking, then we propose that the following criteria be considered in designing assessments:

- Students and teachers work together in establishing the basis for tests and measurements.
- Students produce work that shows the fullness of their thought: essays, portfolios, and performances such as lectures, debates, skits, and exhibits.
- Teachers share fully and transparently their responses to this work.
- Teachers seek to imagine as clearly as possible the distinct associative process in each student so the student feels that her logical arrangements have been witnessed and addressed, resulting in the enrichment of her analytical reach. If the teacher cannot so imagine, then he freely admits this lack and invites further exploration with the student.

When I transitioned back into public school systems from private schools, it was immediately apparent that expectations of academic achievement were significantly lower in public schools. After twelve years, I had become accustomed to giving exam questions that rested on the assumption that students spent much of their social life discussing "Why did the classical Athenians (500–350 BC) arrive at such a degree of autonomy and self-consciousness as evident in their political, philosophical, artistic, and economic lives, when all neighboring civilizations seemed in thrall to their indigenous cultures?" Such questions seemed utterly beyond reach in public schools, especially given that I did not announce the topics of these exams prior to the tests in private schools. After wrestling with this learning gap for awhile, I began to spell out the questions before I gave the exam. I soon found out that public school kids did just as well as private school kids when these "higher-order" questions were announced beforehand. I received the same sense of the quality of their thought, and it gave impetus to serious discussion before the exam and after. There was also much evidence that the kids spent some of their social time discussing the implications of these knotty questions. Moreover, they frequently studied for exams in small groups, pooling, and therefore enhancing, their understanding of cultural legacy. I found that these strategies produced higher-level thinking and more accurate assessments than the secretive, "gotcha"-type examinations that we routinely give. Expectations rose without anyone noticing the ascent, and this higher quality of feeling and thinking invited discussion in my office, in the hall, in the cafeteria, and study halls on an ongoing basis.

VALUING BEHAVIOR

As an individual is aware and directs her images from that awareness by way of feeling into thought, so these three faculties of the whole body require that nerves, blood, muscles, and bone take action aligned with this transfer of images. This action we call Personality, the movement of the body according to the impulsion of feeling and the propulsion of thought. From the flicker of the eye to the galvanized conduct of the whole body, we have agreement of the physical with the Thought and Feeling of a person. The persona behaves in concert with the translated character of the drama in which it finds itself. For millennia, cultures have been at great pains to assure proper behavior or deportment, given the collective assumptions of a culture.

Our focus within the written concerns of this book is not so much on behaviors which serve the needs of conventionality, but rather on behavior congruent with the three faculties. Here again a developmental rubric suggests itself. From earliest childhood we respond to care with behaviors of pleasure, happiness, and contentment, and to neglect with behaviors of pain, misery, and discontent. Throughout childhood our feeling life puts forth images of us as subjects, not objects, as existing beings subjected to that which surrounds us. If we access our inborn awareness, we develop an imagination that is essentially open and actively appropriating more of the surround. We develop language that reflects that vivid state and our personalities find little difficulty in aligning themselves with our feelings and thoughts. Not long ago Marcia was playing a game of Castle with her four-year-old grandson, Jesse. "Grandma! Grandma!" he cried, excitedly. "I know what can happen to the princess. The dragon can fly in and take her off to his secret cave. But Aquaman, who sprays a lot of water, can ask Merlin to use his magic to find the cave. Then Aquaman can spray out the dragon's fire and rescue the princess." This is a child whose language reflects his Awareness imprinting a wide-open imagination, which in turn illuminates his developing analytical life.

If we sense that our environment is hostile or dissonant with our existence—our subjectivity—the feeling life produces discordant images and the thinking life understands neglect as normal. Any gallery of pictures of children in afflicted countries shows faces at once resigned, dazed, and suffering. Whatever the source of a good or bad environment, both outside and inside our bodies, our behavior is only able to respond in kind. Recalling Fred, the sixteen-year-old in my global studies class whose story I told in Chapter 7, from the start, Fred was the teacher and I the student in this arena. This situation produced a new animation and light in his behavior—he seemed amused by my ignorance of trains. He promised me a copy of his independent study addendum to his term paper on the history of the Delaware and Hudson Railroad. Unfortunately, it was never delivered because his intended recipient, Jim, the train-wreck specialist, passed away quite suddenly before completion of Fred's term paper. In spite of this blow, Fred graduated and presumably went to work for the railroad, supported and intact in his Awareness.

As suggested in Chapter 3, there are a variety of scenarios and strategies for perceiving and dealing with congruence and alienation among our four faculties. Of course, temperament plays a crucial role in how children respond to their environment. Some manage to thrive in a hostile surround, while others turn negative within a seemingly broad arena. As with disease, some throw off contagion, while others perish in an otherwise safe climate. For a compelling and thorough examination of violent behaviors, we recommend James Garbarino's *Lost Boys*. His Awareness and delineation of personality formation is enlightening.

In valuing behavior, we suggest the following set of questions regarding the relationship of personality to the faculties:

- Are you, the teacher, prepared to allow your Personal Awareness to shine on any given student, even though such awareness can initially cause you boredom, flight, fright, or freeze you into inaction as the images their behavior produces in your feelings can be quite off-putting? Are you willing to wait as your compassion awakens?
- What is the relationship between the child's personality and her awareness life? Does he allow himself access to extensive awareness? Partial awareness? Extensive awareness will manifest as bright shininess and vivacity, partial awareness as dullness

informed by rejection, neglect, shame, depression, and vulnera-
bility.

- What is the relationship between a child's personality and his
  life? Are the images of her grief balanced by images of kindness?
  Does his sadness run to poetry, depression, or other forms? Is
  her anger tempered by compassion, revenge, or other forms? Is
  anger kindled in increasingly destructive displays of acting out?
- What is the relationship between personality and the thinking
  life? Is ideation directed toward justice and redress of griev-
  ances, or does it lean toward punishment of projected enemies
  and evildoers, or somewhere in between? Is intellect a means of
  exploration or a weapon of alienation? Both?

CONCLUSION

We are not proposing testing procedures; these can be obtained in
numerous manuals and texts. Other expert guidance to methods of
authentic testing can be found in the works of Alfie Kohn and Grant
Wiggins. Rather, we are posing questions about attitudes that produce
results and deeply affect learning outcomes. These questions are
meant to point at a reassessment of evaluation. We hope our questions
will motivate educators to cease being "paperhangers," in the words of
George Patton, and instead will incline them towards exploration and
creative teaching. This will lead to assessments that will enhance
rather than depress learning.

In the final chapter, "Education for the Twenty-First Century," of
his book *What Are Schools For*? Ron Miller writes, "So far, holistic
thinking has appealed to modern society's more sensitive souls—seekers and mystics—who cannot tolerate a meaningless and mechanistic
culture. They are not satisfied being consumers of goods and entertainment, nor do they resist through narcotics and violence; rather,
these seekers hold out hope that cultural transformation can be
achieved" (p. 224). Indeed, if an increasing number of our teachers
become seekers, especially in their early professional training, we hold
out every hope that our society, rather than burning itself out, will
transform its schools into institutions with human shape.

References

Adams, Henry. *Mont-Saint-Michel and Chartres*. New York: Houghton Mifflin, 1963.

Alexander, Samuel. *Space, Time, and Deity: The Gifford Lectures at Glasgow, 1914–1918*. New York: Dover Publications, 1966.

Atkins, P. W. *The Periodic Kingdom: A Journey into the Land of the Chemical Elements*. New York: Perseus Books, 1995.

Bartlett, John. *Bartlett's Familiar Quotations*, 13th ed. Boston: Little, Brown. 1955.

Bennett, E.A. *What Jung Really Said*. New York: Schocken Books, 1983.

Blake, William. "Nurse's *Song*" in *Songs of Innocence and Experience*. New York: Penguin Books, 1961

Dawkins, Richard. *River Out of Eden: A Darwinian View of Life*. New York: Perseus Books, 1995.

Eisner, Elliot. *The Educational Imagination*. New York: Macmillan, 1985.

Fay, Jim and David Funk. *Teaching with Love and Logic; Taking Control of the Classroom*. Golden, CO: Love and Logic Press, 1995.

Freire, Paulo. *Pedagogy of the Heart*. New York: Continuum Press, 1997.

———. *Pedagogy of the Oppressed*, trans. Myra Bergman Ramos. New York: Continuum Press, 1993

Fried, Robert L. *The Passionate Teacher: A Practical Guide*. Boston: Beacon Press, 1995.

Garbarino, James. *Lost Boys*. New York: First Anchor Book Edition, Random House, 2000.

———. *Raising Children in a Socially Toxic Environment*. San Francisco: Jossey-Bass, 1995.

Gardner, Howard. *Frames of Mind: The Theory of Multiple Intelligence*. New York: Basic Books, 1983.

Gilligan, Carol. *In a Different Voice*. Cambridge, MA: Harvard University Press, 1982, 1993.

Hartmann, Thom. *Attention Deficit Disorder: A Different Perception*. Grass Valley, CA: Underwood Books, 1997.

Hudson, W. H. *The Book of a Naturalist*. New York: E. P. Dutton, 1919.

Jarrell, Randall. *The Complete Poems*. New York: Noonday Press, 1969.

Jung, Carl G. *Psychological Types*, trans. R. F. C. Hull. Princeton, NJ: Princeton University Press, Bolligens Series XX, 1976.

Keirsey, David. *Portraits of Temperament*. Del Mar, CA: Prometheus Nemesis Book Company, 1987.

Keirsey, David, and Marilyn Bates. *Please Understand Me*. Del Mar, CA: Prometheus Nemesis, 1978.

Keller, Evelyn Fox. *A Feeling for the Organism: The Life and Work of Barbara McClintock*. New York: W. H. Freeman, 1997.

Kohn, Alfie. *Punished by Rewards*. New York: Houghton Mifflin, 1993.

Krause, Lois Breur. NF Profile from the Cognitive Profile Learning Styles Model. http://www.cognitiveprofile.com (accessed 2007).

Levinas, Emmanuel. *Alterity and Transcendence*, trans. Michael B. Smith. New York: Columbia University Press, 1999.

———. *God, Death, and Time*, Stanford, CA: Stanford University Press, 2000.

Lao Tsu. *Tao Te Ching*, trans. Gia-Fu Feng and Jane English. New York: Vintage, 1972.

Merleau-Ponty, Maurice. *The Visible and the Invisible*. Evanston, IL: Northwestern University Press, 1968.

Millay, Edna St. Vincent. *Edna St. Vincent Millay Collected Lyrics*. New York: Harper & Row, 1969.

Miller, Ron. *What Are Schools For?* 3rd ed. Brandon, VT: Holistic Education Press, 1997.

Morris, Van Cleve. *Existentialism in Education: What It Means*. New York: Harper & Row, 1966.

Murphy, Elizabeth. *The Developing Child*. Palo Alto, CA: Consulting Psychologists Press, 1992.

Palmer, Parker J. *The Courage to Teach*. San Francisco: Jossey-Bass, 1998.

Quenk, Naomi L. *Essentials of Myers-Briggs Type Indicator Assessment*. New York: Wiley, 2000.

Rilke, Rainer Maria. *Letters to a Young Poet*. New York: Norton Library, 1963.

Roethke, Theodore. *On the Poet and His Craft*. Seattle: Univ. of Washington Press, 1965.

———. "The Lost Son—Flight," in *The Collected Poems of Theodore Roethke*. New York: Anchor Books, 1975.

Radhakrishnan, Sarvepalli. *Indian Philosophy: A Source Book of Indian Philosophy*, eds. S Radhakrishnan and C. S. Moore. Princeton, NJ: Princeton University Press, 1989.

Sizer, Theodore R. *Horace's Compromise: The Dilemma of the American High School*. New York: Houghton Mifflin, 1984.

Tift, Larry, John Sullivan, and Dennis Sullivan. *Discipline as Enthusiasm: An Entry in the Recent Discussion on the Moral Development of Children*. Paper presented at the annual meeting of the Association for Humanist Sociology, Pittsburg, November 6–9, 1997

Warshall, Peter. Quotes Ortega y Gassett in "The Great Arsenic Lobster." *Whole Earth*, 98 (Fall 1999): 13.

Washburn, Michael. *The Ego and the Dynamic Ground*, 2nd ed. Albany: SUNY Press, 1995.

Whitehead, Alfred North. "Technical Education and Its Relation to Science and Literature" in *Aims of Education*. New York: Free Press, 1929.

———. *Adventures of Ideas*. New York: Macmillan, 1967.

———. *Modes of Thought*. New York: Capricorn Books, 1958.

Wiggens, Grant. *Assessing Student Performance, Exploring the Purpose and Limits of Testing*, San Francisco: Jossey-Bass, 1993.

Wolf, Aline D. *Nurturing the Spirit in Non-Sectarian Classrooms*. Holidaysburg, PA: Parent Child Press, 1996.

Xingjian, Gao. *Soul Mountain*, trans. Mabel Lee. New York: HarperCollins, 2001.

Annotated
Recommended Reading

Ariès, Phillipe. *Centuries of Childhood.* New York: Vintage Books, 1962.
A compelling history of Western attitudes toward children.

------. *The Hours of Our Death.* New York: Vintage Books, Random House, 1982.
A historical overview of Western attitudes toward dying and death.

Ariès, Phillipe, and Andre Béjin. *Western Sexuality.* New York: Basil Blackwell, 1985.
A historical overview of Western sexual attitudes since Greco-Roman times.

Ariès, Phillipe and George Duby. *A History of Private Life, Vols. I–V.* Cambridge, MA: Belknap Press of Harvard University Press, 1987–1991.
A compendium of attitudes toward private life from Greco-Roman times to present.

Aurobindo, Sri. *A Greater Psychology.* New York: Jeremy P. Tarcher/Putnam, 2001.
A psychology of total involvement without burnout—an attitude of perspective without unattachment.

Banner, James M., and Harold C. Cannon. *The Elements of Teaching.* New Haven and London: Yale University Press, 1997.
Contains most characteristics of teaching, emphatically emphasizing the difference between power and authority.

Bellah, Robert N., Richard Madsen, William M. Sullivan, Ann Swidler, and Steven M. Tipton, *Habits of the Heart.* New York: Perennial Library, Harper & Row, 1985.
Perhaps one of the most penetrating revelations about attitudes and character in actual America.

Bennett, E. A. *What Jung Really Said.* New York: Schocken Books, 1983.
A clear explanation of Jung's main ideas. A good section on typology including the history of its development. References to the typological overlap between Kretschmer and Jung.

Brown, Sally, and Donald McIntyre. *Making Sense of Teaching; Developing Teachers and Teaching.* Bristol, PA: Buckingham, 1995.
Descriptive of the climate of good teaching and the condition in which good teaching can take place.

Bruner, Jerome. *Actual Minds, Possible Words.* Cambridge, MA: Harvard University Press, 1986.
Elucidates two distinct modes of cognition—truth and verisimilitude—in establishing our positions toward learning.

Crowley, Sharon. *A Teacher's Introduction to Deconstruction.* Urbana, IL: National Council of Teachers of English, 1989.
Examines poststructuralist considerations that increasingly underlie reading/writing instruction.

Eagleton, Terry. *Literary Theory: An Introduction.* Minneapolis: University of Minnesota Press, 1983.
Disentangles all the confusion over the different schools of literary criticism, such as hermeneutics, semiotics, reception theory, structuralism and deconstructionism. Lets the reader choose the influences.

Eisner, Elliot. *The Educational Imagination.* New York: Macmillan, 1985.
A significant critique of the forces influencing the educational experience and basic orientations to the curriculum.

Elkind, David. *Children and Adolescents.* New York: Oxford University Press, 1970.
Essays interpreting the work of Jean Piaget.

Erikson, Erik. *Childhood and Society.* 2nd ed. New York: W. W. Norton, 1963.
A classic in childhood and adulthood attitudinal development.

Fay, Jim, and David Funk. *Teaching with Love and Logic: Taking Control of the Classroom.* Golden, CO: Love and Logic Press, 1995.
Represents a mix of behavioral and transpersonal values in exploring efficacious control in the classroom.

Feuerstein, Reuven. *Instrumental Enrichment.* Arlington Heights, IL: Skylight Professional Development, Pearson Education, 1995.
A masterpiece in locating and eliminating learning disabilities—a full witness to an open attitude toward life long learning.

Fiske, Edward B. *Smart Schools, Smart Kids.* New York: Simon & Schuster, 1991.
A review of where education has been and by example where it might go.

Foucault, Michel. *Madness and Civilization*. New York: Mentor Books, The New American Library, 1967.
Any of Foucault's books are instructive about the role context plays in the formation of attitude. This early volume is particularly direct and clear in so doing.

Frankel, Steven A. *Hidden Faults*. Madison, CT: Psychosocial Press, 2000.
In the field of psychotherapy, Frankel represents the precise attitude toward clients that we advocate toward students.

Freire, Paulo. *Pedagogy of the Heart*. New York: Continuum, 1998.
A powerful series of essays on accommodation and relationship shaping an educator's (and politician's) attitude toward education.

Fried, Robert L. *The Passionate Teacher*. Boston: Beacon Press, 1995.
Passionate in the best sense, this is an important contribution to the development of "stance" or attitude conducive to sharing and learning.

Garbarino, James. *Lost Boys*. New York: First Anchor Book Edition, Random House, 2000.
A clear view of the attitudes of violence and of effective intervention.

Gardner, Howard. *Frames of Mind: The Theory of Multiple Intelligence*. New York: Basic Books, 1983.
———. *The Unschooled Mind*. New York: Basic Books, 1991.
Both books offer a penetrating analysis of learning preferences.

Gilligan, Carol. *In A Different Voice*. Cambridge, MA: Harvard University Press, 1982, 1993.
Challenges developmental models that omit the complexity of human relationships.

Gilmore, David D. *Misogyny*. Philadelphia: University of Pennsylvania Press, 2001.
An anthropological study of the pervasiveness of misogyny, even in modern societies. Gilmore hypothesizes a psychogenic basis rooted in the male developmental cycle. Chilling in its implications about institutionalized gender biases.

Glazer, Steven, ed. *The Heart of Learning*. New York: Tarcher/Putnam, 1999.
A collection of voices contributing views on a more capacious attitude toward the condition of learning.

Gould, Stephen Jay. *The Mismeasure of Man*. New York: W. W. Norton, 1981.
Incisively examines how institutional assumptions miscast what they purport to measure, as in intelligence quotient.

Grof, Stanislav. *The Adventure of Self-discovery*. Albany: SUNY Press, 1988.
A healing attitude toward the rigors of human suffering and development.

Grusko, Robin, and Judy Kramer. *Becoming a Teacher.* Bloomington, IN: ERIC, 1993.
In addition to organization, the authors assert the teacher's motivation and broad tolerance as characteristics of good teaching.

Hall, Edward T. *The Hidden Dimension.* New York: Anchor Books, 1966.
An anthropologist's view of the territoriality of human space.

———. The Silent Language. New York: Anchor Books, 1973.
An anthropologist's view of the attitudinal language of the body.

Hartmann, Thom. *Attention Deficit Disorder: A Different Perception.* Grass Valley, CA: Underwood Books, 1997.
A perspective on ADD that parallels descriptors of the SP temperament types in the MBTI. Contains further helpful ideas for teaching children with this label.

Himley, Margaret, ed. with Patricia F. Carini. *From Another Angle.* New York: Teachers College, Columbia University, 2000.
A helpful, case-illustrated outline of the Prospect School's description process for observing and recording children's progress in school. Contains an appendix on Prospect's resources, publications, and activities.

Hoffman, Marvin. *Chasing Hellhounds: A Teacher Learns from His Students.* Minneapolis, MN: Milkweed Editions, 1996.
Addresses the issue of being present, of being one's self, both for teachers and students.

Jenkins, Peggy J. *Nurturing Spirituality in Children.* Hillsboro, OR: Beyond Words Publishing, 1995.
A practical guide in meeting the developmental spiritual needs of children.

Johnson, Eric W. *Teaching School.* Points Picked Up. New York: Walker, 1979, 1981.
One of the best books we have read on practicing excellent teaching in most of its manifestations.

Jung, C. G. *The Development of Personality.* Princeton, NJ: Princeton University Press Bolligens Series XX, 1954.
A collection of essays dealing with child psychology and education.

———. Psychological Types. Princeton, NJ: Princeton University Press, Bolligens Series XX, 1976.
Jung's masterful elucidation of a typology based on normal functions for gathering and evaluating information. The basis for all later extensions of temperament theory (David Keirsey; MBTI)

Kagan, Jerome. *The Nature of the Child.* New York: Basic Books, 1984.
An effective overview of ideas on child development.

Kane, Pearl Rock, ed. *The First Year of Teaching*. New York: Walker, 1991.
A wide range of first teaching experiences toward "getting the feel" of what others have experienced.

Keirsey, David. *Portraits of Temperament*. Del Mar, CA: Prometheus Nemesis, 1987.
In this book Keirsey provides a history and overview of the positions of various temperament theorists. Each chapter describes a type in terms of its interest or goal. The book contains his temperament sorter, useful to anyone beginning an exploration of temperament/type theory.

Keirsey, David, and Marilyn Bates. *Please Understand Me*. Del Mar, CA: Prometheus Nemesis, 1978.
A book that has popularized temperament-type theory and made it accessible to lay readers. Particularly valuable for grouping types into clusters and defining the goals of each cluster.

Koetzsch, Ronald E. *The Parents' Guide to Alternatives in Education*. Boston: Shambhala, 1997.
An accurate review of 22 alternatives to public education.

Kohl, Herbert. *Growing Minds/On Becoming a Teacher*. Cambridge, MA: Harper & Row, 1985.
A narrative on the experiences of teaching as a journey in personal growth wherein one's attitude is enriched and expanded.

Kozol, Jonathan. *Death at an Early Age*. New York: New American Library, 1967.
The classic discussion of the destruction of spirit in an urban public school.

Kohn, Alfie. *Punished by Rewards*. Boston: Houghton Mifflin, 1993.
An accurate picture of the weaknesses of behavioral stimulation when trying to stimulate thought and feeling.

Kretschmer, Ernst. *Physique and Character*. New York: Cooper Square, 1970.
A temperament theory based on physical traits.

Krause, Lois Breur. *NF Profile from the Cognitive Profile Learning Styles Model*. http://www.cognitiveprofile.com (accessed 2007).
I (Marcia) used this Web site when I was teaching at SUNY, as it was free and easily accessible to my students.

Levinas, Emmanuel. *Outside the Subject*. Stanford, CA: Stanford University Press, 1994.
———. *God, Death, and Time*. Stanford, CA: Stanford University Press, 2000.
In both books, Levinas considers the nature of patience and waiting upon the unknown. A major contribution to notions of what constitutes helping others.

Lillard, Paula Polk. *Montessori Today*. New York: Schocken Books, 1996.
A good guide to Maria Montessori's application in education today.

Macrorie, Ken. *Up Taught*. New York: Hayden, 1970.
Glimmerings that there is something wrong in college teaching.

McCourt, Frank. *Teacher Man*. New York: Scribner, 2005.
A vivid collage of teaching experience, at once illuminating and circumscribing attitudes encountered in education in every direction.

Merleau-Ponty, Maurice. *The Visible and the Invisible*. Evanston, IL: Northwestern University Press, 1968.
Considers the intertwining or crossover of mutual perception.

Millay, Edna St. Vincent. *Edna St. Vincent Millay Collected Lyrics*. New York: Harper & Row, 1969.

Miller, Ron. *What Are Schools For?* 3rd ed. Brandon, VT: Holistic Education Press, 1997.
One of the most important books on the cultural roots of American education and holistic responses to reform. Contains critical information on attitude.

Moore, Thomas. *Care of the Soul. A Guide for Cultivating Depth and Sacredness in Everyday Life*. New York: HarperCollins, 1992.
Makes palpable and practical the word soul.

Morris, Van Cleve. *Existentialism in Education*. New York: Harper and Row, 1996.
A lucid discussion of the implications of the philosophy of existentialism regarding teaching and learning. A very useful book on attitudes.

Murphy, Elizabeth. *The Developing Child*. Palo Alto, CA: Consulting Psychologists Press, 1992.
Coauthor of the Murphy-Neisgeier Type Indicator for Children (MNTIC), Murphy gives a clear explanation of how personality develops in children and provides suggestions for how to create "type-sensitive" classrooms. Have used as a text for graduate seminars—a gem!

Neff, Lavonne. *One of a Kind: Making the Most of Your Child's Uniqueness*. Gainesville, FL: Center for Appreciation of Psychological Type, 1995.
A book about typology written for parents, but helpful for teachers in establishing parent-teacher collaboration. Contains a type observation inventory for young children.

Neill, A. S. *Talking of Summerhill*. London: Victor Gollancz, 1968.
One of the most influential reports on essential attitudes in teaching in regard to the care and education of young people.

Nelson, John E. *Healing the Split*. Albany: SUNY Press, 1994.
Presents a healing attitude toward the mentally ill.

O'Hear, Anthony. *Education and Democracy.* London: Claridge Press, 1991.
A straightforward attack on "the posturing of the left establishment" in which elitist and authoritarian culture/education is preferred to child-centered, egalitarian education.

Olwens, Don. *Bullying at School.* Cambridge, MA: Blackwell, 1993.
The pre-eminent authority on aggressive, violent, student behavior, Olwens discusses ways to reduce bullying and victimization in schools based on his studies in Scandinavian countries.

Onenk, Naomi L. *Essentials of Myers-Briggs Type Indicator Assessment.* New York: Wiley, 2000.
Clearly written text and illustrative reference charts explain the MBTI to lay readers. Onenk is coauthor of the 1998 revision of the MBTI Manual.

Palmer, Parker J. *The Courage to Teach.* San Francisco: Jossey-Bass, 1998.
One of the most seminal books on attitude in teaching in recent times. This book includes "A Guide for Reflection and Renewal."

Pollard, Andrew, and Pat Triggs. *Reflective Teaching in Secondary Education.* London: Cassell, 1997.
Comprehensive on most elements in education from a British point of view.

Poundstone, William. *Labyrinths of Reason.* New York: Anchor Books, 1988.
Explores the exigencies of thought applied to knowledge.

Rowland, Stephen. *The Enquiring Tutor: Exploring the Process of Professional Learning.* London: Falmer Press, 1993.
The centrality of controlling one's own learning activity and avoiding predetermined or imposed objectives, if the goal is to seek higher conceptual levels.

Sarason, Seymour B. *You Are Thinking of Teaching?* San Francisco: Jossey-Bass, 1993.
Although delivered as a kind of sermon, the author makes a case for the inner life of a teacher who as a professional has something to profess.

Saunders, Frances Wright. *Katharine and Isabel: Mother's Light, Daughter's Journey.* Palo Alto, CA: Consulting Psychologists Press, 1991.
The fascinating story of how Katharine Briggs and Isabel Briggs-Myers developed a much used personality assessment.

Sizer, Theodore R. *Horace's Compromise: The Dilemma of the American High School.* Boston: Houghton Mifflin, 1984.
A classic story of how teacher and students negotiate learning away for the appearance of success and suggestions of what to do about it.

————. *Horace's School—Redesigning the American High School.* New York: Houghton Mifflin, 1992.
Establishes parameters for genuine reform and elaborates eight attitudinal habits to be cultivated.

Sizer, Nancy Faust, and Theodore R. Sizer. *The Students Are Watching.* Boston: Beacon Press, 1999.
A book concerning the morality of teaching and its implications for value and character formation.

Steiner, Rudolph. *The Essentials of Education and First Steps in Inner Development.* Hudson, NY: Anthroposophic Press, 1997, 1999.
Gives the reader a direct sense of Steiner's vision of child development.

Sullivan, Dennis, and Larry Tift. *Restorative Justice.* Monsey, NY: Willow Tree Press, 2001.
Explores an attitude of restoring rather than punishing our battered natures.

Tift, Larry, John Sullivan, and Dennis Sullivan. *Discipline as Enthusiasm: An Entry in the Recent Discussion on the Moral Development of Children.* Paper presented at the annual meeting of the Association for Humanist Sociology, Pittsburg, November 6–9, 1997.

Tom, Alan R. *Teaching as a Moral Craft.* New York: Longman, 1984.
Examines flexibility in the teaching situation and the absence thereof.

Lao Tsu. *Tao Te Ching,* trans. Gia-Fu Feng and Jane English. New York: Vintage Books, 1972.
A central focus for the inspiration of this book, especially reading #38.

Tuchman, Maurice, et al. *The Spiritual in Art: Abstract Painting 1890–1985.* New York: Abbeville Press, 1986.
Los Angeles County Museum of Art. Records an exhibition in which an open attitude is graphically apparent.

Vygotsky, Lev. *Thought and Language.* Boston: MIT Press, 1986.
Working in the USSR during the 1920s and 30s, Vygotsky proposed theories about the historical and social bases of cognition. His work became known in the United States during the 1980s.

Washburn, Michael. *The Ego and the Dynamic Ground,* 2nd ed. Albany: SUNY Press, 1995.
Represents a cogent interpretation of transpersonal human development, especially regarding the rigors of adolescence.

Whitehead, Alfred North. *The Aims of Education.* New York: Free Press, 1929.
Arguably one of the greatest books on education ever written; essays on the proper shape of education in clear, unequivocal prose.

———. *Adventures of Ideas*. New York: Macmillan, 1967.
Addresses the creative impulse of ideas, the activity of ideas, the nature and life of ideas, and the purpose of philosophy.

———. *Process and Reality*. New York: Free Press, 1928.
The author's masterpiece describing the philosophy of organism.

Wiggins, Grant. *Assessing Student Performance: Exploring the Purpose and Limits of Testing*. San Francisco: Jossey-Bass, 1993.
Precisely challenges assumptions on accountability and measurement of students. A remarkable book.

Wilber, Ken. *The Spectrum of Consciousness*. Wheaton, IL: Quest Books, 1977.
———. *The Atman Project*. Wheaton, IL: Quest Books, 1980, 1996.
———. *Sex, Ecology, Spirituality*. Boston: Shambhala, 1995.
We recommend all of Ken Wilber's works as they pertain to attitude, consciousness, and human development, but especially point to these three works.

Wilkinson, Roy. *Rudolph Steiner on Education, A Compendium*. Gloucestershire, UK: Hawthorn Press, 1993.
An excellent introduction to this pioneer in childhood development.

Wolf, Aline D. *Nurturing the Spirit in Nonsectarian Classrooms*. Hollidaysburg, PA: Parent Child Press, 1996.
One of the few books directly addressing the notion of the tripartite child, that is of the child as a spiritual being as well as a mental and physical one.

Index

Entries beginning with capital letters refer to philosophies discussed in this book or to proper names. Italic page numbers refer to figures.

Read what they are saying about what could be the <u>most</u> important book in Education today . . .

"*In educating teachers, it is far too easy to focus our attention on questions to which we have clear answers, rather than questions that are essential but to which it is more challenging to fashion a clear response. In* Heart of the Matter, *Willis and Greenberg have chosen to tackle questions that are essential to teaching and provide a framework for action: who are my students, and how can I build a bridge that connects me to each student, so that learning can occur? Knowing our students has disturbing, even revolutionary implications, for if we choose to know our students, we cannot also demand compliance or set uniform expectations for all students. Greenberg and Willis draw upon their knowledge of psychology and philosophy, as well as insights from their many years of teaching, to pose alternative routes for teachers. They describe these routes using analysis and stories. All teachers, both novice or seasoned, can be sure that they will learn from the journey they take in reading* Heart of the Matter.*"*

— Lynn M. Gelzheiser, Associate Professor
Department of Education and Counseling Psychology
University at Albany, SUNY

"*If some one has ever described your teaching style as defiant, this book will make you proud to bear the title. Art Willis and Marcia Greenberg have written a book that pragmatically compiles and dissects the common perceptions about how schools work today and how a teacher's Awareness of themselves, and of their students can lead to a level of differentiated instruction that engages the young learner in more than learning just facts and skills. The authors' approach is based on over 60 years of experience between them, as well as help from Jung, Buddhism, and the Tao Te Ching. A great book for the nascent or experienced teacher leader, Mr. Willis and Ms. Greenberg have written a guide that asserts what we do for kids in our classrooms must be first and foremost about the spirit, abilities, and interests of the kids in our classrooms. Teachers must be aware and awake to who these students are, without prejudice, before they can expect success in their classrooms.*'

— Ms. Jennifer L. Wolfe, NBCT, P.P.D.(Honorary)
NYS High School Social Studies Teacher of the Year, 2006
Fulbright Scholar 2004 UK
Social Studies Teacher Oceanside High School